Indirections of the novel

INDIRECTIONS OF THE NOVEL

James, Conrad, and Forster

KENNETH GRAHAM

Professor of English Literature,
University of Sheffield

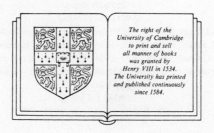

The right of the
University of Cambridge
to print and sell
all manner of books
was granted by
Henry VIII in 1534.
The University has printed
and published continuously
since 1584.

CAMBRIDGE UNIVERSITY PRESS

Cambridge

New York   Port Chester   Melbourne   Sydney

Published by the Press Syndicate of the University of Cambridge
The Pitt Building, Trumpington Street, Cambridge CB2 1RP
40 West 20th Street, New York, NY 10011, USA
10 Stamford Road, Oakleigh, Melbourne 3166, Australia

© Cambridge University Press 1988

First published 1988
Reprinted 1989

Printed in Great Britain at
the University Press, Cambridge

British Library cataloguing in publication data

Graham, Kenneth
Indirections of the novel: James, Conrad
and Forster.
1. English fiction – 19th century – History
and criticism 2. English fiction – 20th
century – History and criticism
I. Title
823'.8'09   PR871

Library of Congress cataloguing in publication data

Graham, Kenneth
Indirections of the novel: James, Conrad, and Forster /
Kenneth Graham.
p.   cm.
Bibliography: p.
Includes index.
ISBN 0–521–34488–3
1. English fiction – 20th century – History and criticism.
2. James, Henry, 1843–1916 – Criticism and interpretation.
3. Conrad, Joseph, 1857–1924 – Criticism and interpretation.
4. Forster, E. M. (Edward Morgan), 1879–1970 – Criticism and
interpretation. I. Title.
PR881.G73 1988
823'.912'09 – dc 19   87–19721 CIP

ISBN 0 521 34488 3

GG

Contents

v

For Sheffield colleagues

Introduction: narratives of the brink

The purpose of this book is to investigate the detailed strategies of three masters of indirection in the early modern novel: James, Conrad, and Forster. Different though the three are from one another, they are linked by this historically crucial development they each represented in the technique of fiction: the deployment of a radically new openness, obliquity, and contradictoriness of narrative forms, both in the large-scale movements of narration and in the smallest details of descriptive language, scene, and dialogue. And what connects them even more profoundly, below this level of technical innovation and virtuosity, is that their innovations articulate, and articulate precisely, a shared response to a world of new uncertainty and danger. They are all writers of the brink. Their narrations waver, take risks, are always on the edge of retraction or contradiction. Private dreams and fears suddenly change the direction of a scene or a paragraph. Intellectual or moral scruple enforces a quick reversal, a renunciation; imaginative desire swells into idyll, or the image of escape and a new start; an impassioned responsiveness to the world-as-it-is produces a cacophony of arguing voices, a quick temporary compromise, a sardonic shrug in the narrating. In each of these three novelists is combined, in the most lambent interplay, the highest degree of artistic, moral, and intellectual awareness with the most self-betraying revelations of unreconciled feeling: control against risk and disarray, sophistication against nostalgia, authoritative assertion against self-testing by irony or by whimsy or, in James's phrase for the form-seeking of the artist, by some 'deep difficulty braved'.[1] Vulnerability is their obsession; the tell-tale vulnerability of their fictional characters, on behalf of all human vulnerability; and, not least, their pressing need as artists to find a form that is clear and definite yet will itself also be vulnerable, in the sense of being perpetually open, pliable, and sensitive to every nuance and change of fictional situation and of narratorial sensibility.

1

Introduction

All three share clear characteristics of transition: different elements that could be called post-Romantic, Victorian, and Modernist. James and Forster at times recall the mode of Jane Austen and Thackeray, even (in James's case) of Congreve. Conrad has an equivocal, dark Romanticism that is at times like Poe or Melville, with here and there a touch of the more sombre Dickens. James and Forster, less black-Romantic (though James has his Gothicism), can often seem haunted by some Romantic dream of an unattainable perfection and harmony, and can juxtapose the headiest nostalgia against the coolest, most worldly irony. They know, and frequently evoke, the Keatsian plangency of loss. They are all moralists in a nineteenth-century sense, with a sardonic high seriousness that only in Conrad's case is not lightened by wit, and they have an Arnoldian commitment to the critical social struggle between culture and anarchy. Like the Victorians, they particularly fear reification, alienation, hypocrisy, loss of will, self-betrayal, and the mechanical. They celebrate, with only some ambiguity (and a more radical doubt on Conrad's part), the value of personal relationships and the fullest play of individual consciousness. They uphold the validity – though hardly the solidity – of Character. And as for their Modernism – they are committed to art and to their profession (particularly James and Conrad) as supreme meaning-bearing activities in a world where other things have failed and where an Armageddon of deadened language, materialism, and fragmentation is never far from sight. Having left the revelations of religion far behind them, they use symbols to provide quizzical glimpses of something more ultimate, sometimes more ravening, than the everyday. Their language is intensely self-aware, even self-subverting, their narrative forms intricate and contradictory, their judgements ambiguous, their innate scepticism enlarged into a whole style of indirection that seeks to challenge fixity, formula, and closure. And they have all, being the antennae of the race, experienced the full terror of vacuity – psychological, social, historical, metaphysical – and pit against that vacuity all the inventiveness of their craft, the invigorating ambivalence of their responses, and their commitment to articulacy.

There is the space of a generation between the two older writers and the younger – James and Conrad born in 1843 and 1857, Forster in 1879. And it might be appropriate to consider the first two briefly as a pair before adding Forster – characteristically – to disrupt, juggle, and reshape them into a trio.

To begin with, they were both exiles, the American and the Pole. Whether that simple biographical fact can be taken as a strict cause of the literary effects I have in mind, or as a general influence, or even just as a suggestive analogy, both these writers do seem to stand somewhat at odds with their world, to ironize it with the cool, half-foreign tones of the *émigré*, to view it with detachment and a contradictory yearning to escape from detachment into commitment and action, and to be haunted by some nostalgic but quickly scotched rumour of a Great Good Place. When James made his long-delayed grand return to the States in 1904 he found he had become an exile there too, and wrote, as a jaundiced 'restless analyst', one of his subtlest and most entangled works out of that experience, *The American Scene*. And when Conrad returned in trepidation to Poland he arrived, by an extraordinary Conradian irony, in August 1914, at the very moment when his homeland vanished once again into its familiar tragic chaos of war and division, and had to retreat frantically, ill, and with difficulty, to Italy. Only in narrative, it seems, was the exile safe; and only there could self-division, anxiety, and the painfully unaccommodated intelligence find containment, within the scrupulous shapings of art.[2]

James's anxiety and self-division were very real. His famously enigmatic trauma of 1861, whether physical or psychological (genital or lumbar!), was only a prelude to a career of intermittent melancholy, recurrent nightmare, and ailment. But for him there was always a stronger countermovement in the form of wit, social ebullience, and an endlessly energizing curiosity about the human scene. And in the novels, for all their characteristic note of impending loss, the chance missed, the fruition not quite achieved, there is an essential confidence in the power of consciousness – that of his protagonists, that of himself as a novelist – which gives his writing a coloration quite different from Conrad's. Both men sound the note of the abyss: a personal abyss that is also the abyss of an old century dying and an ominous new century coming in. The coiling, uncoiling complexity of their narrative method expresses the instability of living in a time when the uneasy activity of consciousness itself has begun to replace externally supported

3

values as the one thing we know. Characters like Maggie Verver and Razumov are beginning to live, to themselves and in the eyes of others, through their febrile faculty of story-making and image-building alone. But compared with the creator of Razumov (and Marlow, and Decoud, and Heyst) James had a somewhat securer (if always self-questioning) grasp of the reality and virtue of the tangible world; and also, within the limits of tragedy and ironic comedy, of at least some of the possibilities of action.[3] Life is rarely a dream for him, as it threatens so often to be for Conrad – though in Conrad, perhaps by a simple reversal of the Jamesian emphasis, the strong drift towards the dream, towards inanition and will-lessness, is in turn almost always challenged from within his narrative by the not-quite-paralysed forces of love, personal and communal, of fidelity, physical battle, yarn-spinning, justified scorn, and, at the very least, of rather grimly holding on.

That life is a dream is hardly to be deduced from most of Conrad's non-fictional prose. The one essay on James, for example, 'Henry James: an Appreciation', sees James and establishes Conrad himself in a distinctly heroic mode.[4] As a performance itself, indeed, the essay is lofty and orotund to an almost mock-heroic degree, its insights half-hidden by its rhetoric. Conrad is full of such awkwardnesses. In terms of style and narrative tact he is by far the most unsteady, the most vulnerable of the three writers I am considering. It is in the inner recesses of his narrations that the real quick and intricacy of his achievement lie. Conrad as exile – figuratively exiled, more than literally – best reveals himself covertly; and where his intricacy of method becomes most overt and self-advertising, as in *Chance*, the result is less a tribute to than a parody of *The Golden Bowl*.[5] Elsewhere, less hampered by artfully self-conscious circumlocution, he can allow the contrary pulses of narrative to articulate more freely the devious nature of his temperament and his outlook. Conrad at his best, I think, writes always on the edge of panic. A sharp note of half-controlled extremism is perhaps the major distinguishing feature between his late-Romantic imagination and the more urbane, elegiac Romanticism of James – though James, too, has his nightmare-images ('The Jolly Corner'), his fear of being overwhelmed, his perturbing fascination with renunciation, his flashes of febrile, cloying morbidity ('The Altar of the Dead' and 'Maud-Evelyn'). For Conrad, more obsessive and less varied than James, it is nevertheless only the edge of panic, not panic itself: he is one of the most icy and rigid of Modernism's starers-into-the-abyss. The tension in his writing between possible hysteria and a meticulous shrewdness is extreme, and, at its best, thoroughly dramatic and creative. He is clearly appalled by nihilism and moral anarchy, and is at his most lucidly critical when he exposes the pettiness and the self-delusions of his numerous tribe of cynics, core-less demoralizers, and bilgerats: Ossipon, Michaelis, and their group in *The Secret Agent*, Donkin in *The Nigger of the 'Narcissus'*; assorted mates, second mates, and engineers like Sterne and Massy in 'The End of the Tether'; Schomberg and his half-mythic quintessence, Mr Jones, in *Victory*; and so on – a sobering list of those who erode, calumniate, cheat, who are the very breath of the pit, but are looked at closely, fiercely, and with a pale, unyielding glare by Conrad, quite assured and unhysterical in his judicious exposure of them. Nevertheless, on the level of feeling, and in various layers of his language and movements of his narration, his fear and dislike sometimes swell up and reveal themselves in strange forms. For example, it appears to me that his exasperation in *The Secret Agent* with his own squalidly ineffectual anarchists, the pompous or devious self-seekers who oppose them, and the feebleness of the good-at-heart (the meek, like Winnie and Stevie, who will never, never inherit the earth) finds peculiar expression through the character of the Professor, who at least utters rage against the smothering world of mediocrity that Conrad himself has exposed:

'You are mediocre [he tells Ossipon at the end]. Verloc, whose affair the police has managed to smother so nicely, was mediocre . . . Everybody is mediocre. Madness and despair! Give me that for a lever, and I'll move the world.'[6]

Conrad condemns the Professor as a 'pest in the street full of men'; but by allowing him to harness to his own words, by quotation, the power and meaning of Winnie's suicide ('an act of madness or despair'), and by allowing him such a sardonic glitter of visage and style, Conrad, I suspect, is creating a vent-hole for some surreptitious passion of his own that the telling of the tale has built up in him. The story sceptically and forcibly judges the anarchists of every social class. But by a characteristic indirection of displaced feeling it comes close to embodying the impassioned nihilism that its would-be anarchists are too mediocre to express.

Time and time again Conrad, so at odds with himself, boxes himself in narrative into an intolerable moral dilemma, a state of intellectually unstable but aesthetically exciting impasse, in that the values he vehemently upholds of love, service, and fidelity are always revealed in stress to have an endemic central hollowness, a lack of total support from the universe, which the human will must nevertheless go on countering with passion and desperate self-delusion. It is this impasse that provokes the obliquity and cross-currents of his narrative modes, his sudden diatribes, or some compensatory excess of lyricism, his perpetual ironic reversals both positive and negative. For both Conrad and James irony, large-scale and small-scale, is not a mere serviceable device: it is the very fibre of their inconclusively speculative imaginations, their personal situations, and their shifting and ambivalent purchase on what they present as a shifting, ambivalent world. Verbal qualification and narrative transposition become for both of them a positive mode of building: of constructing by conscious craft an intricate edifice of aspects, nuances, and narratorial divagations in order to withstand the destructive pull of unleashed relativism, of human perversity, unstable words, loss of will, and 'the horror, the horror' of an ungraspable, nightmarish reality.

James, unlike Conrad, also pits against negation – against stupidity, betrayal, and failure – the vivifying movement of humour and of sheer aesthetic play. Such playfulness is no mere additive, but part of a general strategy for expression and discovery. Indeed, the centre of James's theory of the novel is the principle of movement and interplay, seen above all as a dynamic formal response to that very complexity of pressures that drove Conrad into his more centripetal and self-vexing posture. For James – by far the most articulate theorist of the three, though Forster is no slouch – form is never the imposition of convention and device but always an unfinished struggle and a multiplication of fluid relationships. It is an event, rather than an achieved stillness or an outline, and something closely akin to the two-way nature of perception itself: 'the state of private poetic intercourse with things, the kind of current that in a given personal experience flows to and fro between the imagination and the world'.[7] James's theory of form mirrors the basic drama of his themes: the interplay, sometimes comic, often tragic, between the irresistible stress of the real, the quotidian, and the equally irresistible free play of the shaping, wondering, appreciative mind – between the facts about Gilbert Osmond and Isabel's imaginative version of him, between lumpish Woollett, Massachusetts, the place of duty, provincial innocence, old age, and moral probity, and on the other hand Strether's free responsiveness to Paris, to Chad's youthful opportunity, to the quotidian and the mortal as transfigured, only half-delusively, into glamorous players and painted stage.

It is too easy to cite by themselves such famous instances of James slighting the claims of 'life' in favour of 'form' as these: the critique of the Tolstoian novel as 'large loose baggy monsters, with their queer elements of the accidental and the arbitrary'; his impatience at 'the fatal futility of Fact'; and the attack on 'saturation' and the 'slice of life' in his exchanges with H. G. Wells – 'It is art that *makes* life, makes interest, makes importance.'[8] No less characteristic, however, are those instances where James describes the 'life versus art' issue in terms of something that is moving and incomplete: a perpetual struggle and drama, rather than an equation or a choice to be made. The drama is most clearly, and most appropriately, expressed by James's elaborate images or metaphors describing the very act of creating, the act of struggle between solicitous, sensuous, multitudinous life and the 'sublime economy' demanded by the shaping mind and the 'cold passion of art'.[9] For example, his reminiscences of battling to write *Portrait of a Lady* in Venice, or *The Tragic Muse* in Paris:

The Venetian footfall and the Venetian cry . . . come in once more at the window, renewing one's old impression of the delighted senses and the divided, frustrated mind. How can places that speak *in general* so to the imagination not give it, at the moment, the particular thing it wants? . . . Such, and so rueful, are these reminiscences; though on the whole, no doubt, one's book and one's 'literary effort' at large, were to be the better for them.[10]

And again:

Re-reading the last chapters of 'The Tragic Muse' I catch again the very odour of Paris, which comes up in the rich rumble of the Rue de la Paix – with which my room itself, for that matter, seems impregnated . . . to an effect strangely composed at once of the auspicious and the fatal. The 'plot' of Paris thickened at such hours beyond any other plot in the world, I think; but there one sat meanwhile with another, on one's hands, absolutely requiring precedence . . . there being so much of the confounded irreducible quantity still to treat.[11]

These same two 'plots' represent the stress and the dynamic in James's concept of form: the dangerous stream of experience within which the artist's mind must seek to live, and the contending 'plot' of fictional device, compression, 'discrimination', and 'value'. There can be no adjudication between the two. Between them they make for stress and difficulty — 'the deep difficulty braved' — and between them they make art, certainly James's art, what it is in practice: an act of perpetually self-qualifying duality and indirection, close to the kinetic of consciousness itself, being self-referential in its linguistic textures but also reflective, celebratory, of the resistant world outside that allows, resists, and destroys. It is in the Preface to *Daisy Miller* that he describes most memorably, if congestedly, this creative act of engagement by the novelist which finds its dynamic and its dialectic intensity in the meeting between the disruptive pressures of the real and the passion to confer shape:

the simplest truth about a human entity, a situation, a relation, an aspect of life, however small, on behalf of which the claim to charmed attention is made, strains ever, under one's hand, more intensely, *most* intensely, to justify that claim; strains ever, as it were, toward the uttermost end or aim of one's meaning or of its own numerous connexions; struggles at each step, and in defiance of one's raised admonitory finger, fully and completely to express itself. Any real art of representation is, I make out, a controlled and guarded acceptance, in fact a perfect economic explosive principle in one's material thoroughly noted, adroitly allowed to flush and colour and animate the disputed value, but with its other appetites and treacheries, its characteristic space-hunger and space-cunning, kept down. The fair flower of the artful compromise is to my sense the secret of 'foreshortening' — the particular economic device for which one must have a name and which has in its single blessedness and its determined pitch, I think, a higher price than twenty other clustered loosenesses; and just because full-fed statement, just because the picture of as many of the conditions as possible made and kept proportionate, just because the surface iridescent, even in the short piece, by what is beneath it and what throbs and gleams through, are things all conducive to the only compactness that has a charm, to the only spareness that has a force, to the only simplicity that has a grace — those, in each order, that produce the *rich* effect.[12]

8

Conrad would undoubtedly have subscribed to that eloquent credo, with its evocation of a multiplicity of 'connexions' and 'conditions' all tempered and made expressive by 'compactness' and 'grace' – though he is comparatively unconcerned with the complicating world of manners, of social and personal theatricality, that makes for so much of James's 'conditions' and is reflected in the particular 'grace' of James's surfaces and styles. Conrad's act of engagement is more anxious, and his sense of impending overthrow and chaos more urgent by far. But his faith in himself as artist, and in the voice of the storyteller – and of the storyteller within the story[13] – is at least as strong as James's faith in the impression-taking, shape-imposing struggle of the novelist and of his own super-sensitive protagonists. But novelists, in their essays and criticism, are at their most impassioned, their loftiest, when considering the high calling of their profession. In the novelist's ennobling responsibility to forge the conscience of the race, and in his opportunity for observation, expression, and display, flashing up against the endemic and opposing pressures of disorder, treachery, and wordlessness, both exiles saw the goal which they showed their fictional characters struggling to achieve: the fusion of thought and feeling, idea and action; a realized identity; and a connection with the world, however fluctuating, that might cancel banishment.

Forster would always have tried to deflate such high and solemn concepts – even in the act of subscribing to them. His famous evasiveness – the unexpected whimsy, the sideways shuffle, the dangling disclaimer, what Lionel Trilling called his 'insistence on the double turn' – is very much his own style, his own mode of confronting, and of defining, the same darkness that threatened James and Conrad. The elusiveness in personal manner that could both charm and infuriate – it made Lytton Strachey brand him, for Bloomsbury, as 'the mole' – becomes part of the essence of his art, where it ceases simply to evade or to posture and becomes, instead, his central creative scheme of reconnoitre and ambivalence.[14] Forster's indirections as a narrator keep him, comically in the Italian novels, dialectically in *Howards End*, tragically in *A Passage to India*, as slippery as a fish. He is more quick and darting as a manipulator than James – and a hundred times quicker than Conrad, who is the least playful, the most grimly solemn, of them all. He covers a more dangerous gamut of tones in a smaller compass than either of the other two, and can pass successfully within a few paragraphs from a gleeful smirk to the most solemn diapason or scathing disquisition, a sudden death, a kiss, an outrageous coincidence, a moment of allegory or symbol. He pulls the strings of his plots with even greater virtuosity than either of the others, and is an unequalled master of surprise, reversal, and *reprise*. Like James and Conrad, of course, he is intrinsically, from first to last, an ironist. And it might even be wondered, in this connection, if he, too, is not something of an ironizing exile: sexually a misfit, temperamentally shy yet waspish, essentially English yet excoriating English ways: the subtle yet downcast person in turban and dhoti, from Hertfordshire, squatting in the Maharajah of Dewas's courtyard.

Exile or not, virtuoso or not, what connects him emphatically with the two older novelists is the subtly variable ways in which his highly structured narratives and his humanistic code flex themselves, and controvert themselves, in order to cope with personal or generalized anxiety and with the emanations of chaos. It is a familiar observation that even the early novels – *Where Angels Fear to Tread*, *A Room with a View*, and *The Longest Journey* – are full of violence and unexpected melodrama, with sudden shifts from the operatic to the meditative, from the rhapsodic to the essayistic to the morbid, even to the masochistic. The catastrophe in *Angels*, for example, is dazzlingly assured, even slick, in its handling of nightmare and cruelty, set in a context of Jane Austen-like satire and wittily edged lyricism: a startling amalgam of modes for a first novel, and in many ways a more daring range than Conrad ever or James often attempted (*Angels* appeared in 1905, it is worth remembering, only the year after *The Golden Bowl* and *Nostromo*). The book has begun like *The Europeans*, wittily, ruefully, and zestfully exposing the incompatibility of different cultures and codes of values and the petty problems of hypocrisy, misunderstanding, and falsity to self that beset people seeking to move between worlds. But the death of Lilia, after her premonitory attempt to escape from her false life ends literally and symbolically with her lying smothered and choked by dust in the roadway ('There is something very terrible in dust at night-time'), is a typically sudden darkening of the scene. The outbreaks of seriousness, amid the farce and the high-pitched sounds of the

English abroad quarrelling, soon adumbrate one theme, among others, that James and Conrad would have dwelt on more explicitly, but with the same commitment of personal feeling and personal recognition as Forster: the theme of the will. Philip Herriton, like so many of the characters of James and Conrad, is trapped by some fatal debility of the will. It is the old Jamesian and Conradian terror of the loss of the power to act: in this case, a wry rather than tragic demonstration of the paralysing gap between the contemplative and the active life, between the alert, civilized consciousness and the world, including the world of the body. Quite casually – with what a reader begins to detect after a while as Forster's beautiful and elaborate casualness – Philip has been presented with an image of sacred passivity in the fresco of Santa Deodata in the collegiate church in Monteriano:

So holy was she that all her life she lay upon her back in the house of her mother, refusing to eat, refusing to play, refusing to work. The devil, envious of such sanctity, tempted her in various ways. He dangled grapes above her, he showed her fascinating toys, he pushed soft pillows beneath her aching head. When all proved vain he tripped up the mother and flung her downstairs before her very eyes. But so holy was the saint that she never picked her mother up, but lay upon her back through all, and thus assured her throne in Paradise.[15]

And when all the tensions among the strange little raiding party of the English, intent on abducting a half-English baby to safety, have risen to breaking-point, when repressed desires and senses become heavy in the air, and the night of stormy catastrophe and another death are just at hand, then the full force of what threatens Philip is given unexpectedly clear words by Caroline Abbott in the chapel of the same saint, whose blessed inaction is an ironic comment on the Englishman who cannot live but can only appreciate, and, like Prufrock, will gain no Paradise: 'You appreciate us all – see good in all of us [Caroline cries at him]. And all the time you are dead – dead – dead. Look, why aren't you angry?' And he replies (on behalf, as it were, of all James's scrupulous, fearful observers and Conrad's haunted dreamers and idealists): 'Some people are born not to do things. I'm one of them . . . I seem fated to pass through the world without colliding with it . . . I don't die – I don't fall in love . . . life to me is just a spectacle.' Something violent is always required to break through the carapace of these intelligent drifters or self-deluders or *hommes moyen spirituels*, caught, as by a trance, in the narrow place where two centuries cross. They must be made to confront a horror, an intimate betrayal, a murderous incursion against their protective island. The almost surrealist nightmare of the baby's nocturnal kidnapping and death, with tuneless fragments of Donizetti hanging in the rain, the sudden ghastly face and incoherent babbling of a local idiot, then the 'whole world's sorrow' in the baby's eyes, the crash, the confusion, the mud, the breaking of Philip's arm – it all comprises the first profound echo from Forster's Marabar Caves, a dangerous and chaotic force that, at its best, inadvertently changes a few lives, shaking them into a new confession or an altered relationship. The strangely protracted and lurid scene where the bereaved Gino tortures Philip by twisting his broken arm till the bone grates in the joint, then half-throttling him, with yellings and gurglings, is not just melodrama (though there is more than a touch of melodrama, as well as covert sexuality, about it). It also expresses a powerful, rather hysterical, mixture of the feelings that even so suave a narration has precipitated: feelings of self-loathing, self-pity, the desire to break and to be broken into something new, to shatter the refinements of scruple against something ugly, physical, and primitive, the desire to destroy and subvert in order that something like passion or an imaginable union might flood out so much human divisiveness.[16]

Henry James, whose characters Forster so curiously and wittily criticized as being 'exquisite deformities . . . huge heads and tiny legs, but nevertheless charming', and as indicating James's sacrifice of 'most of human life' in favour of an aesthetic pattern,[17] was just as possessed as Forster by the vision of a harmony, a new fusion of human faculties, and with the same accompanying clear-eyed view of practical possibilities, the weakness, perversity, yet capacity for partial change of the individual psyche.[18] Both writers also express this idea of a new power, a new self, by an image of the impersonal. James's tantalizing symbol of the Virgin in *What Maisie Knew* (like the Maltese Cross in *The Spoils of Poynton* or the Bronzino portrait in *The Wings of the Dove*), resembles Forster's, in *Angels*, of Caroline, the baby, and Gino momentarily tranformed by a magical accident of arrangement into a painting of 'Virgin and Child with Donor'. It is the symbol of a brief

Introduction

intersection of the transcendent with the mundane, answering our ordinary human desire for equipoise and transfiguration. There is always more overt magic of this kind in Forster than in James, more symbols, more unbalancing strangenesses from outside the world of ordinary human affairs – James usually preferring to work the trick more obliquely, by the accumulative effect of extended metaphor or hyperbolic analysis or mannerism in gesture and style. But all three authors have an unempirical vision of richness or of devastation deeply at work, often unexpectedly or melodramatically or romantically at work, within their otherwise humanistic frame of reference – and in the case of Conrad and Forster, strongly challenging that humanism in its most basic precepts.

Forster, quite the most critically deflating in outlook and style of the three, made one memorably damaging comment on Conrad – as damaging, for all the accompanying praise, as his criticism of James that he sacrificed 'most of human life' – which has established itself as a classic obstacle that even Conrad's admirers must negotiate. It is delivered teasingly, trenchantly, with many a witty qualification, and, of course, with a certain obliquity. But what he says about Conrad – perhaps just as in his critique of James – touches on something of his own style and achievement, and in particular of this underlying concern with the transcendent, the impersonal, and what he calls in his fiction 'the unseen'. He seems at first to be commenting only on Conrad the essayist and austerely self-restrictive autobiographer, but it soon becomes clear he is also confronting Conrad the novelist:

Behind the smoke screen of his reticence there may be another obscurity, connected with the foreground by wisps of vapour, yet proceeding from another source, from the central chasm of his tremendous genius . . .

Is there not also a central obscurity, something noble, heroic, beautiful, inspiring half a dozen great books; but obscure, obscure? . . . These essays do suggest that he is misty in the middle as well as at the edges, that the secret casket of his genius contains a vapour rather than a jewel; and that we need not try to write him down philosophically, because there is, in this particular direction, nothing to write.[19]

It is true that Forster then says – in one of his usual quick frisks of indirection – that this question ought not to be raised when we read Conrad's half-dozen great novels; but the damage has been

13

done, very characteristically, for all the disclaimer. And it is therefore fair to point out that Forster, too, 'to write him down philosophically', is cloudy rather than hard-edged; that *Where Angels Fear to Tread* and *A Room with a View* are completely and properly indecisive as to the relation between personal commitment to action in life and the transformative, reality-bearing power of the 'unseen', exemplifying shiftingly as they do that the worldly will and the contemplative imagination each touch on something like 'reality' yet also run counter to one another; that in *Howards End* the Schlegel view is now endorsed, now exposed, and the mysterious primal world of 'nature' and 'sea' appears as alternatively chaotic and constructive; and that in *A Passage to India*, the greatest of the novels, the 'vapour' of obscurity, the changing facets of the infinite (or whatever we must call the voice of the caves), is at its most pronounced. Conrad's misty perception of an all-swallowing horror, or a stony-visaged, unanswering universe, has – like Forster's in the end – none of the precision of a theorem or a syllogism, but all the self-sufficient validity of a nightmare. And the perfectly hard-edged questions – questions, not answers – that come from both Conrad and Forster are, how can we live with such disturbing intimations? How can we hold them at bay or build them into our creative selves or, at least, resist them intensely in a seven-year dispensation of heroic action on our Patusan, or in an assertion of the will to build a flawed new state in our Sulaco, or in a new marriage between Wilcox pragmatism and Schlegel imagination, a new friendship between men, between races? How to go on expressing the mysteriously given energies of self-respect, or of sexual desire and aggression, or of narrating and pattern-making, against everything that is their opposite – so intrinsically opposite as to be their intrinsic, intimate shadow?

But this, as before, is too solemn a note to maintain for very long in the vicinity of Forster. He is witty, and sly, and gimlet-eyed, and distrustful: solemnities appear in his novels, as lustrously as in James and Conrad, but they are in the highest degree unstable, shot through with punctual anticlimax, dubiety, and quirkiness. It is entirely characteristic of Forster's vulnerability and need for independence that he should have marked himself off from the two older practitioners by his critical caveats against them, for all that he admires them and, in his own humorous and open narrating, shares their moral and artistic brinkmanship. In the end, like his characters, he has to be his own man, with his own style of reflecting their shared concern with vulnerability, risk and movement: as elusive, and therefore as deep, as a mole.

In what follows, I wish to study how these crucial moral concerns and shared anxieties are expressed by and produce, in the novels of three of the founders of modern fiction, certain comparable narrative modes of ellipsis, complex modulation and dynamism, subversion, irresolution, and interplay. In some cases I do this by concentrating on local details or selected aspects of the text involved – for example, as regards *The Europeans*, *Heart of Darkness*, and *Nostromo*, or in my examination of one chapter of *The Golden Bowl*. In other cases, for example in the account of *The Bostonians*, *The Shadow-Line*, and both Forster novels, I aim at something rather more comprehensive – though still based on very close analyses of how texture and movement create signification.

For James, I have begun with one very early novel, *The Europeans*, in which the many-layeredness of his later narration is most clearly prefigured in its experimentation with dramatic devices of indirect inference, through gesture, pause, scene, narratorial stance, and shifts of style and tone – coupled with what that manner precisely and subtly begins to express of the major Jamesian themes of a questioning unease about personality, self-projection, withdrawal, and the dangerous duplicities of social and artistic style. I then contrast the succinct theatricality of narrative in *The Europeans* with the completely different discursiveness of one of the typical middle-period works, *The Bostonians*, where the new panoramic descriptiveness and large-scale dialectic of ideas are nevertheless still seen to be engaged, and also much qualified, in the varying dynamics of plot, uncategorical language, and complex local incident – with the unease, revealed in this engagement, taking on a new generality of national and cultural application. Jamesian indirection at its most extended is then represented in two works of his later period, *What Maisie Knew*, at its beginning, and *The Golden Bowl*, at its end, where modulation of narrative mode and of emotion in the former, and the proliferation of nuance and perturbed ambiguity in the latter, are an apogee in James's own career as a stylist and novelist of the brink, and something of a watershed in the development of complexity in the English novel.

In the case of Conrad, rather differently, the focus is deliberately more concentrated, picking out specific problem areas or telltale points of stress in five representative fictions that span his career, from *Heart of Darkness* in 1899 to *The Shadow-Line* in 1917, and thereby overlap the fertile last phase of James's career (including *The Golden Bowl*) and most of Forster's (up to *Howards End*). *Heart of Darkness*, *Lord Jim*, *Nostromo*, *Under Western Eyes*, and *The Shadow-Line* each present striking cases of narrative delay and circuitousness, and of abruptly opposed switches of narrative register, that demonstrate not only the profound involutions of Conrad's method but the dynamic ways in which his more negative moral vision continues to be resisted internally, even covertly, by unexpected assertions of energy and renewal, in ways that at times provoke the highly responsive instability of his texts to a dangerous degree. With fewer stages of stylistic development than James, Conrad in each of these five characteristic works enforces a quite similar attention to how ambivalent, self-testing narration of this kind problematizes in its own intimate movements the relationship between different modes of knowledge, different levels of literary communication, as well as following out its more overt moral concern with the bases of selfhood, will, integrity, and personal and communal action.

The same problematic relationship within language and knowledge, and the same passionately confronted moral issues, are taken into entirely new areas of exploration, and into a new (though still quite Jamesian) style of articulation, in Forster's two major novels, *Howards End* and *A Passage to India*, with which I conclude. In the first of these – published a year before *Under Western Eyes* – there is much of Conrad's fear of general breakdown within the Jamesian wit and the uniquely Forsterian rhetoric of variable tone and recurrent motif, plot-device, and slyly double-edged commentary. And in *A Passage to India*, my whole subject of the willed and the involuntary indirections of intricate narrative, combined with the necessary indirections of language itself, comes to a consummation – at the very midpoint of the great decade of Modernism – in a book that self-consciously looks inward, into its own passages, and outward, for its era, for its genre, into passages to more than India.

Introduction

In describing the pressures, deviations, and surprises within the processes of certain relatable fictions I am clearly indebted in a very general way to contemporary narratological, poststructuralist, and reader-response criticism, which has enormously sensitized our responsiveness to the indeterminacy of texts – I think in particular of some of the writings of Gérard Genette, Hillis Miller, Geoffrey Hartman, Frank Kermode, John Holloway, Wolfgang Iser, and Stanley Fish. But I have very consciously avoided the elaborately self-aware methodologies of that criticism, and also its basic concern to theorize, in an attempt to find instead a more common language – more common to readers but more common also to the novels and novelists I am describing – in which to communicate my reading, which of course can only be my own reading, offered up to the community of other readings and readers, of how these novels function by crosscurrent of narrative movement and texture. When so much narratological criticism has to work within a systematic and difficult vocabulary of its own, and deconstructionists seem so quickly impelled in the direction of metaphysics, if not mysticism, it may be that some things still relevant to our shareable reading experience are left unvoiced, things that can be better expressed in a language that implicates the act of analysis more revealingly within an evoked experience of that reading and within a fuller coloration of the work being discussed. Tentative imputations of meaning, value, referentiality, pleasingness, and even of authorial personality, therefore, might properly be allowed to pervade, contextualize, and anchor our analyses – since they seem in experience to go on unstoppably pervading our readings – of the language and the language-units of texts. In Robert Scholes's phrase – Scholes having apparently become something of a revisionist in matters narratological – 'Narrative is not just a sequencing, or the illusion of sequence . . . narrative is a sequence of something for somebody'[20] – to which one might add, 'and by somebody, and within the world, and within history.' In seeking to deploy something of a critical double focus – that is, by blending and qualifying my concern for textuality with an equal concern for referentiality – I hope to admit to my own discourse a somewhat wider range of still-relevant material and a few more of the innumerable facets that comprise our complex reading experience.

Both here and in the chapters that follow I have no concern to

17

Introduction

engage in full-scale debate with other critics and other schools, and I have tended to restrict to endnotes the demurrals and the politenesses that would interfere with my purpose of a close and, I hope, fresh engagement with the texts in question. The aims of this book are empirical rather than polemical: to offer, by the analysis of shared or contrasted characteristics of ellipsis and contradiction in narrating, some enhancement of the way we read these three masters of subtle and ambiguous fiction, both in their verbal surfaces and in the depths of their common anxiety and resistance; and also, by studying the very particular strategies of individual works, to afford a more general insight into some of the cunning indirections by which the novel (like Polonius) can find directions out.

I · *Jamesian stages*

1. *The Europeans*: acts of style

The Europeans seems a far cry from the abysses of Modernism. Here is a novel published in 1878, the same year as Trollope's *Is He Popenjoy?*, a year before Meredith's *The Egoist*, and only two years after George Eliot's *Daniel Deronda*. It seems full of light and zest, apparently untouched by personal nightmare or neurosis, with no sense of metaphysical crisis or of *fin de siècle*. James himself disparaged it as too slight, and omitted it from the New York Edition. But he was surely wrong – it is, in its own terms, one of his most completely satisfying, and certainly one of his most perfectly achieved novels. It is also – and this is its interest from our present point of view – a striking example of James beginning to deploy that dynamic narrative mode of oblique implication and quick shifts of evaluation and feeling that was to form the basis of his mature style, and was a mode radically different from anything found in other novels of this period, certainly any novels of Eliot or Trollope or Meredith. The narration is fast-flowing, very scenic, and crisply worded, and in its blatant theatricality seems to have all the self-sufficiency and bravura of a perfect gesture. But like any planned gesture of the stage it has its challenging intimacies, its unassertive rhetoric of modulation, surprise, and inwardness. Within its brisk linearity there occur pauses and silences, little pockets of unexpected inference or suggestive stylistic play. And this is the real secret of its energy: that, like a stage gesture, it affirms outwards and onwards, from scene to scene, entrance to exit, yet contradictorily creates a sense of something behind, something receding at another angle.

For example, in one of the darker moments of the plot, when Eugenia, in cold and gloom, confronts the impending failure of her visit, and pleads that she is 'in trouble' to the irritatingly blithe Felix, their relationship is suddenly prised apart for us, and its limitations and incommunications revealed. There is a

characteristic effect of almost tangible dimensionality: a compressed movement from brightly contrasted dialogue, full of ironies, un-
truths, and tangents to a gesture of looking, then to a brief entry
into the thoughts of the two characters, then to authorial statement, undecided speculation, and finally to a blank narrative cut-
off of knowledge:

> 'Well, let me give you some news,' said the Baroness. '. . . Robert Acton
> wants to marry me.'
> . . . 'Accept him, accept him!' cried Felix, joyously. 'He is the best
> fellow in the world.'
> 'He is immensely in love with me,' said the Baroness.
> 'And he has a large fortune. Permit me in turn to remind you of that.'
> 'Oh, I am perfectly aware of it,' said Eugenia. 'That's a great item in
> his favour. I am terribly candid.' And she left her place and came nearer
> her brother, looking at him hard. He was turning over several things; she
> was wondering in what manner he really understood her.
> There were several ways of understanding her: there was what she said,
> and there was what she meant, and there was something, between the two,
> that was neither. It is probable that, in the last analysis, what she meant
> was that Felix should spare her the necessity of stating the case more
> exactly and should hold himself commissioned to assist her by all honour-
> able means to marry the best fellow in the world. But in all this it was never
> discovered what Felix understood.[1]

There is little or nothing directly physical in this passage: it is
analytic, even abstract. But the movements of it are quite intricate,
in that limited scope, and its different directions − its subtle indirections − combine to create a type of narrative signification not
only of great technical originality in its period but one that is adum-
brating, after all, some of that unease about communication, about
language, about the depths of personality and relationships, that is
to become the expressive focus of James's later and more modern
writings.

The dialogue, at the outset of the passage, creates its own quizzical echoes. Beneath her words, we know the Baroness has no real
justification for saying Acton is 'immensely in love' with her, and
is putting on a brave face to her brother. Felix's reference to
Acton's 'large fortune' reverberates with a snide knowingness. And
Eugenia at once brings the knowingness, the implication in Felix's
remark, into the open, then appends to it her claim to be 'terribly
candid' − which even in these few lines she has obviously failed to

be. As these nuances in the dialogue are perceived, they take on an almost visual quality: they seem to be tabulated on the page, little lines and boxes drawn beneath the plain running of the speech. The one actual physical movement then confirms this graphic presence, and focuses our own stare on the growing significance of the encounter: 'she left her place and came nearer her brother, looking at him hard'. But the narration does not allow us to rest in this one point of view – Eugenia's, as she stares – but at once, very sharply, becomes omniscient and detached: 'He was turning over . . . she was wondering . . .' Having 'seen through' the dialogue, having seen Eugenia move then stare, having looked at the mental posture of each character, we are now offered, in a very different analytic mode, three stances. They are almost chalked up on a blackboard: three lines, one above the other. 'What she said', we have already grasped. 'What she meant', though only probably, the narrator goes on to tell us in the next sentence. But the third way of understanding – 'something between the two' – is not filled in for us. It is left casually blank, like a guiding passage of untouched white paper in a watercolour sketch. What is this third position for understanding, somewhere halfway between Eugenia's words and her meaning, and where does the hint of it lead us? And as if to confirm the presence of (at this point) unarticulated complexity, of free space in narration, and the inadequacy even of so-called omniscient analysis, we are told in the last sentence, in effect, that we cannot be told what Felix's thinking was, since – and there is a typical authorial jokeyness in this – 'it was never discovered'. That trace of whimsy, lightly drawing attention to the make-believe of the whole affair, is the last quite new direction and dimension of the little passage; and yet it manages not to detract from the seriousness of represented feeling – Eugenia indirectly asking for help, Felix being positive but reserved and even evasive – that dominates the exchange.

Not only can the overall artfulness of expression in *The Europeans*, of which this is an example, be figured as a single large gesture, uttering an inward life through concise outward action, its detailed articulation also frequently takes the form of specific gestures, sometimes quite balletic in their wordlessness and their complementariness to dialogue.[2] One of the commonest of these has the effect of emphasizing the significance of a pause in conver-

21

sation. For example, when Charlotte approaches Gertrude in the garden on a Sunday morning in May:

> 'Gertrude,' she said, 'are you very sure you had better not go to church?'
> Gertrude looked at her a moment, plucked a small sprig from a lilac-bush, smelled it and threw it away. 'I am not very sure of anything!' she
> answered.   (p. 14)

Gertrude's pause clearly outlines the inner reservations that separate her from the normal flow of Wentworth life, and the gesture of plucking the lilac, smelling it, and throwing it away is an assertion – and a sensuous one at that – of her independence. Then when Acton has taken Eugenia out driving in the country, and she tells him about her morganatic marriage which she can annul simply by sending the Prince a document (a controlling hypothetic event that keeps appearing), we have this:

> 'Well,' he reflected, audibly, 'I should like to see you send his Serene Highness – somewhere!'
> Madame Münster stooped and plucked a daisy from the grass. 'And not sign my renunciation?'
> 'Well, I don't know – I don't know,' said Acton.   (p. 72)

The pause in this case expresses, for both Eugenia and Acton, her possible sexual availability to him. And the stooping to pick a daisy is both self-display (Eugenia knows well how to manage a graceful and revealing bending of the body) and a coyly mocking irony (the daisy being by tradition the simplest and most unassuming of flowers).

Again, when Felix takes Gertrude boating on the Wentworths' pond, a simple gesture – that of stepping into a boat – becomes an implicit statement of a woman's independent decision to accept a man's love. Felix, with his extravagant irony, pretends to see advantages for him in the possibility of Gertrude being engaged to Mr Brand:

> 'I could tell you how much I admire you, without seeming to pretend to that which I have no right to pretend to. I should make violent love to you,' he added, laughing, 'if I thought you were so placed as not to be offended by it.'
> 'You mean if I were engaged to another man? That is strange reasoning!' Gertrude exclaimed.
> 'In that case you would not take me seriously.'

'I take every one seriously!' said Gertrude. And without his help she stepped lightly into the boat.

Felix took up the oars and sent it forward. (p. 88)

When Gertrude says 'I take every one seriously' she firmly disposes of Felix's levity and his *doubles entendres*, and is implicitly conferring on his half-concealed declaration a serious and overt status. Then by deliberately stepping into the boat that he stands holding for her, and submitting to the action of the oarsman, she appears to make a gesture of accepting that declaration. And the delicacy of this mute exchange takes place underneath their continuing badinage, their planning to marry off Charlotte and Mr Brand, and, not least, the surrounding sense of physical movement, the 'pink and yellow gleams in the water', and the quick, long strokes of Felix's urgent oars.

Even when the space-opening gesture is of the briefest and slightest kind, the reader can be drawn into it imaginatively, so that it fills out with suggestiveness. For example, when Felix first tells Gertrude about his sister's peculiar marriage arrangements Gertrude's cry, 'She must be very unhappy!' is spontaneous, innocent, and a very inadequate account of the worldly Eugenia's feelings – all of which is faintly hinted at in Felix's delicate response of physical self-restraint:

Her visitor looked at her, smiling; he raised his hand to the back of his head and held it there a moment. 'So she says,' he answered. (p. 24)

The gesture – the dramatized pause – of Felix putting his hand to the back of his head cannot be said directly to 'signify' his reservations. But it does seem to suggest, by indirection, that whole dimension of self-consciousness, private caution, and partial withholding that exists like a necessary echo beneath the words of all conversation.

Similarly, in the grand theatrical scene where Felix asks Mr Wentworth for Gertrude's hand, he is obliged to touch his head once again:

'I leave [Gertrude's future], in the last resort, to a greater wisdom than ours,' said the old man.

Felix rubbed his forehead gently. 'But *en attendant* the last resort, your father lacks confidence,' he said to Gertrude. (p. 146)

Here, in the briefest of self-steadying gestures, is something of the tension of a whole scene: Felix straining to call on his reserves of tact and confidence to cope with Mr Wentworth's dignified opposition, and to control his own perhaps slightly hysterical inclination to laugh at this baffling and very foreign invocation of the Deity in such a matter – which he then does manage to deal with by private elliptical humour, sidestepping Mr Wentworth's God as 'the last resort', and from behind a protective French phrase. So many of the scene's currents and tremors – when the beset Felix has already had to talk in so many directions at once that Mr Wentworth and Charlotte have 'looked at him as if they were watching a greyhound doubling' (p. 145) – can be identified within and around this one instant, shaped by Felix rubbing his forehead.

And lastly, in the scene where Felix invites Mr Brand into his studio and suggests that Charlotte is in love with him, an equally brief hesitation serves to bring to a new focus the confused feelings and motives of the encounter, and to leave us, as so often, with a sense of openness and unresolved possibility:

> Mr. Brand eyed his strange informant askance again; but he said nothing. At last he turned away, as if to take leave. He seemed bewildered, however; for instead of going to the door he moved toward the opposite corner of the room. Felix stood and watched him for a moment – almost groping about in the dusk; then he led him to the door, with a tender, almost fraternal movement. (p. 127)

In that moment when Felix watches Mr Brand blunder in the darkness there is a sudden reminder of the manipulative quality of Felix's moustachio'd, gimlet-eyed brilliance; and a gap is created in which, for once, some sympathy for the solemnly fumbling Mr Brand can flow, only at once to be complicated by the 'tender, almost fraternal movement' by which Felix quickly asserts himself again. That gesture is no doubt as much patronizing as fraternal, but the point is that we are left unsure what to make either of such benignly efficient manipulation or such insidiously superior tenderness. The scene has been splendidly visual and precise, filled with the crimson glow of the sunset, the gleam of Felix's 'surprising' sketches and paintings, and the sound of the two men's voices intently crossing then awkwardly veering away from one another. And the little pocket of narrative surprise and hesitation created at the end adds a different but corroborative effect of space and richness.

To talk of the inwardness of *The Europeans*, as enforced by pauses and gesturing, is, however, only half the story. What is most characteristic of this novel is the way it makes the reader partake of its outwardness − its mannered surfaces of language and deployment, and the evoked surfaces of its characters' lives and styles − at the very same time as being drawn into that other narrative dimension of silent implication, contrary resonance, and dubiety. Such basic interpretative questions as whether Eugenia is more a predatory adventuress than a creative and life-enhancing actress, or whether Felix is to be judged superficial and inadequate or as the perfect compromise between the Wentworth and the European attitudes, or whether Acton is simply a sexual prig and provincial moral coward or a very understandably and naturally hesitant man faced with far too daunting a gamble − all these issues are articulated and fully subtilized only by the reader being drawn into the full choreography and complex enactment, both outward and inward, of the narration.[3] That enactment is an affair in which speed, lightness of touch, and a perpetual surface brio of verbal humour and coloration are in continual interplay with other levels of expressiveness. For one thing, there is a strongly linear quality to the plotting: an aspect of the book's dynamic that depends, archetypally, on our impulses of curiosity and desire.[4] We are curious to know from the very first chapter what will happen when such incongruously worldly figures as Eugenia and Felix encounter their puritan cousins; we are curious as to whether Eugenia will get what she seems to want; whether Acton's doubts and nervousness will prevail over his attraction; whether Gertrude − the New England princess locked in the tower − will escape from her family and from Mr Brand's black gloves; whether all will end in explosion, embarrassment, and recrimination, or in laughter and orange-blossom. Eugenia and Felix are adventurers, on a journey, and we are eager to see the outcome of that journey. As readers we watch our own eagerness and curiosity, as well as the devices by which they are aroused and satisfied. We watch these feelings projected into the form and movement of the narration, and see them objectified, to our own view, in the shape of provocative curtain-like endings: 'Felix burst out laughing, and Mr. Brand stood staring, while the others, who had passed into the house, appeared behind him in the open doorway' (p. 24); and in freshly energizing, tantalizing beginnings: 'The first Sunday that followed Robert Acton's return from Newport witnessed a change in the brilliant weather that had long prevailed' (p. 115). Partly by ancient literary (and folk-tale) convention, partly by all the narrative tricks-of-the-trade being worked by James, we are made to desire that the immured Gertrude should cast off Brand and escape with Felix (the 'Happy' one who is also Young). And we are made to desire, by an amalgam of cultural convention and natural instinct, that restraint (as in the Wentworths) will be challenged and leavened by the bold and the aesthetic (as in Eugenia and Felix), but that it will also uphold itself and expose the limitations of what challenges it. As for the relationships between Eugenia and Acton, or Felix and Mr Wentworth, the reader's actual desire probably goes no further than for a continuation of the pathos and comic percussiveness that the very different encounters between them provide — and this, too, is the kind of desire that puts a premium on forward movement of action, progressive time, and the prolongation and anticipation of pleasure.

Just as this forward-moving linearity proves compatible with the other direction of the narrative — its gestural pausing, its sudden brief drops into stiller areas of irresolution or contrapuntal ambiguity — so, too, the book's strong pictorial quality seems to act in a double way. The descriptions of house and decor — the Wentworth house, with its 'large, clear-coloured rooms, with white wainscots' (p. 18), its white classic exterior, its uncurtained openness to wind and light; the Europeanized boudoir-clutter of Eugenia's cottage; the Acton house with its glimmering chinoiseries and porcelains and the large oriental rug in the hall, where the sunlight falls richly yellow on the white walls — these descriptions are vividly mimetic in effect, create the dimension of 'real' objects and places among which the characters move, and offer clearly referential suggestions about the differing nature of the inhabitants (or their visitors). There is a continual sense of weather in the book, of sunsets ostentatiously grand, a 'strange white light', a 'far-away blue sky', of breezes and sudden snowfalls democratically bestowed upon everyone, of the sudden first autumn chill that suggests departure. We are given stony fields with apple trees and grass, simple gardens with roses and geraniums, execrable roads to stumble along, enormous vistas of woods, rivers, hill-tops, and very

American horizons. Yet this illusive pictorialism is such that its mimetic effect is almost always accompanied by something that seems to be its opposite. The reader's attention is continually being drawn to the very painterliness of these devices – to their aesthetic nature *as* devices – and to a descriptive technique that can also be seen self-consciously reducing its characters and their places to a pleasing arrangement that is therefore *unreal*, reduced in scale, charmingly well made – in fact like the 'Nuremberg toy' that Felix chooses as his analogy for the Wentworth house. The 'painting' of the narrative, that is, is so pointed, so precisely chosen, and imbued with such pervasive and such 'placing' humour that it gives a distinct tone of the fairy-tale, the pastoral, and the artistically mannered ('How shall I describe it? It's primitive; it's patriarchal; it's the *ton* of the golden age', says Felix) to a presentation that also, *per contra*, achieves the cinematic, the embodied, the naturalistically visualizable. That the 'events' have a clearly announced aesthetic, as well as a referential, dimension is exemplified in the scene where Felix takes Gertrude boating:

Felix passed through the garden toward the house and toward a postern gate which opened upon a path leading across the fields, beside a little wood, to the lake. He stopped and looked up at the house; his eyes rested more particularly upon a certain open window, on the shady side. Presently Gertrude appeared there, looking out into the summer light. He took off his hat to her and bade her good-day; he remarked that he was going to row across the pond, and begged that she would do him the honour to accompany him. She looked at him a moment; then, without saying anything, she turned away. But she soon reappeared, below, in one of those quaint and charming Leghorn hats, tied with white satin bows, that were worn at that period; she also carried a green parasol. She went with him to the edge of the lake, where a couple of boats were always moored; they got into one of them, and Felix with gentle strokes propelled it to the opposite shore. The day was the perfection of summer weather; the little lake was the colour of sunshine; the plash of the oars was the only sound, and they found themselves listening to it. They disembarked, and, by a winding path, ascended the pine-crested mound which overloooked the water, whose white expanse glittered between the trees. The place was delightfully cool and had the added charm that – in the softly sounding pine-boughs – you seemed to hear the coolness as well as feel it. Felix and Gertrude sat down on the rust-coloured carpet of pine-needles and talked of many things.   (p. 84)

The appeal to the senses here is superlatively handled: a seduction of the sympathetic, and therefore mimetic, imagination. But so is the appeal to our distancing sense of art and artfulness: we do not only watch the scene, we watch the narration shaping the scene, patting it into place, dropping the perfect pigments in the perfect places, orchestrating the various sensory responses, and generally holding the whole in an enhancing and attention-concentrating frame. We begin by watching, from above, Felix's movement of approach and invitation; then we enter, more narrowly, into his vision of the one significant window where Gertrude (princess-like once again) will appear. When she appears it is not only with charm but with several distinctly individuating touches: the Leghorn hat (which we are at once made aware of historically, in terms of 'that period' — another distancing, 'framing' effect), the vivid colour spots of the white bow and the green parasol. White and green, two figures in a boat, they row across light itself, the colour of sunshine. Then sound succeeds sight: the 'plash of the oars' is now the focus, the focus by sound. And when they land on the mound, all the senses are drawn climactically together: the water glittering white between the pine trees, where it *feels* cool, and 'you seemed to *hear* the coolness as well as *feel* it' — with perhaps (as the subtlest emanation of what the description has been building towards) a covert appeal also to the accompanying sense of smell in the repeated reference to the pine-boughs and the pine-needles on which they sit and talk. Nothing else is needed. The paragraph is extraordinarily intimate: all the private feelings of Felix and Gertrude are contained, delicately and indirectly, within these outlines of other things. It is memorably vivid: a complex image that remains throughout the rest of our response to their little affair. But as well as being intimate and dramatic, it has also the publicity of a perfectly judged and ostentatiously controlled act of painting: an act of style, an act of narrating. And for all its genuine lightness of touch, this whole paragraph might seem to the contemplative–analytic reader to tremble just a little from the precarious balancing of its varying forces, a tremor which is deeply characteristic of Jamesian narration at its best, whether early or late, and gives the act of keen reading that James enforces a very particular edge of excitement.

The implied voice of the narrator is another of the crucial modes of control, another of the acts of style, in this book, and in itself perpetuates complexity and contrariety as well as acting as a single harmonizing medium. At times, the narrating medium is almost a transparent one: a direct recounting of facts, movements, visits, other people's voices. At times, as in the opening sentences of the novel, it is very much a narrator's voice, deducing generalizations, appealing directly to the listener, and, virtually for the sake of the fun, being deliberately pompous:

A narrow grave-yard in the heart of a bustling, indifferent city, seen from the windows of a gloomy-looking inn, is at no time an object of enlivening suggestion; and the spectacle is not at its best when the mouldy tombstones and funereal umbrage have received the ineffectual refreshment of a dull, moist snow-fall. If, while the air is thickened by this frosty drizzle, the calendar should happen to indicate that the blessed vernal season is already six weeks old, it will be admitted that no depressing influence is absent from the scene. (p. 1)

As the book progresses we begin to infer certain similarities between this particular narrating tone – ponderously if temporarily elaborate, theatrical, wittily self-displaying, and as wittily self-reserving – and the tone of Eugenia herself: a stylistic alliance (though not an identity) that is significant for our overall reading of the novel. For example, there is the 'style' of converse Eugenia adopts when she arrives *chez* Wentworth:

Charlotte was walking beside her; she took hold of her hand again, smiling always. 'And you, *cousine*, where did you get that enchanting complexion?' she went on; 'such lilies and roses?' The roses in poor Charlotte's countenance began speedily to predominate over the lilies, and she quickened her step and reached the portico. 'This is the country of complexions,' the Baroness continued, addressing herself to Mr. Wentworth. 'I am convinced they are more delicate. There are very good ones in England – in Holland; but they are very apt to be coarse. There is too much red.' (p. 31)

Such self-display appears frequently in the device – it can only be seen as a device, not as a lapse – of the self-revealing narrator; as in this:

Gertrude, however, had to struggle with a great accumulation of obstructions, both of the subjective, as the metaphysicians say, and of the objective, order; and indeed it is no small part of the purpose of this little history to set forth her struggle. (pp. 37–8)

Or, far more extravagantly, this:

29

As I have had the honour of intimating, she had come four thousand miles to seek her fortune; and it is not to be supposed that after this great effort she could neglect any apparent aid to advancement. It is my misfortune that in attempting to describe in a short compass the deportment of this remarkable woman I am obliged to express things rather brutally. I feel this to be the case, for instance, when I say that she had primarily detected such an aid to advancement in the person of Robert Acton, but that she had afterwards remembered that a prudent archer has always a second bow-string. (p. 97)

This familiar trick and mannerism works, as always, in a double way. It stops the flow of events and reminds us − just as the pictorial and theatrical 'framing' did − that this is all an aesthetic ploy, a game of words. But paradoxically, by distancing the narrator from the narrated-about − by suggesting that there *is* something larger than 'this little history', a 'real' original which the narrator has 'the honour' of talking to us about − the device also confers a strange kind of independent status and reality on those distant originals, a status which, in effect, reflects back favourably on the highly stylized art-work and word game that is thus seen to be reporting them, and not just inventing them. It is apparently the most unmimetic and anti-illusive of mannerisms, and one that James so often attacked in his criticism precisely on that ground. Yet − just as is to be the case when used later by Forster − one of its effects is to confer an indirect touch of existential independence, some illusive three-dimensionality, on the otherwise notably aesthetic objects of the fiction.[5]

The relations between the reader's varying levels of response to this book's narrative are therefore subtle and crucial in ways that are hardly to be found in earlier English fiction, not even in Jane Austen, who perhaps comes closest at times to anticipating the Jamesian mode of indirection. It is important to recognize, as we read, the ubiquity of a distinctive narrating presence, sometimes adopting purely decorative postures, frequently outlining and evaluating action or character by irony, comparison, or straightforward commentary, manipulating a flowing system of sentences (often surprisingly short in this novel, with clauses like single brush-strokes, separated by semi-colons), and all the time giving an infinitely reassuring sense − one of the most notable features in the reading experience of any James work − of supreme *savoir-faire*, tact, and a self-delighting disposition that is also specifically

friendly to the reader. Within this presence, which itself is varied
in its tones and operations, there also exists, as we have seen, the
sense of quasi-independent scenes, figures, motives, and utterances; and other senses too, those of the aesthetically pictorial and
theatrical, of the linear drives of plotting, and of the areas behind
gesture and behind style, filled by the significance of silence.
Through all these varying and interrelated modes *The Europeans*
pursues its concern with the relation between style and experience,
between the surface of manners and the inner resonances of private
desire or timidity or personal integrity. What is explored so
scrupulously and so provisionally in such terms – Eugenia's
dangerous but vital self-advertising, self-concealing, self-expanding
role-playing and sophistication; Gertrude's discovery that truth-to-
self can sometimes best be expressed in the form of social lying; Acton's mathematical eagerness to detect lying, and his distrust of the
'lying' that determines Eugenia's life-by-style; the slightly hardening cruelty that can (and perhaps must) lie in any self-liberation like
Gertrude's; the more dangerous cruelty by which an Acton, lover
of algebra, porcelain, and charming women, defends his half-
estimable scruples and his sexual timidity; the insufficiency yet
dignity and style of the Puritan, the insufficiency yet predatory
flair and stylishness of the Worldling; life as a stage, where to act
and to do anything worthwhile is necessarily to adopt a style and
create a falsity; manners as a mask and a betrayal, manners as
enhancement and imaginative expansion[6] – all of these issues for
debate and for ambiguous evaluation are explored more fully for
being acted out in the histrionic to-and-fro, the masks and manners
of the narrative's stylistic levels. It is with the details of the latter
that I have been explicitly concerned, rather than these larger
thematic matters. But the movement of Jamesian ideas has to be
followed, characteristically, along with – and neither subsequent
nor prior to – the movement of his narrative in its revealing textures and strategies. What that Jamesian narrative activity enacts
by style is what the reader's act of interpretation – the irrepres-
sible, unconcealable act of interpretation – may also spell
out in the more extrapolative, more moral terms of an author's
governing perceptions and themes. And these perceptions, which
arise in *The Europeans* and develop throughout James's *oeuvre*,
point also to what will activate the narrative and stylistic

31

complexities of the two novelists, Conrad and Forster, who followed him, in indirection and unease, to the brink: the perceptions that there is no secure judgement or word available to anyone concerning another person, in social or in private life, that there may indeed be no integral self, only an idea of the self plus a repertoire of roles and gestures; that life-style and language-style are necessary for survival and communication, for knowledge and for pleasure, but always contain reverberative pauses and echoes that call these things radically into question; that life itself betrays, just as the fitful will to act betrays; that people nevertheless go on, with difficulty, taking their chance; and that only in unsteady movement and dialectic, in the perpetual creating and challenging of relationships, can the mind try to make terms with the world, or the actor with the stage.

2. Stresses of *The Bostonians*

It is not just in its title that *The Bostonians* (1886) is a revealingly opposite case to *The Europeans*. The scale of things has utterly changed. The brief highlighted scene and significant gesture have been replaced by the extended encounter filled with debate-like dialogue and elaborate commentary; pointillism of descriptive method has been replaced by a Balzacian naturalism and by a patient, witty, and weighty exposition. But even though *The Bostonians* − like *The Princess Casamassima* and *The Tragic Muse*, also of this period − seems to flaunt its ideas on the outside, compared with the more restrained suggestiveness of the earlier novel, its narrative is still essentially a drama rather than a statement.[7] Much more powerfully than *The Europeans*, its large rhetoric of scene, language, feeling, and plot-movement is a response to the pressures and anxieties of a general insight into crisis and the threat of cultural and national breakdown, and the narrating of it is full of conflicting pressures and changes of mode that perfectly express that crisis of contending wills to power, of sexual conflict and perversity, of opposing forces of desire and manipulation, impassioned search, and deadening impediment.

Olive Chancellor, for example, for all the particularity and vividness of her portrayal, quickly points to a general idea, and is inextricably linked with a whole society of cant, eccentricity, and exploitation. Olive is Boston – or Bostonia, rather, its state of mind – and Bostonia is Olive Chancellor; with the rider that to a degree, though only a minor degree, she is its victim as well as its collaborator. Almost a formal parody of the typical 'fine central intelligence' of other James novels – like Isabel Archer, Hyacinth Robinson, and Maisie, like Fleda Vetch and Strether – the energies of Olive's consciousness and conscience, her testing of herself and the world at every turn, her baffled search always, in Jamesian fashion, for a higher, for the highest synthesis, have turned destructive, and self-destructive. In her desperate self-contradiction and fragmentation – her taste opposing her theories, instincts against principles, shyness against aggression, and, by implication, femininity against maleness – feelings in Olive have turned into, or almost into, abstraction, and sexual passion into soul-hunger. Alembicated by an over-refined, over-closeted culture, her passional self (and she believes urgently in the *concept* of passion) can be brought to a focus, fatally, only by a ruling Idea – and by the one young woman, Verena, who seems to offer embodiment and language for that Idea of freedom, but who also, perversely, thereby becomes her possession, to be exploited and smothered by Olive's intense emotionality, and fought over with her rival manipulators and power-seekers like Matthias Pardon and Mrs Burrage. The directness of the senses has been replaced by the distancing of the mind; the dream of a 'union of soul' is pursued by the exercise of a personal hegemony that can only destroy the dream and the relationship; and passion becomes twisted into the cold formulae of a disembodied idealism, a displaced sexuality, and a transcendent will to power. Somewhere behind the apparent Balzacian panorama of *The Bostonians*, James is deploying that recurrent nightmare of the nineteenth-century imagination: the conglomerate nightmare of the machine, dehumanized philanthropy, Hard Facts, and the drying-up or diversion of the personal sources of feeling. As well as *Hard Times* and *Bleak House*, it points to the example of John Stuart Mill, describing his rescue by music and by Wordsworth's poetry from the aridity of analysis – his Bentham-inspired obsession to be (like Olive) 'a reformer of the world'[8] – and to George Eliot's Wordsworthian critique of narrow doctrine, of 'notions' as against 'feelings', in *Adam Bede* and *Silas Marner*. And closer to James's own intellectual tradition, it is the Unpardonable Sin of Hawthorne's Ethan Brand: intellectual experiment, self-isolation, and the death of the heart.[9] James's vision in *The Bostonians* of the self-destructiveness of human action is distinctly Conradian – though without Conrad's ultimate bleakness – in its demonstration of how the highest idealism (like Kurtz's, like Gould's and Nostromo's, or even Jim's) in the name of an idea like freedom, expansion, or heroism, can quickly turn into its own travesty: self-aggrandizement, obsession, narcissistic self-delusion, and the constriction of others. Conrad's futilely declaiming anarchists and *émigrés*, living by ideas and gaseous words but battening off others all the time, could have lived and talked in this Boston as well as in the London of *The Secret Agent* or the Geneva of *Under Western Eyes*. Conrad, too, with a more devastating recognition of his own personal demon, knew the perils of retraction from the world of committed feeling, and the eroding delusiveness of a private utopianism – a Heyst's island of self-protection. And James's fear, part personal, part intellectual, at the etiolation of passion and the general breakdown of communication between the sexes, between human faculties, between the power-groups of a society, prefigures very clearly the anxieties of *Howards End*, with its picture, too, of a male–female rift, a Wilcox–Schlegel antipathy of values, that characterizes a society on the brink of war and dissolution. The dangers that face Boston as a culture are the same as those that threaten Olive personally, for all that she despises the people and the apparatus of her cause: the dangers of a life in which mere words and notions – the American lecture, the American hotel lobby, the newspaper, the self-exposure of speechifying in the gas-lit vastness of the Boston Music Hall – have become as deadly to the self (especially to the hitherto over-closeted self) as is pure abstraction and dogma to the humane imagination. Matthias Pardon the journalist, strangely effeminate, unnaturally white-haired, eager to break the integrity of the private self and convert it – to 'manage' it – into the abstracted pabulum of newspaper clichés and into money, together with Selah Tarrant, the venal and betraying father, charlatan mesmerist and faith-healer, who scavenges on the fringe of any radical cause, who worships the newspaper interview, and has a smile 'as noiseless as a patent hinge' – these two men are the nodding, mechanical heads of James's Coketown, James's Geneva, and Olive's Bostonia.[10]

Basil Ransom, too, casts the shadow of his century and his culture − through explicit narrative commentary, association, and the pervasive use of ironic counterpart and juxtaposition. Much more clearly than Hyacinth Robinson he is that archetypal nineteenth-century hero whom Lionel Trilling identified, in his essay on *The Princess Casamassima*, as the avatar of Napoleon, the ambitious young man from the provinces.[11] Ransom is a would-be conqueror from Mississippi − perhaps the Corsica of America − and he has an almost unshakeable will that gives something of its own direction and representative energy to a whole narrative concerning wills in conflict. Olive, for example, has a notable will, though it is uneven in its concentration. Verena, by contrast − and this is her *donnée* and fate − has no will whatsoever: she is pliant, generous, sensuously aware, but in need of, one might say in unconscious search of, a will. The traditional will to power is very evident in Mrs Burrage, genteel matriarch and schemer; the sexually predatory will in Mrs Luna; the etiolated, emasculated, but still active will in Matthias Pardon, the publicizing child of his age. Even more emasculated, the will droops in Selah Tarrant, the pariah, and in Henry Burrage, the likeable man of taste and charm, but with far less masculine will than his own mother. Ransom has the will to oppose, to seize what he wants, and to make good − and Bostonia and New York are evoked by the narration as tangible obstacles to his nineteenth-century will. He is the penniless patrician who must carve his place in the foreign city, and find a way of earning a living. The weight of a shapeless, enormous, and inhospitable New York opposes him − and we feel the significant weight of it in the long description of a sordid and congested Second Avenue that opens chapter 21, where the narrative first moves from Boston to New York. We even feel the burden of impediment in another way when he seeks to enter the fashionable world of Mrs Burrage's Wednesday Club, in pursuit (as always) of Verena:

. . . people behind him pressed him forward. He yielded to the impulsion, and found himself in a great saloon, amid lights and flowers, where the company was dense, and there were more twinkling, smiling ladies, with uncovered bosoms. It was certainly the fashionable world, for there was no one there whom he had ever seen before. The walls of the room were covered with pictures − the very ceiling was painted and framed. The people pushed each other a little, edged about, advanced and retreated, looking at each other with differing faces — sometimes blandly, unperceivingly, sometimes with a harshness of contemplation, a kind of cruelty, Ransom thought; sometimes with sudden nods and grimaces, inarticulate murmurs, followed by a quick reaction, a sort of gloom. He was now absolutely certain that he was in the best society.[12]

The individual instance of Ransom, or, in its first extension, the representative role of Ransom as sexual pursuer and sexual antagonist, is further enlarged by the fact that we are never allowed to forget he is a postwar refugee from a failed and crushed society, and in consequence has 'a deep aversion to the ineffectual'. He must succeed, he must make a living. The urgency of his financial plight, added to his memory of the recent 'immense national fiasco' of the Civil War that hangs over the whole book as an effective image of futility and loss, is kept before us as a challenge to his pride and to his will. His opposition to the world of Olive Chancellor is not all personal, sceptically conservative, and philosophical, with his belief that a woman can best fulfil herself in private not in public life: his opposition is also economic. And his sexual will to win Verena is given a fine edge of bitterness by his perpetual sense of exclusion from the comfortable world of Charles Street and of Mrs Burrage's fine rooms. James pictures New York so as to remind us — as his contemporary, Howells, was to do very effectively in *A Hazard of New Fortunes* in 1890 — that American society is a rough sea in which the non-swimmer can only drown. Ransom must grasp, he must rise, he must be militant; for behind him is a broken South, and all around him is a formless, seething New York where, as a warning to him, 'groups of the unemployed, the children of disappointment from beyond the seas, propped themselves against the low, sunny wall of the Park'.

The baffled dynamism which Ransom exemplifies as an individual and as a representative character — and which is partly expressed, as we shall see, in the alternating surge and fall of the narrative's unfolding — is a fine complex, then, of the typical Jamesian urge personally to know and to grasp strongly, to arrive at what Ransom believes to be true integrity to self as opposed to the vaporous self-delusions of the reformers, a strongly implied personal sexuality, economic and family motives, and his whole intellectual and moral drive. But disappointingly — it is a peculiar lapse for such a connoisseur of multiple aspects as James — this complexity is not then mirrored in a complex ambiguity of attitude to such a protagonist.

For all his qualifying ironies against Ransom, James loses the opportunity here for the fullest deployment of his usual indirection and openness, and, instead, can be felt basically to endorse Ransom's position. The little sardonic volte-face of the novel's last words is somehow not quite adequate:

'Ah, now I am glad!' said Verena, when they reached the street. But though she was glad, he presently discovered that, beneath her hood, she was in tears. It is to be feared that with the union, so far from brilliant, into which she was about to enter, these were not the last she was destined to shed. (p. 433)

Marriage to Ransom may indeed bring some tears; but the gesture seems only a casual one, almost a negligent or merely habitual irony on James's part, compared, say, with the subtler and far more reverberative doublenesses that mark the endings of *Howards End* and *A Passage to India*. James for once oversimplifies, tends towards the categorical rather than the dramatic method, by not allowing a stronger element of validity to the feminists' case (the affectionate portrayal of Miss Birdseye, made possible by her antiquity and fragility, is the very opposite of an intellectual endorsement); and also by not fully facing up to the fact that Ransom's desire for Verena is potentially as restrictive and possessive as Olive's, and that Ransom's Carlylean views, especially when in the end he goes in for theorizing and (like Matthais Pardon!) for publishing, are as abstract and at least as open to cant as those of the reformers.[13]

On the other hand, the complaint sometimes voiced against Verena — that she is too much of a *tabula rasa*, merely charm, red hair, and a good speaking voice, for us to believe there should be such a battle, such a second civil war, to win her[14] — is easier to answer and to answer precisely in terms of those large-scale pressures of fictional debate and portrayed cultural crisis that have been seen to activate so much of this narrative. All the way through, Verena is seen and realized through the desires and the needs of others: the conflicting desires of Ransom, Olive, the Tarrant parents, Matthias Pardon, Mrs Burrage and her son, and the desires of her sympathizers and her public who make possible her brief national éclat. In such a formless, centreless, jostling society, urgent for publicity and novelty, driven by futilities of different kinds and dominated by the memory of war and the hope of

37

a thousand different utopias, Verena represents what others feel they lack. She is their personal or their public holy grail, a beautiful empty vessel, vaguely religious, vaguely supernatural, that will give shape and meaning to their own dreams and restlessness. She is in danger of becoming a provincial Madame Blavatsky, not a Mrs Pankhurst. She has, as we are frequently told, a 'gift', a 'talent', and an impersonal 'power'. She has words, and is their Word. And this is what they all search and contend for, this society of comically lost souls, fearful of their own inner hollowness and twisted by the displacement of their personal energies into a rabble of freaks and charlatans, buyers and sellers, media-men and mediums. They are as grotesque and American in their way as the Hollywood menagerie in Nathanael West's *Day of the Locust*: mesmerists, vegetarians, faith-healers, spiritualists, primitive communists, suffragettes, prohibitionists, old Abolitionists, revivalists, inspirationists. It is the whole traditional ragged army of America's neurotics – though still genteel, still Bostonian – seeking to be born again through the word, and to hear Verena's golden voice, at the book's climax, fill the emptiness of their lives and the significantly Roman and abstract void of their own – their very own – Boston Music Hall. But what she offers to the void – it is the most Jamesian, the most modern and Conradian and Forsterian of all ironies – is itself empty: the reverberation of mere words, which is the most telling of a novelist's nightmares, like the hollow philanthropic eloquence of a Kurtz or an Ivan Ivanovitch, like the engulfing 'ou-boum' of an Indian cave.

As a narration, *The Bostonians* articulates all these stresses and dilemmas through local variations of rhythm, scene, texture, narratorial stance, and modes of language that are in themselves more fluid and less categorical than the terms of a cultural debate. For one thing, this is a novel with a very pronounced and characterizing tempo. For much of its extent it moves with great slowness – which, however, only occasionally verges on sluggishness, as just before the much-needed switch of scene from Boston to New York in chapter 21. This slowness, perfectly characteristic of the other middle-period and of some of the later-period novels, worried James himself, who, in a typically inhibited letter to brother William, attributes it to 'knowing terribly little about the kind of life I had attempted to describe . . . I should have been much more rapid, and had a lighter hand, with a subject concerned with people and things of a nature never near to my experience'.[15] But even without its many alleviations and contrasts of tempo, which I shall turn to shortly, this very slowness has a function, an indirect communicativeness of its own that belongs to the *donnée* of the subject itself, and is a reflex of the creative act that renders it. If James had known his Bostonians better in life, we might have known them worse, and certainly differently, in his fiction. The slightly exasperated, overladen voluminousness of his descriptions achieves a suggestiveness like that of Conrad in *The Secret Agent* and *Under Western Eyes*, where there is a similar heaviness, a continual note of irritation and even of reluctance, a repetitiousness that expresses simultaneously a lack of full self-confidence about such subject matter and an overwhelmed fascination with it. The effect in both writers − there is nothing like it in Forster − can be hypnotic, claustrophobic, and totally relevant to the subject matter. Conrad, of course, though sardonic enough, lacks the leavening effect of James's wit: a pervasive activity of mind and language that is enough in itself virtually to redeem the tempo and certainly to change the character of a narration. Nevertheless, rather like Conrad, one can detect James in this book labouring creatively against an obstacle: a mass of rebarbative and resistant material; an oppressive panorama of human self-delusion and falsity that can only be expressed, understood, judged, and brought fully into presence by an involving narrative movement that is itself − like the movement of the narrator's mind − deliberate, heavy-footed, and quivering with wittily controlled distaste.[16] The very weight of a perverse Boston and New York can be felt in the resultant narrative tension, just as the archetypal weight, 'the heavy and the weary weight', of the nineteenth-century metropolis is made by style and by allusion to loom over the fragile sensibilities of Hyacinth Robinson in *The Princess Casamassima* (as over the less sensitive perambulations of Verloc or the Assistant Commissioner in *The Secret Agent*). The tension is expressed in the slightly malevolent over-extension, and in the almost obsessively minute details of description, in the picture of Ransom's surroundings at the beginning of chapter 21. This is often cited as an example of James at his most objective and Balzacian; but there is something too nervously uneasy and variable about its tones throughout (for example, in the faintly discordant sophistication of the concluding ironic phrase):

Basil Ransom lived in New York, rather far to the eastward, and in the upper reaches of the town; he occupied two small shabby rooms in a somewhat decayed mansion which stood next to the corner of the Second Avenue. The corner itself was formed by a considerable grocer's shop, the near neighbourhood of which was fatal to any pretensions Ransom and his fellow-lodgers might have had in regard to gentility of situation. The house had a red, rusty face, and faded green shutters, of which the slats were limp and at variance with each other. In one of the lower windows were suspended a fly-blown card, with the words 'Table Board' affixed in letters cut (not very neatly) out of coloured paper, of graduated tints, and surrounded with a small band of stamped gilt. The two sides of the shop were protected by an immense pent-house shed, which projected over a greasy pavement and was supported by wooden posts fixed in the curbstone. Beneath it, on the dislocated flags, barrels and baskets were freely and picturesquely grouped; an open cellarway yawned beneath the feet of those who might pause to gaze too fondly on the savoury wares displayed in the window; a strong odour of smoked fish, combined with a fragrance of molasses, hung about the spot; the pavement, toward the gutters, was fringed with dirty panniers, heaped with potatoes, carrots, and onions; and a smart, bright waggon, with the horse detached from the shafts, drawn up on the edge of the abominable road (it contained holes and ruts a foot deep, and immemorial accumulations of stagnant mud) imparted an idle, rural, pastoral air to a scene otherwise perhaps expressive of a rank civilization. (p. 195)

And as a clearer instance of these slight excesses and awkwardnesses — evoking the scene but suggesting the distortions of a half-understood subjectivity — we find in the very same huge paragraph the surprisingly Gothic image of the Elevated Railway. It is Dickensian in its way, but it is also like some of Conrad's peculiarly unprepared grotesqueries of description and incident (or, by inversion, Forster's occasional telltale outbursts of obliquely compensatory lyricism). The effect is not quite the mere lightness of fantasy intended but also one of accumulating menace and alienation:

These [houses] were also painted red, and the bricks were accentuated by a white line; they were garnished, on the first floor, with balconies covered with small tin roofs, striped in different colours, and with an elaborate iron latticework, which gave them a repressive, cage-like appearance, and caused them slightly to resemble the little boxes for peeping unseen into the street, which are a feature of oriental towns. Such posts of observation commanded a view

40

of the grocery on the corner, of the relaxed and disjointed roadway, enlivened at the curbstone with an occasional ash-barrel or with gas-lamps drooping from the perpendicular, and westward, at the end of the truncated vista, of the fantastic skeleton of the Elevated Railway, overhanging the transverse longitudinal street, which it darkened and smothered with the immeasurable spinal column and myriad clutching paws of an antediluvian monster. (p. 196)

Even less extravagant exercises in description have something of the same nagging, fixated quality, with a self-relieving tendency towards the sudden grotesque, accompanied by a lack of economy – as in this account of Mrs Tarrant receiving Olive's visit to her house in Cambridge, where the details are a little too insistent, and there is at least one sentence too many:

Mrs. Tarrant, with her soft corpulence, looked to her guest very bleached and tumid; her complexion had a kind of withered glaze; her hair, very scanty, was drawn off her forehead *à la Chinoise*; she had no eyebrows, and her eyes seemed to stare, like those of a figure of wax. When she talked and wished to insist, and she was always insisting, she puckered and distorted her face, with effort to express the inexpressible, which turned out, after all, to be nothing. She had a kind of doleful elegance, tried to be confidential, lowered her voice and looked as if she wished to establish a secret understanding, in order to ask her visitor if she would venture on an apple-fritter. She wore a flowing mantle, which resembled her husband's waterproof – a garment which, when she turned to her daughter or talked about her, might have passed for the robe of a sort of priestess of maternity. (pp. 129–30)

These are the excesses of detail that add up to the slowness of general movement – but they also gradually accumulate an expressive load of feeling which parallels, and at times passes into, the feelings of oppression, resentment, and frustration that activate the protagonists, Olive and Ransom. The reader becomes aware of a particular effect in *The Bostonians* that arises from the occasional resemblance between Olive's desire for expansion, reformation, and 'a union of soul', Ransom's struggle to understand and to break open a social and personal situation that opposes him, seems foreign, perverse, and diseased to him, and James's struggle, as creative consciousness, to reveal an inner truth and to impose form on his swelling and recalcitrant material. Each of them – character and creator – seeks to possess and liberate something central, to penetrate a resistant mass of social and psychological experience: 'penetrate' being that significantly recurrent verb in James's Prefaces to describe his own struggle for artistic conception and shaping. And here we have the characteristic energy of *The Bostonians*: a pressure that comes from the encounter between a searching force and a threatening obstacle, and that seems to echo some very intimate pulse of the book's creative conception. The rhythms in the narration are of collision and repulsion, a slowly prowling circling (so typical of James), interrupted here and there by a scene of delusive but powerful idyll; then a sudden aggressive pursuit and entry, an outburst, a peroration; a strangely piercing laugh, a quick shedding of tears. These rhythms in their extension are more like *The Golden Bowl* than either *The Europeans*, which does not work at all by alternation or by massiveness, or *What Maisie Knew*, where the rhythms of change are far quicker and stagier, more expressively irregular; and are far more like the brooding circuitousness of Conrad in *Nostromo* or the first half of *Lord Jim* than anything in Forster's nimbler and more linear plotting. They are how this book confronts and projects the complex dilemma that it has also analysed in the other language of commentary and analysis. The oppressive pyramid-building of its narrative disquisitions and summaries, which can convey as well as elucidate the sense of stalemate that so enrages Ransom, collapses on occasion into the vividness of physical pursuit and challenge, as the visual succeeds the discursive, or as Ransom finds his own clear, urgent voice in Central Park, or as he hunts angrily for the hidden Verena through the thickets of Bostonia near the end. And the mounting effect of social concussion and of intellectual and temperamental opposition – again, a refought Civil War – produces a tension of feeling that is suddenly released, and made understandable, by contrasted scenes of elegiac peace or of tranquil intimacy, such as the momentary 'truce' in Henry Burrage's rooms in Cambridge, where firelight shines on precious objects while Burrage plays a little Schubert, a little Mendelssohn ('harmony ruled the scene; human life ceased to be a battle' – p. 166). *The Bostonians* is *about* the contrasted directions of human feelings: its perversities, its damming-up, its urgency, its private and its national crises. And the book expresses much of that drama of ideas through its own narrative dynamic of pressure, resistance, and release – 'proving' the play of ideas upon the pulse of the reader's response.

All this becomes clearer and stronger after the already-mentioned change of scene to New York in chapter 21. Up to that point, the movement of the narrative has been strongly centripetal and enclosing, with Verena at its centre – certainly as a prize and a focus of contention, if not as a centre of analytic interest or elaboration. The terms and the feelings of antipathy between the two unlikely cousins, Olive and Ransom, have been starkly established; Henry Burrage and Matthias Pardon have briefly joined the besieging suitors around Verena; and Ransom has been forced to retire from the fray, leaving the narrative to concentrate on the picture of Olive subtly and passionately weaving her 'fine web of authority', her 'suit of golden mail', around the ductile, bright-eyed figure of Verena. The suffocating intimacy and pressure of their life together, from the moment Olive masterfully wraps her cloak around the girl in the emblematic cold night of Bostonia outside the Tarrants' home ('a sparkling wintry vault, where the stars were like a myriad points of ice. The air was silent and sharp, and the vague snow looked cruel' – p. 147) is expressed in details and images of an overwhelming, obsessive privacy: their turning domestically inwards away from the squalid winter scene of the city to the concentrating firelight where they study together, their urgent talk, here in a narrow but comfortable room (with its 'glittering tea-tray'), of an endured tyranny, an ecstatically shared martyrdom:

. . . [Olive] had made up her mind that it was women, in the end, who had paid for everything. In the last resort the whole burden of the human lot came upon them; it pressed upon them far more than on the others, the intolerable load of fate. It was they who sat cramped and chained to receive it; it was they who had done all the waiting and taken all the wounds. The sacrifices, the blood, the tears, the terrors were theirs.(p. 191)

The sudden switch to a new spaciousness – 'Basil Ransom lived in New York, rather far to the eastward, and in the upper reaches of the town' – is at first a welcome and diametric change in direction and expectation, away from the 'cramped and chained'. But it becomes clear before very long that what we have now is also a study in stress, not just the stress of an unyielding New York upon a struggling and alien lawyer but sexual stresses, too, particularly those as powerfully exerted on Ransom by the widowed Mrs Luna. The constricting, moulding pressures exerted by Olive on Verena in their lamplit Boston parlour are now transposed, by an elegant irony, to the tempting comforts and the warmly expectant sympathy deployed against Ransom's susceptibilities and depression by Olive's sister in her 'little back drawing-room'. At times it becomes a parody of Boston intimacies, Boston tea-trays, Boston stresses:

[Ransom] seemed to see himself, to feel himself, in that very chair, in the evenings of the future, reading some indispensable book in the still lamp-light – Mrs. Luna knew where to get such pretty mellowing shades . . . Mrs. Luna said, with her sociable manner, 'There is nothing I like so much, of a winter's night, as a cosy *tête-à-tête* by the fire. It's quite like Darby and Joan; what a pity the kettle has ceased singing!'   (p. 206)

The power of the temptation to succumb is expressed in Ransom's hasty departure (as in *The Europeans*, this is a narrative syncopated by pointed exits and arrivals) and in his abrupt foray to Boston, there to try for the first time to break out of his own unproductive stasis by penetrating the magic circle that protects and hides Verena from him. And there, in one of the book's significant motifs, we find him, not for the first or the last time, wandering on the streets (as restless as a novelist!), seeking information, quizzing the numbers of houses and the colour of approaching street-cars – opposed by the felt will, hanging formidably in the air, of the unvisited Olive, and (for a little time only, and very charmingly) by the soft, anxious vagueness of Miss Birdseye, who holds the key to his denouement, the 'secret' of Verena's address.

Ransom's half-surreptitious visit to Verena in Cambridge brings the first moment of intimacy between them – the moment, half-way through the book, where the solid wall of Bostonian resistance (reinforced by the pressures of New York and of Mrs Luna) first begins to yield to Ransom's independent persistence, his journeying, his politely sceptical, insistent questioning, which creates a trajectory for the whole narrative.[17] And the first yielding occurs, exactly as will happen in the more prolonged wooing at Marmion, within a paradoxical ambience of elegy. This is a quintessentially Jamesian touch of indirection: the use of a heightened mood of loss, often touched by religiosity, through which stored-up feeling is suddenly enabled to flow, providing an effect of positive turning point and revelation. Coming in the midst of the usual ironies and polemical exchanges, the naturalistic detailing of buildings, horse-cars, and shabby domestic interiors,

Ransom's and Verena's little expedition to Harvard and its Memorial Hall is a highlighted moment of transcendence and calm (like the 'momentary truce' in Henry Burrage's hedonistic rooms) – a calmness created by the thought of death and the memory of war, of *the* War:

> The effect of the place is singularly noble and solemn, and it is impossible to feel it without a lifting of the heart. It stands there for duty and honour, it speaks of sacrifice and example, seems a kind of temple to youth, manhood, generosity. Most of them were young, all were in their prime, and all of them had fallen; this simple idea hovers before the visitor and makes him read with tenderness each name and place – names often without other history, and forgotten Southern battles. For Ransom these things were not a challenge nor a taunt; they touched him with respect, with the sentiment of beauty. He was capable of being a generous foeman, and he forgot, now, the whole question of sides and parties; the simple emotion of the old fighting-time came back to him, and the monument around him seemed an embodiment of that memory; it arched over friends as well as enemies, the victims of defeat as well as the sons of triumph.
>
> (p. 246)

Their everyday contentious voices – those of Ransom and Verena, male and female, South and North – then quickly break the spell, and their little war breaks out afresh. But the overarching moment has done its work. Ransom's feelings, her new sense of inner 'perturbation', are suddenly in honest confrontation. The issue of whether or not to tell Olive about their walk together focuses it all, and provides the shape and convention of a shared secret to put the seal on their new sense of closeness:

> 'I tell her everything', said the girl; and now as soon as she had spoken, she blushed. He stood before her, tracing a figure on the mosaic pavement with his cane, conscious that in a moment they had become more intimate. They were discussing their affairs, which had nothing to do with the heroic symbols that surrounded them; but their affairs had suddenly grown so serious that there was no want of decency in their lingering there for the purpose.
>
> (p. 247)

That first discovery of the private bond leads on at once to the contrastedly 'public' event – extravagantly public, indeed – of Verena's performance to the social élite of New York in Mrs Burrage's rooms; and to the whole central New York section of the plot where that private bond is put to the test, and where the city itself, Olive, and Mrs Burrage do all in their power to overcome it by other pressures. The Memorial Hall, with its elegiac softening and directly personal benediction, is replaced by the 'great saloon, amid lights and flowers, where the company was dense, and there were more twinkling, smiling ladies, with uncovered bosoms' (p. 215). The *grosse welt*, with its burden of worldly motive, interposes once again between Ransom and his goal, his 'secret':

> The company – such of it as did not immediately close together around Verena – filed away into the other rooms, bore him in its current into the neighbourhood of a table spread for supper . . . He heard the popping of corks, he felt a pressure of elbows, a thickening of the crowd, perceived that he was glowered at, squeezed against the table, by contending gentlemen who observed that he usurped space, was neither feeding himself nor helping others to feed. He had lost sight of Verena; she had been borne away in clouds of compliment.   (p. 270)

Olive, white with the intensity of her self-consciousness, is again on the scene, vibrating with resistance and resentment. And to add to the thickening atmosphere of opposition, there is also Mrs Luna, doing all in her power to prevent Ransom escaping from her coquetry towards the ever-receding figure of Verena; then Henry Burrage, dangling urbanely but persistently in Verena's vicinity, with 'a splendid camellia in his buttonhole'; and the forceful Mrs Burrage, anxious to please her son, beginning to manipulate Olive and Verena, by the power of money and skilled innuendo, in the direction of her wishes.

By another of those rhythmic contrasts in narration that so dramatize the book's areas of analysis and debate, Ransom, in crisis, makes his supreme appeal to the personal, to the 'secret' of feeling between him and Verena, in the most public place imaginable: in the middle of New York's Central Park. The mounting sense of burden and bafflement which he seeks to overcome for himself and Verena by his new directness is kept before us right up to the Central Park episode by our seeing its exact counterpart in the mind of Olive, who, after her memorably barbed and nuance-laden tussle with Mrs Burrage over the future 'ownership' of Verena, is also nearly at breaking point. Olive, always white-faced and shaking, recognizes that she is 'face to face with a crisis of her destiny', a crisis of sheer crushing dread at the idea of Verena slipping from her, at Mrs Burrage's arguing and wheedling with worldly cunning, and always at the shadow of Ransom hanging over

everything, sardonically encountering her in drawing-rooms, looking up at her in the form of his little notes and visiting-cards left
in the hall of her boarding-house in West Tenth Street. But what
crushes Olive even more — and we are made dramatically to experience something of her weight of dread, despite the balance of
argument being clearly against her — is precisely what Ransom
must do to lift the burden of oppression and falsity from himself
and the unknowing Verena. That is, Olive's knell is figuratively
sounded by the words with which Ransom, the searcher, debunker,
and man of will, opens up the prison-house: 'Come out with me,
Miss Tarrant; come out with me. *Do* come out with me' (p. 311).

The expedition to the publicity of Central Park means, after all,
something very different from either Ransom's purposeful street-
walking or the crush of the salon. The movement it brings, so different from other movements in the book — but once again so an-
ticipative of the pace of life in Marmion — is one of aimlessness,
of multifariousness without form and purpose, and therefore
without pressure. All at once, the change of motion and place, as
in the different kind of change in the Memorial Hall in Harvard,
allows personal directness of feeling to break through the falsifying
forms of habit and abstract dogma — the breakthrough to which
the whole thrust of narrative, imagery, and idea has been
dedicated. The new freedom that the Park confers, the whole relaxing indiscretion of the expedition, reminds Verena of being a child
'in the woods and fields, looking for raspberries and playing she
was a gypsy':

They visited the animals in the little zoological garden which forms one of
the attractions of the Central Park; they observed the swans in the orna-
mental water, and they even considered the question of taking a boat for
half an hour, Ransom saying that they needed this to make their visit complete. Verena replied that she didn't see why it should be complete, and
after having threaded the devious ways of the Ramble, lost themselves in
the Maze, and admired all the statues and busts of great men with which
the grounds are decorated, they contented themselves with resting on a
sequestered bench, where, however, there was a pretty glimpse of the
distance and an occasional stroller creaked by on the asphalt walk.(p. 320)

By way of these disorienting ramblings and sequestrations, far
from 'the land of vapours, of dead phrases', far from the mechanical whirring of New York and Olive's fixed Bostonian stare, comes

47

Ransom's peroration on behalf of 'love' – and on behalf also, it seems, of Thomas Carlyle. For the striking thing about James's management of this climactic encounter between Ransom and Verena, where Ransom at last speaks totally what he believes, without irony or even politeness, is that the general argument of it is clearly more than a little preposterous, yet the personal part of it rings true. When Ransom apparently claims that a woman's highest destiny can lie in her being agreeable to a man and in remaining firmly at home, that women are always 'weak and second-rate' in public affairs, or that the whole age has already become over-feminized ('nervous, hysterical, chattering, canting'), we are left uneasy, to the degree that James's ironic quip against 'these narrow notions' seems at best half-hearted and disingenuous, and Verena's ripostes lacking in force. But it is the personal outburst that bears the weight and is backed so conclusively by the whole accumulation of the book's unfolding rhetoric of structure and language thus far:

'. . . you ought to know [Ransom tells Verena] that your connexion with all these rantings and ravings is the most unreal, accidental, illusory thing in the world. You think you care about them, but you don't at all. They were imposed upon you by circumstances, by unfortunate associations, and you accepted them as you would have accepted any other burden, on account of the sweetness of your nature. You always want to please some one, and now you go lecturing about the country, and trying to provoke demonstrations, in order to please Miss Chancellor, just as you did it before to please your father and mother. It isn't *you*, the least in the world, but an inflated little figure (very remarkable in its way too) whom you have invented and set on its feet, pulling strings, behind it, to make it move and speak, while you try to conceal and efface yourself there.'   (p. 330)

The appeal to the need for truth to self has a powerful resonance, echoed by the whole surrounding apparatus of alternative falsity and possessiveness that the narrative has built up in our minds:

That description of herself as something different from what she was trying to be, the charge of want of reality, made her heart beat with pain; she was sure, at any rate, it was her real self that was there with him now, where she oughtn't to be.   (p. 331)

But so typically of the movement of this novel, the liberating vision of the 'real self' sends the character – here, Verena – at once swerving off in panic, back to Olive's tragic face, to flight, conceal-ment, and resistance.[18] The apparatus clicks shut around Verena. And Ransom's rhetorical appeal amid 'the artificial lakes and cockneyfied landscapes' of the Park has to be renewed and transformed – and made more ultimately effective – in the truer pastoral surroundings of Marmion.

That pastoral is an elegiac one; and its mood of natural drowsiness and decay not only slackens the rigours of Bostonia, and those imposed by some Bostonians on others, but also allows the narrator his most expansive, self-delighting, and colourful writing in the whole novel. New York, with its strenuous expeditions, its plottings and defences, its swarming, purposeful soirées, seems a world away – though the narrative has passed abruptly, without a transition, from Verena sobbing in Olive's arms in West Tenth Street to Ransom strolling in the late-summer night through the sandy roads and the earth-smelling air of the New England littoral. Everything about Marmion seems pointedly opposite to almost everything that has gone before, and to almost everything about both New York and Boston. The life of the inhabitants (mostly retired sea-captains) is sedative, run-down, ineffectual. It reminds Ransom of the South (and it will further the interests of this Southerner). The buildings straggle, 'slightly collapsing'; the roads peter out; sea slides invisibly into estuary, into blurred fields, then faint woods. The outlines of life are smoothed away. There is space and time for the wry mirthless humour of Dr Prance to set up a little relationship with (in his scepticism at least) her counterpart, Ransom. The decayed quality of the little town, its crumbling memorials everywhere of its vanished shipbuilding industry, open a vista into the past rather than into the uncertain future of the reformers, and inspire – or insinuate, mistily – resignation and half-melancholic indulgence. Miss Birdseye, in the cottage taken by the Bostonians, is flickering out in the gentlest of deaths, like the landscape:

At the end of her long day's work she might have been placed there to enjoy this dim prevision of the peaceful river, the gleaming shores, of the paradise her unselfish life had certainly qualified her to enter, and which, apparently, would so soon be opened to her.   (p. 352)

And even the presence of the complete writings of George Eliot, brought to the cottage by these most serious of holidaymakers, is not enough to brace the feminists (or Verena at least) against Ransom's persistence – a persistence now backed overwhelmingly by sensuously pleasing climate and surroundings.

If the Marmion episode is memorable for how it evokes the senses and the feelings as they are wooed away from false rigours by touch, atmosphere, tempo, and natural description, it also, by an entirely characteristic counterturn, precipitates the greatest experienced agony in the novel. Intriguingly, the book's only prolonged idyll proves to be the catalyst of these two opposed extremes: the relaxation of constraint and the despair of a frustrated and betrayed passion. The episode holds both of these opposites within a virtuosity of controlled tone and structure, and sets one against the other to bring a climax to the whole narrative's prolonged unfolding of tension, debate, and opposition. Here is the former – relaxation – as Ransom, for a whole month, meets Verena for an agreed hour every day:

> They wandered along the waterside to a rocky, shrub-covered point, which made a walk of just the right duration. Here all the homely languor of the region, the mild, fragrant Cape-quality, the sweetness of white sands, quiet waters, low promontories where there were paths among the barberries and tidal pools gleamed in the sunset – here all the spirit of a ripe summer-afternoon seemed to hang in the air. There were wood-walks too; they sometimes followed bosky uplands, where accident had grouped trees with odd effects of 'style', and where in grassy intervals and fragrant nooks of rest they came out upon sudden patches of Arcady. (p. 373)

But for Olive – in the very same paragraph – 'it was war to the knife'. And similarly, the death of Miss Birdseye, which in its manner of narration catches the relaxing Arcadian tone (a sunset-touch of harmony, resignation, and fulfilment), produces dramatic discordance from Olive:

> 'Good-bye, Olive Chancellor,' Miss Birdseye murmured. 'I don't want to stay, though I should like to see what you will see.'
> 'I shall see nothing but shame and ruin!' Olive shrieked, rushing across to her old friend, while Ransom discreetly quitted the scene. (pp. 388–9)

Tension in James's fiction is often expressed in the act of waiting; and the great scene of Olive waiting for Verena to return from her significantly prolonged boating-trip with Ransom, which virtually concludes the Marmion episode, concentrates all the inner tensions of one woman, and many of the book's ramifying stresses

of idea and judgement, into one moving image of tragedy, touched
by mystery and articulated by a new intensity and complexity of
language. Olive, 'dumb and cold with despair' at Verena's
treachery, is outlined pacing in her misery against the familiar blue-
and-gold ease of the landscape:

She went very far, keeping in the lonely places, unveiling her face to the
splendid light, which seemed to make a mock of the darkness and bitterness of her spirit. There were little sandy coves, where the rocks were clean,
where she made long stations, sinking down in them as if she hoped she
would never rise again.   (p. 396)

The strong hint of crucifixion in the 'stations' Olive makes is given
quite without irony. Intermittently, through the earlier part of the
novel, we have already been prepared to see her, for a while, as victim. As well as a manipulator, we have also had glimpses in her of
that other powerful nineteenth-century archetype, the woman of
thwarted energy, sensibility, and thoughtfulness, like Maggie
Tulliver or Dorothea Brooke, seeking to be free or to move the
inertness of the world. But now Olive's own vision is into a darkening vista that goes far beyond her particular situation or even the
situation of women, a vision (Jamesian through and through) 'that
the world was all a great trap or trick' and 'human effort' all
'barren and thankless':

These hours of backward clearness come to all men and women, once at
least, when they read the past in the light of the present, with the reasons
of things, like unobserved finger-posts, protruding where they never saw
them before. The journey behind them is mapped out and figured, with its
false steps, its wrong observations, all its infatuated, deluded geography.
They understand as Olive understood, but it is probable that they rarely
suffer as she suffered. The sense of regret for her baffled calculations
burned within her like a fire, and the splendour of the vision over which
the curtain of mourning now was dropped brought to her eyes slow, still
tears, tears that came one by one, neither easing her nerves nor lightening
her load of pain.   (p. 398)

As in traditional tragedy, suffering brings its moment of transcendence – or perhaps, in Olive's weird case, of a suitably inverted
transcendence: downwards, into darkness and dissolution. For
Olive, too, has a brief ecstasy of liberation, of her dreamed-of
union – such as she has up till now denied others and denied
herself. Marmion momentarily relaxes even Olive – into its

51

darkness. Moaning with what is by now openly 'a wild personal passion', haunted by the image of a Verena drowned and disfigured, she rushes into the unlit parlour (so many tight parlours that hold these Bostonian lives!) where Verena is after all sitting waiting for her in total silence:

Olive took her hand with an irresistible impulse of compassion and reassurance. From the way it lay in her own she guessed her whole feeling — saw it was a kind of shame, shame for her weakness, her swift surrender, her insane gyration, in the morning. (p. 399)

That phrase, 'it was a kind of shame', comes once: as a simple analogy from Verena. Then in a brief, intense litany, quite extraordinary in a novel so unstylized in its prose, the phrase comes quickly twice again. Thus:

[Olive] would just sit there and hold her hand; that was all she could do; they were beyond each other's help in any other way now. Verena leaned her head back and closed her eyes, and for an hour, as nightfall settled in the room, neither of the young women spoke. Distinctly, it was a kind of shame.

The shame has at once grown around them, far beyond the terms of blame or apology, into something impersonal, something desolating though conjoining. And for the third time, in the same paragraph, to end the scene:

After a while the parlour-maid, very casual, in the manner of the servants at Marmion, appeared on the threshold with a lamp; but Olive motioned her frantically away. She wished to keep the darkness. It was a kind of shame. (p. 400)

And so shame swells into a darkness to be embraced and kept, a dissolving consolation — almost a union, to be seized, in death. From the varying elegiac stands of the Marmion episode, some merely sleepy, some comic, or wistful, or seductive, or plangent, there is no stranger outgrowth than this, the image of Olive's brief *liebestod*.

The final direction of *The Bostonians*, after such intensities of idyll and despairing passion, is suddenly back into the fully social, the lamentably social world — and back to what is surely the dominant movement of the whole book, that of pursuit, obstacle, and tug-of-war, beginning with a whole chapter of rattling dialogue between Ransom (questioning, seeking, challenging), Mrs Luna (concealing, pouting), and Matthias Pardon (interviewing, cliché-mongering). Perfectly, too, it returns firmly to the comic mode, in what is probably the nearest approach to farce in the novel. It is startling, and highly effective, that a narrative that began so weightily, with argument and exposition, changed its direction of debate and collision in its New York setting, then switched to a radically different mode in Marmion, should now, at the very end, plunge into the animation and even slapstick of the events in the Boston Music Hall. Public exposure, abstraction of the personal, and the public hunger for a Word have after all been dominant among those large general issues that are borne along by the narrative rhythms I have just been examining. And to that extent it is right that the book should end with two figures set against a mass: Ransom struggling to extract Verena from her last place of conceal-ment and perversity, which proves to be the proudest and largest, most echoing, most crowded public building in Boston. The sense of the pullulating city by night passes into the description of the Hall, and catalyses Ransom's resistant will. The individual private lover − whether or not he is an antediluvian conservative − is defined heroically, 'apart, unique', against 'the mighty multitude', his sceptical hardness and confident personality against the half-commercial 'claptrap' of 'a great popular system', the 'noise of many throats'. And so, amid the disembodying cacophony of those same Bostonian voices with which the novel began, in vaporous talk, prattle, and harangue − with Mrs Tarrant having hysterics, Olive pleading in agony, Verena frantically yielding to her nature, Mr Filer the agent lamenting the worth in dollars of each lost minute, Selah Tarrant unctuously regretting, Mrs Farrinder haughtily disparaging, Mrs Burrage ironizing, the mob stamping and clapping − amid, in Dickensian phrase and with something of the Dickensian meaning, the 'usual uproar' of 'the noisy, and the eager, and the arrogant, and the froward, and the vain',[19] Ransom memorably damns aloud the whole vociferous city of Boston, plucks away the imprisoned maiden into gladness (qualified by the prospect of tears), and leaves Olive to what is no doubt not her last perversity: seeking martyrdom before the unap-peased Boston audience whose innate respectfulness, however, now seems likely to cheat her even of the final pleasure of being humiliated.

There have been some imperfections in a book that falls short of being among James's greatest novels – particularly as regards the unusual degree of *parti pris* that surrounds its portrayal of Ransom and of the feminists. But in that noisily comic and touching confusion of the last scene, with its complex ironic nuances and reversals, and its lovers fled away into the storm, we are left with an overriding sense of how narrative transformation and narrative persistence have combined to vivify the book's great bulk, to compensate for its areas of narrowed vision, and to convey far more deviously and intricately to the imagination than mere naturalism or disquisition could ever do its troubled and premonitory vision of people, a culture, and an era in stress.

3. Crossing the Channel with Maisie

Compared with the middle-period expansiveness of *The Bostonians*, *What Maisie Knew* is a strange, quick, jumpy book with the introverted strangeness, the almost expressionist excesses of linguistic mannerism and theatrical distortion of tone and character that typify so much of James's later fiction – the period of his career that one might even regard, bearing those Jamesian traits in mind, as the period also of late Ibsen, Maeterlinck, and early Conrad. It is as though the book achieves the feat of combining much of the quizzical gaiety and self-conscious stylization of *The Europeans* with the underlying sombre diagnosis of personal dishonesty and cultural decay of *The Bostonians* – yet, along with the closely related *Spoils of Poynton*,[20] it also creates, out of this succinct combination of the comic–theatrical and the morally perturbed, something quite new in James's method. This is part of its fascination: that it marks a turning point in James's career, and in more than James's career. It appeared in 1897, in the same year (and indeed in the same periodical, Henley's *New Review*) as *The Nigger of the 'Narcissus'*, and like Conrad's first mature fiction *What Maisie Knew* seems to represent a new dimension of radical ambiguity of technique and of discrimination, touched (lightly, in James's case) by symbolism, in the development of the modern novel. Its fluctuating openness of narration – its peculiar intertwining of movingly tragi-comic effects with a puppet-like characterization – problematizes James's method of indirection with a new vividness, and foregrounds the play of consciousness itself as a narrative-cum-moral strategy in a way that points straight to the ultimate in that mode, *The Golden Bowl*.

The problem, above all, is one of modulation: the ways in which contrasted literary manners overlap one another, or a sensibility contradicts a prevailing narrative convention, elusively, fluidly – and hence strangely. It makes for a witty and idiosyncratic little drama: partly naturalistic, partly dream-like; very touching, very absurd, solemn and playful, acerbic yet *risqué*; full of oblique emotionality, quaint flickering lights, marionette-like gestures, and sudden directness of appeal. There is something challengingly simple about the narration, even *faux-naif* at times; yet is it also kaleidoscopic and perpetually mobile.[21] For example, halfway through the book Maisie's climactic flight with Sir Claude, first to Folkestone then to Boulogne, initiates an extraordinary intensification of all the delicate oddities and shiftings that have already characterized the narration up to that point. The change of scene to France (like that to New York in *The Bostonians*) brings new dynamism and interest; but it also highlights the problems one faces in reading a book that, by the crossing of a channel, moves from the mode of Congreve and Wycherley to a mode more like Chekhov, or even, in moments, like the abstract and half-symbolic manner that James admired in *Little Eyolf* and *John Gabriel Borkman*.[22]

While the transition from London to Boulogne is of major importance in terms of plot as well as of mode, it might be helpful to approach it by first examining closely one earlier episode – that between Maisie, Sir Claude, Ida, and the Captain in Kensington Gardens – which could be taken as representing all the typical smaller-scale transitions, the ubiquitous slight crossings of the channel of style, narrative voice, and feeling, that lead up to and are then suddenly intensified in that halfway turning point.

The episode begins in a characteristically stagey archness with the narrating voice consciously imitating the class solecisms of Susan Ash the maid ('he do look beautiful', 'them wandering "airs"', etc.), and making a knowing appeal to the reader, well over the head of the half-comprehending Maisie, by ironies at Sir Claude's shuffling and dilatoriness – he has been for some time 'on the point of making arrangements for regular [music] lessons', and has now, instead, laid out a whole five shillings on a piece of sheet music for Maisie. The reference to Beale having spent the night away from home (Maisie thinks she knows where, but perhaps is mistaken), and to Maisie consciously imitating a duchess-like grandeur in her reproof to Sir Claude, are all part of the prevailing style of innuendo and play-acting. The style, as well as being elegantly arch (in the Congreve manner), also throws up sentences and perceptions like these:

Even she herself almost knew how it would have expressed the strength of his empire to say that to shuffle away her sense of being duped he had only, from under his lovely moustache, to breathe upon it. It was somehow in the nature of plans to be expensive and in the nature of the expensive to be impossible.[23]

The idea of the child *almost knowing* what the rest of the sentence articulates is finespun, though acceptable as a reflection of experience: knowledge *can* exist at a level below such elaborate verbalization. 'The strength of his empire', however, after the momentary double-take forced on the reader by the intricate 'almost knew', bulges up as a metaphor of unexpected fulsomeness and suggestive warmth; only to be as quickly hedged about by the mannered comicality of 'his lovely moustache' and of the delayed mixed metaphor, 'shuffle'/'breathe upon'. After which, in the second sentence, on top of everything else we have a neo-Johnsonian antithesis to add a final flourish of deliberate pomposity and abstractness.

Again, after Sir Claude has surprised Maisie (and the reader) by his cry of 'the dear old soul!', which is an incongruous and hardly natural epithet for him to use about Mrs Beale, we have this:

She clung to his hand, which was encased in a pearl-grey glove ornamented with the thick black lines that, at her mother's, always used to strike her as connected with the way the bestitched fists of the long ladies carried, with the elbows well out, their umbrellas upside down. The mere sense of it in her own covered the ground of loss just as much as the ground of gain. His presence was like an object brought so close to her face that she couldn't see round its edges.   (p. 115, ch. 15)

The elaborate association of the glove is partly naturalistic: the child's mind, focusing on a minute detail in this way, bounds off naturally and even affectingly, at a tangent. But for the reader, the vignette of 'thick black lines' suggesting 'bestitched fists of the long

56

ladies' carrying upside-down umbrellas is also bizarre: a half-arbitrary caricature in the margin. And it is characteristically followed at once by two figures of speech, related to each other, that seem to create as much abstraction as concreteness: the 'ground of loss' and the 'ground of gain' presumably signifying that Sir Claude's presence was enough simultaneously to redeem any past sense of deprivation and to leave no imperfection in Maisie's present sense of fulfilment; and then Sir Claude as an 'object' filling all of her vision being a typical elaboration, slightly incongruous but distinctly uncomic, of the preceding figure.

Yet the scene, all this while, is also acting itself out quite briskly, even rattlingly, despite these minute convolutions and stylistic whorls on the way. In a theatrically spotlighted irony, Sir Claude's fancy of an artistic idyll – 'It's the Forest of Arden' – is shattered by the (stagey) reality of the erring Ida arm in arm with the Captain. And there follows the familiar interplay of a jocose and slangy dialogue ('Right you are, my duck!'), concussive movements and sharply outlined gestures like stage directions ('Sir Claude threw away his match'), and facetiously implied strong feelings behind the gestures ('he was looking at her, she thought, rather queerly. "What do you know about Lord Eric?"'). The wit that governs and energizes the whole complicated display continues to make the language rear up in unexpected tricks and figures: 'Mama looked terrible from afar, but even under her guns the child's curiosity flickered . . .'; or, very extravagantly, 'Maisie received in petrification the full force of her mother's huge painted eyes – they were like Japanese lanterns swung under festive arches'. There is something rather dehumanizing about such clever wit, a tendency in the direction of pure style and even fantasy (fantasy of the period: Wildean or even Beardsleyan). But the extraordinary effect of this scene – the one effect, really, that I wish to emphasize as being significant for our reading of the whole narrative – is that the Yellow Book preciosity, glittering and a little metallic, coexists exactly with its opposite: a growing urgency of repressed, then of uttered feeling. The feeling is first wonderfully parodied in Ida's *grande dame* affectations:

. . . her mother opened a pair of arms of extraordinary elegance, and then she felt the loosening of his grasp. 'My own child', Ida murmured in a voice – a voice of sudden confused tenderness – that it seemed to her she heard for the first time.

Those elegant maternal limbs creak open like an instrument —
perhaps a nutcracker. And 'tenderness', which Maisie yearns for —
and which we are made more and more to see her need of, and her
whole milieu's urgent need of — is converted, by the wit's sleight
of hand, into Ida's self-regarding materiality:

The next moment she was on her mother's breast, where, amid a wilderness
of trinkets, she felt as if she had suddenly been thrust into a jeweller's
shop-front, but only to be as suddenly ejected with a push and the brisk
injunction: 'Now go to the Captain!'[24]   (p. 120, ch. 15)

The feeling that *does* flow suddenly, even in a different language,
out of such a shop-front of conceits — they have been James's as
much as Ida's — is dramatically direct: Sir Claude's vituperative
anger against Ida, and Maisie's immediate response of horror: 'It
was enough, it was too much; she fled before it, rushing even to
a stranger in the terror of such a change of tone' (p. 121).

The episode in Kensington Gardens is really *about* this discovery
and expression of feeling 'amid a wilderness of trinkets', and enacts
the shock, the pathos, and even the bizarreness with which feeling
comes to life in such a context. The second chapter of the episode
focuses with a new intensity on the intimacy of Maisie's emotion
in relation to the Captain and his inspiringly affectionate idea of
her mother — while around this uncovered intimacy, where feeling
flows more freely than in any preceding part of the narrative, the
'trinkets' of the adult world continue to gleam and rattle insidiously. The physical contact of the Captain and Maisie is emphasized.
Much less quizzically than with Sir Claude's 'lovely moustache', we
are given a new sense of direct relationship with the Captain's
'bright and kind' face, his 'blue eyes' like 'little pale flowers', his
smell of cigars, and the 'big military hand' that frankly takes
Maisie's and keeps it covered protectively. He provides for her a
totally new image and channel for tenderness by arguing (in-
genuously, as *we* can see from our different standpoint) on behalf
of her mother's essential goodness, her 'mysterious grace'. As so
often for Maisie, her encounter with experience, even the
experience of unexpected tenderness, has to be accompanied by
play-acting, the conscious adoption of roles as demanded by the
trinket-world of adults: she judges she has to express her new affection for the Captain by imitating the manner of 'young ladies . . . in

58

the intervals of dances'. It is all an outgrowth, though certainly an exotic and ominous outgrowth, of the concept of style and role-playing as it was first presented, with more than a little ambivalence of its own, in *The Europeans*. In Maisie, here and elsewhere, there is a moving – or will it be redeeming? – fusion of Gertrude's first innocence and Eugenia's stylish duplicity. Our perpetual awareness of how radically *style* has entered into Maisie's consciousness and mode of utterance adds tension to our perception of her freer, less mediated feelings – her blushing, her 'sudden surge of deprecation', her panting in response, her feeling 'something tremble within her'. The little climax of this scene is remarkable for its contrast of these extremes: extremes of style in narration as well as extremes of represented experience. The Captain's naivety and his misjudgement of Ida are blatant to our eyes: there is the note of high comedy in the way he chooses to praise Ida to her daughter – 'She has the nerve for a tiger-shoot – by Jove I'd *take* her!' (p. 126, ch. 16). And we are kept coolly aware of the irony of the Captain just beginning to squirm as Maisie's directness of appeal to him increases and she asks him if he really loves her mother. Yet through the continuing texture of these worldly ironies and detachments, Maisie's crisis of unalleviated feeling is overheatedly, almost fulsomely, conveyed: 'the intensity of her response, throbbing with a joy still less utterable'; 'something strange and deep and pitying surged up within her'; 'The tears filled her eyes and rolled down her cheeks'; '[She] presented to her companion, soundlessly but hideously, her wet, distorted face'; and:

He called her by her name, and her name drove it home. 'My dear Maisie, your mother's an angel!'
It was an almost incredible balm – it soothed so her impression of danger and pain. She sank back in her chair; she covered her face with her hands. 'Oh, mother, mother, mother!' she sobbed.   (p. 127, ch. 16)

Then the climax abruptly passes – as it must, being poised upon a delusion, a lie. The blur of high, grand emotionality, empathetic in its momentary unrestraint, is suddenly replaced by the narrative's clear-eyed view of the Captain suddenly nervous and embarrassed, 'whacking his leg with his stick', dodging the issue with jocosity and conventional laughter – 'the immemorial note of mirth'. The scene has not changed but the stage has – the very terms of the little drama. And the whole episode concludes where it began, with our smiling down uneasily at Maisie's lack of full knowingness (telling the Captain as she leaves him not to love her mother 'for just a little − . . . like all the others'), then our watching her, faced by Sir Claude's curt questioning and her own 'horror' of further emotion and exposure, re-adopt her self-protective role of childish ignorance − a mask she consciously dons for the social stage with the self-congratulating expertise (and the pathos) of a little worldling.

The little worldling's flight to the other world and the other style of France − representing, we are told, 'a crossing of more spaces than the Channel' (p. 168, ch. 20) − is ushered in by a quaint but significant litany between Maisie and Sir Claude celebrating freedom, the words of which will continue to sound ironically through the book's second half. 'I'm free − I'm free', he tells her, standing 'under the stars' in the grounds of the Folkestone hotel. 'You're free − you're free', she chimes. Then again, 'I'm free − I'm free!', he says, out of 'the agitation of his soul'. And: 'She repeated her form of assent. "You're free − you're free."' (p. 191, ch. 21). It is all very grave and solemn after the grand farce of Ida's Positively Last Appearance as dignified mother casting off her daughter. And this suddenly intrusive tone of mysterious seriousness 'under the stars', together with the recurrent words and challenging concept of 'freedom', strikes the very keynote of what I wish now to investigate: the indirections in narrative mode highlighted by crossing that new 'space' in the narrative, the Channel.

Across the Channel, 'freedom' is at first extravagant and novel, in a life that has been so far, for Maisie, one of comparative restriction: a London life of being owned, resented, and exchanged. Now, the world of 'abroad' is all expansiveness: 'the great ecstasy of a larger impression of life'; an 'initiation', 'a consciousness much quickened', a 'multitude of affinities and messages' − 'it appeared to her that no one since the beginning of time could have had such an adventure or, in an hour, so much experience'.[25] There is one determining feature of the whole French section in the novel that makes it spring out challengingly from what precedes it. It presents among other things, as part of its sense of new place and new space, the dangerous exaltation of fresh possibilities, fresh knowledge, a greater personal power − 'freedom' in the most evocative and

Jamesian sense, like the freedom that Gertrude Wentworth sought in love and in escape, and Basil Ransom fought for against principled bigotry and economic circumstance. And very quickly, to strain contradictorily against that sense of expansion and create the full tension of the Boulogne narrative, there is the declaration of exactly the opposite principle. Embodied in the long-expected and now landed Mrs Wix we find responsibility, constricting disapproval, and her peculiarly heated, almost neurotic, advocacy of propriety and restraint: in the disapprovingness at least, it is the return of Bostonia.

But incongruously – and almost everything by now has its accompanying incongruity and doubleness – Mrs Wix brings the message and the word of 'freedom', in that Ida has called on her in London to convey to Sir Claude and Maisie their 'freedom'. That incongruity is compounded by the half-grotesque comedy that always plays around the absurd figure of Mrs Wix, with her eternal optical 'straighteners' that beam out a dark reproachfulness, or 'roof over' Maisie protectively, her awkward clothes, her strident ugliness, and the red glow of her complexion, now fuelled by a succession of restorative *petits verres*. And when her announcement of their 'freedom' is given in a dauntingly unnaturalistic style and tone, so that dramatic roundness is partly lost within a more stylized and even abstract Jamesian idom, then the reader's growing sense of dislocation is complete:

It was as if, with this scruple, [Mrs Wix] measured and adjusted all that she gave him in at last saying: 'What she meant was to make me know that you're definitely free. To have that straight from her was a joy I, of course, hadn't hoped for: it made the assurance, and my delight at it, a thing I could really proceed upon . . . You already know what, so long, we have been looking for and what, as soon as she told me of her step taken at Folkestone, I recognised with rapture that we *have*. It's your freedom that makes me right' – she fairly bristled with her logic. 'But I don't mind telling you that it's her action that makes me happy!'   (pp. 203–4, ch. 23)

The full ambiguity of Mrs Wix's 'happiness', and of the narration's half-expressionist, half-farcical extravagance, produces one strikingly problematic episode later that evening. The air in the Boulogne hotel is now full of aggression: though for the first time in this novel of contention it is a specifically moral, or moralistic, aggression, emanating from Mrs Wix. She too has undergone a sea change by crossing the Channel. She quite suddenly begins to dominate the action, after having played a very restricted role in the English section. And this suddenness, too, plays its part in disorienting the reader. Where have Mrs Wix's rhetoric and grandeur come from? What kind of transition is it between the sections and between the settings of this novel that has so galvanized and transformed a Mrs Wix? And what exactly is the effect of this new note when combined with the continuing former note of broad comicality? When Mrs Wix attacks Sir Claude over the scandal of his continuing connection with Mrs Beale, and concludes 'with an unparalleled neigh of battle', what we have is almost a return of the *grande dame* manner of the now abdicated Ida. And these transformative quirks in the writing now produce the crux in question, focusing on the ambiguous use once again of the word 'free'. If Mrs Beale is now 'free' as a result of Beale Farange casting her off, does this freedom extend to allowing her to live with Sir Claude? Sir Claude, trying to be bland, tackles the termagant Mrs Wix on 'freedom':

'Then why the deuce do you grant so – do you, I may even say, rejoice so – that by the desertion of my own precious partner I'm free?'

Mrs. Wix met this challenge first with silence, then with a demonstration the most extraordinary, the most unexpected. Maisie could scarcely believe her eyes as she saw the good lady, with whom she had never associated the faintest form of coquetry, actually, after an upward grimace, give Sir Claude a great giggling, insinuating, naughty slap. 'You wretch – you *know* why!' (p. 213, ch. 24)

There are many surprising turns and twists in *What Maisie Knew*, but none stranger than this one, this outlandish 'freedom' taken by the previously straightlaced Mrs Wix. The obvious 'explanation' of the incident – which causes only momentary 'stupefaction' to Sir Claude – is the naturalistic and psychological one often offered, that Mrs Wix has by now become infatuated sexually with Sir Claude. Within the book's more realistic mode this is acceptable, and has been prepared for by evidence earlier on of the deprived Mrs Wix's star-struck response to Sir Claude's glamorousness and courtesy. The infatuation itself need not be seen as indecent or as in some way clinical – it would seem to be quite 'natural' for an emotional widow of her kind, suddenly and dazzlingly raised from her straitened circumstances to a position of confidence, and surrounded by a social situation (and now, suddenly, a geographically foreign situation) of extraordinary 'freedom', to become infatuated and also to give all the more stress to her conventional moralistic position in order to compensate for her surreptitious emotional involvement. Her moral position for the rest of the novel is certainly not destroyed because of this other possible motivation − though the abstract principles of that position are clearly shown to be only one aspect of a more complicated and dynamic whole. So much would seem to be perfectly compatible with everything else we know, from his other novels and from his essays, of James's fluid and un-absolutist view of what constitutes 'morality'.[26] But 'explanation' in terms of hidden motivation of character and the Jamesian concept of morality does not entirely resolve the whole incident (tiny though the incident is). As it comes to us in the act of reading, it retains, and goes on retaining, a certain vitalizing quality of shock and high colour. For the book's hallmark − perhaps to a degree that is uniquely Jamesian − is that its qualities of truth-to-experience and attachment to recognizable moral values and ideas are mediated, compatibly yet under strain, by a stylistic excitement based on intermittent contortion, aesthetic and intellectual surprise, and even a willed ungainliness. When Mrs Wix acts so strangely − though also, of course, in part so 'explainably' − it is as though the narration itself suddenly coils up insinuatingly, gigglingly, even tastelessly, and briefly flaunts its capacity to convert character into caricature, moral probity into a naughty leer, and a serious situation into a game and a curlicue.

What happens here is only one further expression of those other elements in the writing, those stylistic or modal changes, 'freedoms', and 'crossings' that we have already detected. The unglamorous, lower-class Mrs Wix so coquettishly and outrageously slapping Sir Claude (gently, one presumes) comes out of those very same imaginative impulses, part satirical, part self-flaunting, that converted Ida's maternal bosom into a jeweller's shop-front or made Maisie sob for love beside an embarrassed Captain whacking his leg with a stick. It is the kind of sophisticated, self-propagating *maniera* − quite foreign to Conrad, but handled with aplomb, if sparingly, by Forster − that seems to generate much of its own dynamism and its own frisky attractiveness, as well as feeding into the more humane and lifelike burden of feeling and actions that it bears along on its inforeseeable current.[27] And when the scene ends with Mrs Wix's grand harangue to Sir Claude against Mrs Beale, with its tearful supplication and physical absurdity, anger, pathos, and vulgarity, all in one, we detect the instability, as well as the complexity, of this *maniera*, which can use the vocabulary of passionate feeling along with a sexual grotesqueness, an unfunny comicality, and a conscious theatrical bombast to create an effect more bizarre, more 'camp', than almost anything else in the entire novel:

'I beseech you not to take a step so miserable and so fatal. I know her but too well, even if you jeer at me for saying it; little as I've seen her I know her, I know her. I know what she'll do – I see it as I stand here. Since you are afraid of her it's the mercy of heaven. Don't, for God's sake, be afraid to show it, to profit by it and to arrive at the very safety that it gives you . . . You stay here with Maisie, with the carriage and the larks and the luxury; then I'll return to you and we'll go off together – we'll live together without a cloud. Take me, take me,' she went on and on – the tide of her eloquence was high. 'Here I am; I know what I am and what I ain't . . . I owe you everything – that's just the reason; and to pay it back, in profusion, what can that be but what I want? Here I am, here I am!' – she spread herself into an exhibition that, combined with her intensity and her decorations, appeared to suggest her for strange offices and devotions, for ridiculous replacements and substitutions.

(pp. 218–19, ch. 24)

It is entirely characteristic of this narrative, with its odd veerings and crosscurrents, its puzzling switches of mood, sometimes delicate, sometimes harshly abrupt, its outbursts of feeling, its teetering on so many diverse edges, that it should now, in a climax of waiting and inaction, arrive by indirection and surprise at the quintessential Jamesian vision of a healing harmony. The effect of waiting replaces the earlier effects of travelling and rebounding – that experience of waiting, waiting for a decision and a change to come (as in Chekhov), which is so often the pressurizing milieu within which James's climaxes of the spirit come slowly to a head.[28] Under such pressure – the contradictory pressures for Maisie, in the two days she spends alone with Mrs Wix in Boulogne, of responding acutely to the warm, rich details of the present moment and simultaneously to the mental image of Sir Claude and Mrs Beale in England, presumably parting for ever – under such pressures, Maisie comes for the first time into

possession of a vision. Having so thoroughly crossed the Channel
and entered into a life of apparent expansion and novelty, free
from her ghastly parents, she now finds her imagination, in the
enforced days of waiting, taking full possession of the possibility
of peace: peace now, peace for the future. The vision is very subtly
handled: it consists of little phenomena rather than of anything
portentous or abstract. It consists of the new fine weather, the
'little yellow-faced houses', the 'brown old women in such white
frilled caps and such long gold earrings' sitting on the 'friendly
benches'. It consists of the perpetual thought, shared with her companion, of the absent, benign, too blessedly weak Sir Claude. It
consists also, most remarkably, of 'the high gilt Virgin', 'the great
golden Madonna' of the church that hangs over the scene: never
filling it with overt symbolism but always just one element among
the others, seen out of the corner of the reader's eye, and of
Maisie's eye. If the Madonna is to be called a symbol, it functions
as the most discreet and even tangential symbol possible – far less
announced than either Conrad's or Forster's epiphanic objects and
events, and indeed very different from James's own Golden Bowl
which becomes an interpretable emblem even in the conversation of
the characters of that novel. It simply is there: something shining
on top of a church, with its own religious symbolism of hope and
sacrifice directed *away* from the world of this novel, yet just allowing a faint colouring of it to seep into our secular, our tourist's view
of it. The secularity of its possible meanings, and the indirectness
and delicacy of its treatment in the narrative, come out in the
significant combinations and elisions of such a passage as this, as
Maisie broods over her half-conscious reluctance to think of Mrs
Beale being broken with by Sir Claude:

The very sweetness of the foreign life she was steeped in added with each
hour of Sir Claude's absence to the possibility of such pangs. She watched
beside Mrs. Wix the great golden Madonna, and one of the ear-ringed old
women who had been sitting at the end of their bench got up and pottered
away.

'Adieu, mesdames!' said the old woman in a little cracked, civil voice
– a demonstration by which our friends were so affected that they bobbed
up and almost curtsied to her. They subsided again, and it was shortly
after, in a summer hum of French insects and a phase of almost somnolent
reverie, that Maisie most had the vision of what it was to shut out from
such a perspective so appealing a participant. It had not yet appeared so

vast as at that moment, this prospect of statues shining in the blue and of courtesy in romantic forms.

'Why, after all, should we have to choose between you? Why shouldn't we be four?' she finally demanded. (pp. 224–5, ch. 25)

The Madonna, while inevitably eminent, is subtly diminished at the end of that passage into a mere statue 'shining in the blue'; and the vision of peaceful harmony and all-inclusiveness, while it bulges towards the transcendent, is brought firmly back to the worldly and charming phenomena that most comprise it: old ladies offering greetings, 'courtesy in romantic forms', the hum of insects, and the mental image of an 'appealing' Mrs Beale becoming one of the 'four' companions and therefore one of the constituents of peace, of relationship, and – so far beyond the channel of divisiveness – of a radiant, summery, and humanly expansive France.

But shattering the vision – again, the quick reversal that is typical of this book, and also of James's whole creative sensibility – Mrs Wix's moral outrage (more than tinged by personal jealousy of Mrs Beale) breaks loose. And the word 'free' sounds out again – 'Free, free, free?' – in all its doubleness, as a call to battle: 'Mrs Wix had never been so harsh; but on the other hand Maisie could guess that she herself had never appeared so wanton.' And the strongly evoked moment of peace on the rampart of the old town collapses into the shrill voices of a suddenly violent altercation between the girl and the woman: a sudden new realism of dialogue, and a sharp, almost embarrassing directness of opposed feeling between the two friends to show the vulnerability of harmonizing visions. The Mrs Wix principle, distinctly un-Jamesian, that the 'moral sense' into which Maisie must be initiated is a faculty of condemnation, now rides roughshod over those very phenomena of the French scene that previously comprised Maisie's richer, uncondemning perceptions. Their conversation, later in the day, is closely focused on the moral sense; but the setting, like Marmion in *The Bostonians*, is active in a quite opposite direction, enters in a more relaxed and sensuous language, and continues subtly to obtrude into the narrative its qualifying counterpoint as a memory of vision and of madonnas 'shining in the blue' – even though at one point Mrs Wix tries to convert it, pervert it, into a mere 'fulcrum' for the rigid moral lever of her mission towards Maisie:

The beauty of the day only deepened, and the splendour of the afternoon sea, and the haze of the far headlands, and the taste of the sweet air . . . The bathers, so late, were absent and the tide was low; the sea-pools twinkled in the sunset and there were dry places as well, where they could sit again and admire and expatiate: a circumstance that, while they listened to the lap of the waves, gave Mrs. Wix a fresh fulcrum for her challenge. 'Have you absolutely [no moral sense] at all?'   (pp. 232–3, ch. 26)

The tense relationship between these two fundamental modes of apprehending experience, the imaginative-sensory and the ethically discriminating – a relation that would seem to be, at a deep level, the *primum mobile* of this novel's whole drama of people and of styles – produces at this point, in a way very different from the explicitness of any intellectual formulation, some strikingly involved displacements of language and mode. For example, as Mrs Wix continues to instruct Maisie in the formulae of moral discrimination – and we are never shown this jangling process directly, only refracted and hence deprecated by James's elliptical rendering of it – Maisie's awareness of the nature of this moralistic instruction, of being made to give clear names to the sexual situations of her elders, comes up against the style of her contrary awareness, that of instinct and forgiveness, associated with her vision on the rampart, and now deplored by Mrs Wix. We follow, first, the impressive analytic and inductive processes in Maisie's mind when she works out how exactly Mrs Wix sees her and how the mentor has been herself educated by having to deal with her (Maisie's) unconventional half-knowledge of the world. Then her inductive processes – which are presumably more akin to the kind of moral sense that Mrs Wix wishes her to attain – are quickly translated, or redeemed, into something else: something almost visionary in her former way, synoptic and imaginative rather than analytic. The whole thing is done with wit, very much in the Donne manner, the transposition of Maisie's modes of perception being conveyed to us by the transpositions of the narration's odd humour:

She judged that if her whole history, for Mrs Wix, had been the successive stages of her knowledge, so the very climax of the concatenation would, in the same view, be the stage at which the knowledge should overflow. As she was condemned to know more and more, how could it logically stop before she should know Most? It came to her in fact as they sat there on the sands that she was distinctly on the road to know Everything. She had not had governesses for nothing: what in the world had she ever done but learn and learn and learn? She looked at the pink sky with a placid foreboding that she soon should have learnt All. They lingered in the flushed air till at last it turned to grey and she seemed fairly to receive new information from every brush of the breeze. (pp. 233–4, ch. 26)

The very progress in that quotation from the Wix-like opening words, 'She judged that', to the last aesthetic phrase, 'every brush of the breeze', confirms this subtle transference from one mental pattern to another, and the subsuming of private 'judgement' within a larger, world-related 'sensation'. And the climactic advance, done with humorous mock-solemn capitals, from Most to Everything to All, and from personal history (with its internal 'stages') to the external stages of the 'sands', 'the world', 'the pink sky', and 'the flushed air', is a kind of parodying transmutation of what Mrs Wix is didactically striving for (seeking to string neat 'pearls of intelligence' on a 'long, tense cord') into the richer, more dissolving mode of poetic vision.

The drift towards synoptic vision, as opposed to the 'long, tense cord' of ethical judgement and logic, is confirmed when the interlude of Maisie and Mrs Wix alone in Boulogne ends next morning with the two of them back on their bench once again gazing 'at their gilded Virgin' and bursting out mutually not in their previous discord, and not any more in the categorical mode of condemnation ('Branded by the Bible'), but with unprecedented frankness and in the language of passion: their shared jealousy of Mrs Beale, their terror at what she might be doing to *their* Sir Claude, and their conjoined cries of 'I adore him' and 'Oh, I know'. On their bench, under that just-hinted-at presence that evoked harmonies the day before, the two of them (just for a moment like Olive and Verena in their 'shame') now come together in the dissolving humiliation of loving Sir Claude to the point of rage – Mrs Wix giving a quite unmoralistic 'wild grunt' of selfish involvement, and Maisie abandoning the search for required answers in favour of the 'brightness suffusing the scene' and the blending of tears:

Their hands were so linked and their union was so confirmed that it took the far, deep note of a bell, borne to them on the summer air, to call them back to a sense of hours and proprieties. They had touched bottom and melted together. . . (p. 240, ch. 26)

The language suddenly throbs hotly in sympathy, a little religiously, rather preciously, a little erotically. Then in one of those theatrical *tours de force* that can make James's narrative spin like a top, a raucous crash of worldly irony closes off this episode of exalted feeling, and Mrs Beale, for whom no golden Madonna will ever loom in the blue, stands glittering in the hotel room, crying out triumphantly the book's eternal, ambiguous refrain of 'I'm free, I'm free!'

The hypnotic effect on Mrs Wix of Mrs Beale's consciously chosen grand style – her daring assumptions and extravagantly deployed charm – reintroduces the note of percussive high comedy, as Mrs Wix's moral outrage flickers lower and lower (like the Wentworths succumbing to Eugenia) and Maisie watches to see whether Sir Claude, returning to Boulogne, might after all make up the 'four' that comprised her vision of unity. The behind-the-scenes discussions between Maisie and Mrs Wix reach a new racy explicitness. And they both agree – as if to prepare us – that the morning's advent of Sir Claude, whether or not he is *with* Mrs Beale (and we are given a broadly comic nudge in the ribs – *'Et pour Madame?'* the *patronne* asks him – to the effect that he has indeed come to the hotel to live with her), has ushered in the book's last crisis. 'It's tremendously grave', says Mrs Wix, weeping again; and Maisie solemnly agrees.

The last crisis – Maisie's breakfast and morning stroll with a serious, nervous Sir Claude – is enacted amid those warmly evocative details of the French scene that have already been seen to play a crucial role in suggesting a happier setting, a richer possibility for life than can be achieved by the mode either of moral condemnation or of social persiflage and display. The hotel is left behind, containing the representatives of both these rejected modes. Maisie and Sir Claude must leave Mrs Wix and Mrs Beale till they have discovered what possible future situation can be constituted between the two of them – or among the three of them, or the four of them. As quickly as it had disappeared, intensity of feeling returns to the narrative, increased by the clear signal which so often gives an almost Conradian urgency and darkness to James's denouements, that if a vision is to be grasped, there is only one chance in life to do so, and that an insecure one. And – equally Conradian, equally Forsterian – what the crisis reveals more clearly than ever before is that at the very centre of charm like Sir Claude's, and of his whole being, as a man and as a quasi-hero, is weakness and passivity:

Why was such a man so often afraid? It must have begun to come to her now that there was one thing just such a man above all could be afraid of. He could be afraid of himself. His fear at all events was there; his fear was sweet to her, beautiful and tender to her, was having coffee and buttered rolls and talk and laughter that were no talk and laughter at all with her; his fear was in his jesting, postponing, perverting voice . . .   (pp. 272–3, ch. 30)

With this highlighted perception, such a feature of Jamesian tragedy, that a personal weakness, especially male weakness, can be the very object of love, and hence the mark of its doom – the mark of Owen Gereth, of Vanderbank, of Merton Densher, of Chad, even of the Prince – we begin to feel the shadowed inevitability of the novel's ending. Across the frothing hot milk poured by the waiter, so dexterously and Frenchly, Maisie and Sir Claude, in a scene of wonderful sardonic insight, begin to search one another out, telling lies and half-lies, defensively, embarrassedly, and with troubled affection and need. The hollowness can be detected now, like a flaw in the core of everything that takes place between them. For the impossible terms of what he proposes – that Maisie should live, minus the scandalized Mrs Wix, along with the cohabiting Sir Claude and Mrs Beale, being loved and cared for, but inevitably being used and manipulated by the two lovers, even if not quite consciously, to give a gloss of respectability to their liaison – the impossibility of that situation, compounded by the growing sense of distance between Maisie and her stepmother, can now be felt almost physically like a weight on their relationship. And how Maisie recognizes this impossibility – the kind of knowledge she always brings to bear in a crisis – is not by logic or moral scruple, not by any inductive 'pearl of intelligence', but by an extreme instinctual emotion: in this case a cold 'terror' at herself and her all-too-human weakness when faced by such terms and by such a gamble.

Confronting the utter loss of her vision of unity – not just the breach in the unity of the four but, far worse, in the unity of the two, herself and Sir Claude – Maisie's idea of escape to Paris, around which so many theories have been woven, is rather less complex, or surely at least less sexually suggestive, than has often been said.[29] It seems more consonant with what we have read so far that Maisie's fear – she and Sir Claude exchange many looks of fear – should be seen not as a guilty fear felt by each at the

70

possibility of some sexual relation between them, but simply as Maisie's fear of having to lose Sir Claude, all chance of surrogate parental love, and everything that the 'space' across the Channel seemed to promise; and Sir Claude's fear of the increasingly formidable Mrs Beale (perfectly compatible with his loving her in his way), fear of Mrs Wix's outrage, genuine fear of losing the child's affection, and fear, simply, of so much impending 'fuss' and awkwardness. His fear represents James's perception of the limits to personal charm and of the flaw that, more often even in his philosophy than in Conrad's or Forster's, is tragically innate to the male will. 'Freedom' (just as in another more famous idyll: in Eden) seems to have brought only responsibility, the necessity of fateful choice, and the prospects of banishment:

The strangest thing of all was what had really happened to the old safety. What had really happened was that Sir Claude was 'free' and that Mrs. Beale was 'free', and yet that the new medium was somehow still more oppressive than the old. (p. 285, ch. 31)

The drama of escape to Paris is a subterfuge: a mere procrastination. And hence it is almost a parody − or rather, perhaps, a rueful conclusion − of Maisie's desireful vision beneath the gold Madonna. If the account of what happens in the railway station is full of tension, it is a tension we respond to in terms of everything that has gone before, the narrative's established ebb-and-flow of tone and feeling, rather than in terms of some new, startling sexual electricity passing between the girl and her stepfather. It is true that we found sexual infatuation with Sir Claude on Mrs Wix's part; but that was controlled stylistically by comedy, by touches of farce, and by other aspects of narrative *maniera*. No such alleviating absurdity could cover Maisie and Sir Claude now; and the presence of overt sexual feeling between them here would surely be an incongruity, an embarrassment beyond the capacity of even this daringly variable narrative mode to absorb. The incident of the train − the train almost taken, the train missed, the train helplessly watched as it leaves the platform − touches closely on one of the most familiar kinds of anxiety dream. Even Maisie's strange telepathic understanding of the French spoken by the porter and Sir Claude fits in with the events of dream and the dream-terror of mysterious half-communicative words − 'It was the most

71

extraordinary thing in the world.' He stands white-faced; her fear is greater than she has ever felt in her life. The incident expresses, with the indirection but all the compression of a dream-image, the stresses of their situation; the idea of escape, of expansion, of at least one clear kind of decision made to catch a train, buy a ticket, find a key verb (' *"Prenny, prenny. Oh prenny!"*), anything to break the impasse of four figures helplessly locked together, helplessly straining apart, almost travelling, looking for strength, waiting for the word of choice, waiting for the moment (*'Ah, vous n'avez plus le temps!'* – p. 288, ch. 31). And the incident, again as a dream does, slightly changes the situation it has expressed. It passes very quickly; the narration does not brood on it; it is almost, though not quite, ordinary and naturalistic. But at the end of it Maisie's fear has disappeared: the loss of the train has released her ability to choose and, working as ever by instinct, to venture across some inward Channel towards the possibility of resolution. She will give up Mrs Wix if Sir Claude gives up Mrs Beale. It is almost a return to the practice and to the deadly style of London life: the style of tit for tat, a blue-eyed Captain against a slightly hairy Countess, the style of billiards, a stepmother for a stepfather, a child bounced from adult to adult like a shuttlecock.

Maisie's last invocation (and the narrative's last devastating invocation) of the Madonna comes as a signficantly hollow gesture. While Sir Claude, as she hopes, breaks with Mrs Beale, and Mrs Wix, in exchange, is packed off in the boat, Maisie will return to the place of inclusiveness and healing (where she need never miss a train, or catch a steamer, or learn, by some 'moral sense', to condemn). But the very vagueness of an echo – not the echo, yet, of a cave, but of a personal and social emptiness – hollows out the place, the thing, the gold symbol, and the words:

'I'll stay out till the boat has gone. I'll go up to the old rampart.'
'The old rampart?'
'I'll sit on that old bench where you see the gold Virgin.'
'The gold Virgin?' he vaguely echoed. But it brought his eyes back to her as if after an instant he could see the place and the thing she named – could see her sitting there alone. 'While I break with Mrs. Beale?'
'While you break with Mrs. Beale.'
He gave a long, deep, smothered sigh.   (p. 291, ch. 31)

Mrs Beale will never go. And, back now in the hotel, the narrative turns away from lost visions or half-illusory trains, and with its old virtuosity shifts quickly into the mode of loud challenge, abuse, social comedy, and stagey, even melodramatic action, with Maisie's lambent sense of loss in the centre of it all, amid the clattering, shrieking voices fighting over her. 'You're free – you're free' is a tribute to her from the anguished Sir Claude; but the words have all their familiar ironic resonances, as devastating as an echo, and signalize more a burden and a deprivation than a liberation. It is a grand theatrical *scène à faire*, full of comically strident denunciations, appeals, confessions of strong feeling, with faces flushing up, and exclamation marks galore; Maisie being clutched, pulled, and pushed, Mrs Beale blocking the exit like a dragoness, Mrs Wix ranting, Maisie watchful, careful, and monosyllabic, Sir Claude dauntlessly announcing his Micawberish intention of never deserting Mrs Beale; then a chorus of good-byes, some gentle and some harsh, and a quick last rush to the harbour. Like the ending of *The Bostonians* and some scenes of *The Europeans* – only much more so – it is all a highly arranged and Feydeau-like performance: so very performed, so last-scened and final-curtained, that Maisie, though still touchingly, rather recedes from our perception as the narrative recedes, returning across her Channel with her inviolability retained and her future, with or without Mrs Wix, undisclosed. There has been just the making of a very human tragedy in all this: the consciously precarious gilding over of a flawed golden bowl, for two or three individuals and for the end-of-century world they inhabit. But the possibility of tragedy is now moved off wittily, though not quite definitively, into the wings. Without the careful mannerisms and elisions of the last few lines – Mrs Wix and Maisie on the ferry hesitant, waiting, 'silent awhile', then easing one another off with, respectively, 'a sidelong look' and 'Oh, I know!'; and then the book's title brought in, like an artful signature, as its last three words – without the final mitigation of these self-reflexive gestures to keep up a style in the narrating, there might well have been too great a weight of feeling for it, or us, to bear.

4. The *Bowl* restored

Precariousness and the keeping up of a style; the anticipation of dissolution and the passion to construct and restore − *The Golden Bowl* is, after the miniaturism of *Maisie*, a prose epic of these contrary principles and effects. James's imagination of disaster − the phrase is used by him of Fleda Vetch in *The Spoils of Poynton* − has never been far beneath the surface even of his more comic, or more stagey writing, as we have seen. And while *The Golden Bowl* is unusual in the positive possibilities − optimism is hardly the word − of its actual conclusion, compared with that of *The Ambassadors* and *The Wings of the Dove*, it does represent in many ways the consummation of James's darkest doubts about his world, and also of the swarming, constructing indirections of style by which he tries to confront and contain disaster. It is the last and the most unsparingly extreme of James's major fictions, and, in 1904, its complexly elliptical language, its method of submersion in the labyrinthine processes of consciousness, and its sombre reverberative ironies seem symbolically to usher in the post-Victorian era. The art of Conrad and Forster − the first by now in the middle and most successful period of his writing career; Forster at the outset of his, with short stories in print, and at work on both the Italian novels − is nowhere more significantly prefigured in *The Golden Bowl* than in its combined sense of an architectural, fabricative confidence and of something apparently opposite: a self-questioning unease and ambiguity that riddles its narrative textures as well as the fictional world it examines.

Through the novel as a whole, as through *The Bostonians*, there is a detectably progressive narrative thrust: the endless multiplications and ramifications, the cutting of facet against facet, do point forwards, create enquiry and suspense, cause a sense of wonder. Something is being built to some end, ever so painfully, scrupulously − often maddeningly. How will it turn out? Meanings and connections slowly but imperturbably unfold, strand leading into strand. Will the meanings disintegrate, or be re-made? Will knowledge ever become hard and revealed − or revealed to us indirectly by image and intuition, as Maisie's was? Fictional human relationships are being built up stage by stage, in all their fluctuations. We participate, for example, in the sense of the making −

the inventing, the dangerous fostering – of Adam's marriage with Charlotte. We participate in the slow, enforced, yet unresisted conjunction of Charlotte and the Prince, and recognize the climactic nature of her visit to him in the rain at Portland Place. Then, as on a graph, we see the point where Maggie, sitting in her drawing-room at the fulcrum of the novel, has to start again from the beginning, determined to put things right by influence and suggestion – by *making* things right, by building up and protecting the 'precious equilibrium' of them all. This line of progression, so essential for the toiling reader and so integral to the aesthetic effect of pattern and harmony, is assisted by recurrent symbol and motif, by sharply illustrative scenes and dramatic crises – the bridge-players at Fawns observed by Maggie through a window, the first public gesture of Charlotte staying on with the Prince on the Embassy stairs – by the structured alternation of drama, panorama, commentary, and restrospect; and, among other things, by the unravelling, interpretative agonizings of Fanny Assingham, who functions as a mode of knowing and coping as much as she does as a character. It is a perfect jigsaw of authorial voice and projected event, of solemnity and playfulness, of an interest in one character or aspect that rises, then fades, and is succeeded by another.

This sense of deep purposiveness cannot be underestimated: it vitalizes the mannered massiveness of the narration. And the purposiveness is given its edge by an underlying awareness of what threatens purposiveness and the whole sought-for 'equilibrium' of the bowl. For the narration also creates, and indeed depends upon, the very Jamesian perception of precariousness: a conveyed experience of the tightrope, of the knife's edge. There are so many pauses and silences to subvert, and not just as in *The Europeans* to extend, the act of confident narration itself. Even the instability of a single word, 'buried', as we shall see in the novel's last sentence, is dizzying, and repeats the many other instances of something in this language that resists, though it can never destroy, the act of building and creating. Even the elaboration of linguistic conceits – those pagodas-cum-ivory-towers of mixed metaphor, like the famous one in chapter 25, that rise and bristle so frequently – is simultaneously an assured constructiveness and a dissolution into unease. The style is full of swaggering self-delight: the pleasure of pure decoration, as well as of underlying scrupulous expression. But it also pushes itself frequently to a point of extravagance where it suddenly stops itself short, allows a voice (of differentiated dialogue, of parody, of unexpected bluntness) to challenge this extravagance and, by inference (as in *Maisie*), to expose the double-edgedness of the higher style. Unrestricted decoration can turn into a vortex; and the endlessly proliferating divisions and self-divisions of hair-splitting analysis can become a mirror reflecting a mirror. Something there is in such narration that does not love its own pagodas – and should not love them, at least not un-qualifiedly, any more than Maggie loves the complex marital 'situation' for which she (and James) deploy the pagoda-image over three pages:

> This situation had been occupying, for months and months, the very centre of the garden of her life, but it had reared itself there like some strange, tall tower of ivory, or perhaps rather some wonderful, beautiful, but outlandish pagoda, a structure plated with hard, bright porcelain, col-oured and figured and adorned, at the overhanging eaves, with silver bells that tinkled, ever so charmingly, when stirred by chance airs. She had walked round and round it – that was what she felt; she had carried on her existence in the space left her for circulation, a space that sometimes seemed ample and sometimes narrow; looking up, all the while, at the fair structure that spread itself so amply and rose so high, but never quite making out, as yet, where she might have entered had she wished . . .
>
> So it was that their felicity had fructified; so it was that the ivory tower, visible and admirable doubtless, from any point of the social field, had risen stage by stage.[30]

'Stage by stage', section by section, clause by clause, revelation by revelation, obliquity by obliquity, *The Golden Bowl* builds itself up against its own evocation of what unbuilds and tears down: formlessness, brutality, unresisted betrayal, loss of will and awareness, failure to be ingenious or to change – and, in addition, the moral blindness, the blank spot in the very centre of the spiral of style, of civilized elegance, and of the Princely manner of the one ex-emplary *galantuomo*. This is very much the final Jamesian stage: the daunting stage of supreme super-subtlety, self-analysing refinement, and the multiplication of aspects; the stage where the divergence of critical response will always be at its sharpest, and where the reader's confidence in being able to trawl such a myriad of nuances into his consciousness is at its lowest. A single representative chapter, closely examined, might offer more hope of gaining a purchase on such a work, and of fairly typifying some of the complications of its techni-que. Being the last chapter, the last scene of this culminating Jamesian stage, it is filled with the climactic pressures of what this whole particular fiction has built up painstakingly in all the poetical and analytical crosscurrents of its method: that method of assertive yet mistrustful narrative-building by which Conrad and Forster, too, on the brink of the most precarious of centuries, expressed the fear, like James's in this book and all his books, that with the failure of love chaos might come again, and the perennial desire of the artist that the bowl, the *Bowl*, might by the act of narrating be restored.

Maggie Verver, in her last scene, then, is seated in her drawing-room, watchful and apprehensive. The whole house is held in an autumnal hush, while her husband paces nervously beside the glittering tea-table. The end of *The Golden Bowl*, so expressive of James's most developed mode of indirection and inward stress, opens on the tension of waiting. Indeed this had been prepared for, in the scene immediately before, by a characteristic Jamesian litany on the very word, 'Wait': the Prince, in his bafflement, offering it to her as his urgent promise of sexual restitution; Maggie then repeating it to him, and to herself, as a curb on her own capacity for surrender.[31] Such waiting is permeated by the pressures – 'the great sea' – of desire. Only after waiting, and by waiting, can the bowl possibly be restored, and filled.

What they are waiting for is also, of course – the incongruity is essential – a mere social visit. These private urgencies must always run counter to – and yet, so typically, be expressed and moulded by – the social event. Everything that Maggie has striven for through the second half of the action – to preserve the 'precious equilibrium' of the two couples while effecting radical unseen changes in the relationships among all four individuals – can be seen as represented in this farewell visit at tea-time by the Ververs *en route* to America. The forms have to be preserved – 'the form of their reunion'. If visits are no longer to be paid, or familiar public phrases to be exchanged around the tea-table, then everything the social forms mask and contain – feelings, pressures, betrayals, promises – will spill over into formlessness and disaster. Restitution and new growth will be possible only if feelings are harnessed into shapes, into the articulate elisions of mannered behaviour, mannered language.

Waiting itself is one form of containment. The reader from his own vantage point watches this form draw its lines between and around the Prince and Maggie. She pretends to read; over there, he paces; the bright-flowered room, with the balcony at the end, gives the dimension of space; their self-awareness grows in it, and gathers towards utterance in conversation. As well as the reader's direct view — 'a spectator sufficiently detached' is how James invokes the reader — we share Maggie's view as it makes shapes, some of them playful, some interpretative, around the implications of the scene in which she is placed. Her mind, artistically, 'even played a little with the prospect'; sees a humorous irony in the formality of their *ménage* and postures ('We're distinctly *bourgeois*!'); and by remembering a similar event, when she waited, full of her climactic sense of discovery and threat, for the Prince to return so late from Matcham (part 4, first chapter), she activates the device of significant repetition as a part of interpretative form ('there hovered in her own sense the thought of other occasions when she had cheated appearances of agitation with a book'). It is then directly the narrator himself, rather than Maggie, who uses repetition and reminiscence to effect a resonant connection in our minds by the allusion to this balcony being the very one from which the Prince and Charlotte had gazed down months before on the upturned faces of Maggie and her father. And the event is further moulded by another, and ubiquitous, mannered device, the decorative extravagance by which the narrator, without seeking to interpret, 'places' the scene as well as wittily embellishing it, the sentence of his commentary having in itself something of the mannered pomp and glitter of a tea-visit:

They might have been ready, on the word passed up in advance, to repair together to the foot of the staircase — the Prince somewhat in front, advancing indeed to the open doors and even going down, for all his princedom, to meet, on the stopping of the chariot, the august emergence.

Like Mrs Ramsay in *To the Lighthouse*, who struggles at the beginning of her paradigmatic dinner party to recreate the shaping forms of consciousness against the raw darkness of tiredness, misunderstanding, and ill-feeling, so Maggie, before her last social testing in this visit of the Ververs — her dinner party, as it were, of human arrangement and of social covenant — has to flare out in a brief assertion of necessary authority. The apparently sacrificial creature can also sharply command by 'lucid firmness' when she has to preserve the precarious forms for living she has been forced to devise. For the Prince suddenly, as conversation between the two of them breaks out of so much waiting, threatens inadvertently to bring everything crashing down. After such model tactfulness, he now suggests at the critical last moment that he must tell Charlotte certain truths about the situation — as if the whole agonizing logic of Maggie's long wait and travail had not been that certain truths can be too destructive, too self-indulgent by far. This last encounter among them all, to be a consummation, *must* continue in the tense mode that Maggie has established of evasion, delicacy, and tautly mannered high style. It is all a matter of a knife edge: and of narrating the knife edge. With the Prince's uncharacteristic directness — ' "I shall tell her I lied to her" ' — the narrative momentarily subjects Maggie's chosen way of ellipsis, which it mostly endorses, to the test. His voice, almost strident in the drawing-room, is a relief to us, after so many thousand words of honeyed nuance and withholding. James allows us to feel the strain, to feel the temptation of the other way, the way of the outraged cry: not restoration but the bringing down of an elaborate house of cards with violence and relief. Then having given it voice — and it must have its full voice in the narration — he makes Maggie triumph quickly, dangerously, once again, like Mrs Ramsay rising from her dinner party and exiting like a queen (*too* like a queen):

After which, while he quite stared for it, as it was the very first clear majesty he had known her to use, she flung down her book and raised a warning hand. 'The carriage. Come!'[32]

Maggie's brief regality is only a prologue to Charlotte's, which, much more, is the real, if enacted, thing. If Maggie's firmness and perceptiveness have acted so as to prepare the scene, then Charlotte proceeds to round it out. Maggie's creative preservation of appearances is succeeded by Charlotte's pure theatricality, and in the role of the latter the Baroness Munster, just for a second, makes her return to the stage, evoking Acton's unanswerable question, 'Is she honest, is she honest?' It is also the question that James played with more extensively and searchingly in *The Tragic Muse*: in acting, and in life, which is the role and which the actress?[33] There is more than a touch of this quizzicality in the portrayal of Charlotte now, in her grandest manner, giving 'so resplendent a show of serenity' that 'the difficulty now indeed was to choose, for explicit tribute of admiration, between the varieties of her nobler aspects'. The fulsomeness is distinctly, indeed opulently, ironic:

The shade of the official, in her beauty and security, never for a moment dropped; it was a cool, high refuge, like the deep, arched recess of some coloured and gilded image, in which she sat and smiled and waited, drank her tea, referred to her husband and remembered her mission.

Yet we recognize only too clearly that Charlotte is, in part, acting out the role that Maggie — innocent little Maggie — has created for her; and is adopting exactly the social forms that Maggie has chosen and, to a large extent, redeemed by her choosing them. Indeed Maggie feels a 'richer relief' in recognizing at once that Charlotte has decided, not like the Prince in a rough moment to tell truths, but like Maggie herself to make 'the occasion easy', and to be 'conjoined'.

However, there is no escape from the knife edge. Even as the narrator swells with amused admiration at Charlotte as *grande dame*, and even as Maggie draws comfort from the spectacle, there is a very sudden, brief drop. Charlotte's capacity to manipulate her aspects — all acting, all social manners and form-making being an affair of more or less benign manipulation — is very 'consummate', as Maggie, somewhat provincial in her vocabulary of appreciation, praises the way Charlotte so blandly accepts a *petit four*. But quite unexpectedly the other side of manipulation is abruptly brought before us, without preparation, halfway through a sentence (describing the overshadowed presence of Charlotte's husband) that seems to have begun in the mode of wit and 'consummate' celebration:

But Adam Verver profited indeed at this time, even with his daughter, by his so marked peculiarity of seeming on no occasion to *have* an attitude; and so long as they were in the room together she felt him still simply weave his web and play out his long fine cord, knew herself in presence of this tacit process very much as she had known herself at Fawns.

The reminder is very deliberate on James's part — as pointed as his earlier allusions to the ominous past associations of the balcony overlooking Portland Place, and to Maggie's memory of having sat once before pretending to read. All the strange, cold unpleasantness of the former incident at Fawns — the 'silken noose' of authority that Maggie had seen her father hold there around the neck of his humiliated and unenlightened wife, leading her 'by the neck . . . to her doom', with the 'high coerced quaver' of Charlotte's voice as she guiltily fears but never knows the extent of her husband's suspicions (part 5, fourth chapter) – rises up almost incongruously into this present incident. This interweaving, so endemic to *The Golden Bowl*, of bland worldliness and cold fear is a very intricate one, and often difficult to read. The phrase 'simply weave his web and play out his long fine cord' sounds harmless. But the pointed allusion back to the very different tone of Fawns makes the difference; for there, previously, we had not only the 'silken noose' but the 'silken halter', 'twisted silken rope', 'immaterial tether', 'long cord', 'gathered lassoo', and in control at the other end 'the hooked thumb' of Adam. And the whole complexity of evaluation which determines the reader's relation to Adam Verver is exemplified now in the fact that he is an 'overshadowed' figure without so much as an 'attitude' yet still plays out the Fawns 'cord' of a harsh authoritativeness;[34] in the fact that he is 'the dear man' (the phrase is dropped into its sentence parenthetically, as if to emphasize that this is Maggie's evaluation of him) though in moving about the room 'noiselessly' he is not just blandly effacing himself but also expressing an 'intention' with 'a certain sharpness'; and the fact that leaving his wife 'to her devices' is shown to imply towards these devices 'as actually exhibited in their rarity . . . a settled appreciation of their general handsome adequacy'. This latter appreciativeness, with its vocabulary of mingled connoisseurship, financial power, and a collector's possessiveness, adds a darker dimension to his 'faint contemplative hum': the Pooh-like hum, as well as being a comic, childlike, and endearing trait, also hints at the contemplativeness of the aesthete and the reserved man of power. Little wonder that with such doubleness running through almost every sentence, we should be told (though this particular point is made with surprising directness) that the 'right quiet lustre' and sustained 'harmony' of the present scene in Portland Place is only 'superficial', and that one moment of silent awkwardness between the Prince and Adam is an 'approach to a break in it'.

The foregrounding of the overtly aesthetic aspects of the encounter – they were already latent in Charlotte's adoption of an 'official' role like that of 'some coloured and gilded image' – now precipitates the one explicit and commanding art-image of the whole scene. From watching the aesthetic display of Charlotte's 'consummate' manners, Maggie is 'floated' by 'the slow surge of a vision' to join her father in looking at the early Florentine painting which was his marriage present to her. The coming together of the father and daughter now for the first – and indeed for the last – time, gathered in contemplation (almost a 'vision') around a precious picture of a religious subject, which is also an explicit token of their past relationship and of her marriage, is a richly freighted moment, and comprises the most emphasized element of the whole episode: the two related conversations between Adam and Maggie, once before the picture, the other immediately after, on the balcony.

The focus provided by the painting is almost too intense. James's quasi-religiosity, never far from the surface, now suddenly wells up, and after 'the slow surge of a vision . . . floated her' we have 'tenderness', 'sacrifice', 'treasure', 'infusion', 'immortal expression', 'beauty of his sentiment', 'spiritual face', 'clasping arms', 'abiding felicity', and 'speech failed them'. Here is one of the notable ways by which (in the phrase from the chapter's very first sentence) 'the form of their reunion' is to be filled out, almost to overflowing, by intense personal emotion – the form here being the precarious shape, the bowl, of their relationship as father and daughter, as giver and receiver of the gift of picture, of selfhood, of past, present, and (though separated) future love. And the form for these feelings is also a continuingly social and temporal one: two people simply touching one another in a room, bending over a picture, among other objects and people in that room, and at a specific time.

The formal and social setting first intensifies then at once qualifies the private feeling, and provides an extraordinary example of how this narration can move between opposed extremes. Only a triumph of manipulation of tones, of precise cadences of language, can effect transitions with as many implications as this one – the modulations of *What Maisie Knew* seem almost simple in retrospect. The moment of near-ecstasy between Maggie and Adam is at once scaled down by the suggestion that their failure of speech might also be seen as merely resembling the awkward lapse of shared topics of conversation between old but separated friends. And the laconic shorthand of their congratulatory exchange about both the painting and the whole story of their marriages − '"It's all right, eh?" "Oh, my dear − rather!"'' − diverts our attention from the father and daughter to the surrounding context of situation and place that contains the signs of those marriages and of their being 'all right'. What the reader finds in that context is not the near-religious exaltation of a moment before but a detaching irony completely opposed to it. The Florentine picture, which we have been 'floated' into sympathetically as part of the throb that united Maggie and Adam, now becomes quite external, part of a room full of precious collectable things that 'stood out . . . consciously, for recognition and applause'. With a sudden detachment we watch father and daughter appraising their possessions, ticking them off one by one. Charlotte and the Prince are 'high expressions of the kind of human furniture required, aesthetically, by such a scene'; they are 'decorative elements', contributing significantly 'to the triumph of selection'. And in a startling, indeed jarring, change to a externalized narrative point of view, we have this:

. . . to a lingering view, a view more penetrating than the occasion really demanded, [Mrs. Verver and the Prince] also might have figured as concrete attestations of a rare power of purchase. There was much indeed in the tone in which Adam Verver spoke again, and who shall say where his thoughts stopped? *'Le compte y est.* You've got some good things.'

In this passage, James twice juggles insinuatingly with his narration. 'A lingering view, a view more penetrating than the occasion really demanded' suggests partly the opposite of what it says: it *is* demanded that Charlotte and the Prince be seen representing the power of Adam's money to buy them (and to marry them off), though the occasion, socially and psychologically, *also* demands the turning of a blind eye. Narrative penetration therefore takes place in the very act of denying its appropriateness. And the narratorial archness of 'who shall say where his thoughts stopped?', when the thinker (Adam) sums up the people and things they are admiring as blatantly and commercially as he does − *'le compte y est'* meaning literally 'the account is correct' − is to suggest, with careful vagueness, that Adam might be capable of a bottomless and materialistic cynicism. These two sudden minute twists of narrative strategy seem coy, as did a similar narrative cut-off in chapter 10 of *The Europeans*, analysed earlier: the peculiarly Jamesian feature is that the coyness is an integral part of the strategy.[35] By being coy, James has his cake and eats it. He reminds us — as in the allusion to the 'long fine cord' round Charlotte's neck both here and at Fawns — of the price that has to be paid for refusing the easy, if 'honest', way of rupture, anger, and separation: the tarnishing presence of manipulative consciousness necessary to sustain most human relationships. And simultaneously, the witty indirection of his phrasing endorses that rejection of open rupture by being itself an instance of mannerism, discretion, and elegant decoration. To adapt the metaphor, he draws attention to the profound crack in the bowl by a device of narrative and of commentary that simultaneously gilds over that crack — just as his protagonists at their tea-table, for all their individual awareness, are also engaged, with James's sympathy, in a gilding operation. And as if to demonstrate the extremes of discrimination that this kind of narrative is attempting to hold together in suspension, we are told that the Prince and Charlotte, as Maggie-the-collector murmurs 'Ah, don't they look well?' to her father, are like 'a pair of effigies of the contemporary great on one of the platforms of Madame Tussaud' — only for that risky *reductio ad absurdum* of the whole endeavour (not to mention the possible moral rebuke) to be at once gilded over by the emotional appeal of Maggie's elegiac 'I'm so glad — for your last look' and by the quite uncoy directness of the comment that for once almost sums up all these divagations:

Yes, this was the wonder, that the occasion defied insistence precisely because of the vast quantities with which it dealt — so that separation was on a scale beyond any compass of parting. To do such an hour justice would have been in some degree to question its grounds — which was why they remained, in fine, the four of them, in the upper air, united in the firmest abstention from pressure.

The narration itself must convey that pressure and sharply question these grounds; but must also work on a level where it does not seem to do so, in that it also conveys the experience of characters as they necessarily abstain from destructive realities — from what Maggie fears, beneath their silences and avoidances, to be 'the hard, the truer voice'.

James, with his ambivalent view of the nature of truth and of lying, often makes the ambivalence central to his dramatization of the social and the private life. A life without falsity is hardly a life at all, since life demands development and change, and development seems possible only by extensions of the self through artifice, manners, and complicating, untransparent communication: above all, extension into the realm of society, of relationships, and of ramifying consciousness. But, as for Conrad (and Conrad's Marlow), there is always a little death in even the most enriching lie: some loss of integrity, a betrayal of others, at best a coarsening. There is a paradigm of romantic tragedy in this single paradox of James's concerning duplicity, that a mode of behaviour which makes us fuller human beings must also by definition diminish and destroy us. But in *The Golden Bowl*, at least, the paradox takes us only to the brink of tragedy; and while, on the other hand, the effect of a consummating redemptiveness, I think, is not really apposite to this conclusion (though many, like John Bayley, Dorothea Krook, and Laurence Holland, would argue otherwise) the esteem and the desire for survival certainly are. In the conversation that ensues between Maggie and her father on the balcony, the principle of survival is paramount, is tested out by a few threatening echoes from 'the hard, the truer voice' beneath, and is articulated in the form of a key discovery by Maggie: that Charlotte's uses at the hands of Adam and his daughter are not yet exhausted, and include providing them with a fiction, a way out, a stylish allusion that contains at least some truth in it, and will ease all four through the ritual of farewell. Underneath the saving half-fiction that will now hold them all just sufficiently together we are made to detect the continuing echo of menace that gives the half-fiction its strain as well as its preciousness. Maggie 'asked herself but for a few seconds if reality, should she follow [Adam on to the balcony], would overtake or meet her there' — and though it is 'but a few seconds' it is enough to remind us just a little of her experience by night on the terrace at Fawns, where 'reality', in the shape of an aggressively forthright Charlotte, pursued her like a creature escaped from its cage. And the very thought of any truly open confession between herself and her father affects Maggie here with a hyperbolic terror of violence, almost animal violence: 'such a passage . . . would have torn them to pieces, if they had so much as suffered its suppressed relations to peep out of their eyes'.

The saving half-fiction is inevitably extravagant and incongruous: it consists in offering to her father the notion that

Charlotte's greatness as a character is what she, Maggie, will most miss through their separation, and that the growth of Charlotte's greatness has been the justification of all their ventures. The rest of the passage between Maggie and Adam consists in an almost musical elaboration of this conceit. The two of them, aware of 'suppressed relations', aware of the deep flaw in what they are engaged in reconstituting and celebrating, aware of the dark echo beneath their decorous and courtly wordplay, toss the idea from one to the other like jugglers hiding some private grief or unease. It is the high social game, the golden lie, at its most developed; and the narrating of it is itself a feat of the sophisticated consciousness and style. By not uttering the 'truth' of her grief at losing her father – Fawns without *him*, not Charlotte, is her 'suppressed' agony for which the name of Charlotte is 'a bold but substantial substitute' – Maggie achieves something heroic as well as refined. Their communicative indirectness, their using the 'substitute', is to behave 'in a manner exaltedly, sublimely' – a sacrifice of full communication verging on one of those acts of abnegation to which James so often attributes nobility in his novels. But the tension of the exchange also contains a contrary aspect, in that the conceit, the 'lie', of lauding Charlotte also has a truth in it. This truth is, as it were, something other, something found – and the order and the internal syntax of three sentences subtly emphasize the serendipity of truth, moving from its determining, abstract strangeness (far at first from conclusive 'words') to Maggie's more intimate observation of its 'sincerity' at work within her, then to her conscious adoption, articulation, and manipulation of what she has discovered:

Nothing was stranger moreover, under the action of Charlotte's presence, than the fact of a felt sincerity in her [Maggie's] words. She felt her sincerity absolutely sound – she gave it for all it might mean. 'Because Charlotte, dear, you know', she said, 'is incomparable'.

On this mingling of truth and artifice a 'basis' is achieved – though only after a tiny and precisely timed drama of gesture and silence which lasts for thirty seconds, then for another minute. In that thirty-second pause – like one of the pauses of *The Europeans*, though far more tense – Maggie and Adam turn away from the street and lean their backs on the balcony rail; Adam's eyes shine; then he asks, taking out his cigarette case, if he can smoke.

For another minute he lights his cigarette. In such highly concentrated theatricality we almost hear the sound of the match, while
the 'basis' of their peace-preserving 'lie' forms itself precariously
in the air between them, then is put to the test of their nervous
silence filled with the threat of 'suppressed relations', and
culminates in Maggie's deliberate hardness — 'not in the least to
falter' — of reiteration: 'Charlotte's great!'

Their earlier self-congratulation, 'It's all right', is now capable
of being extended. On the basis — the stretched tightrope — of a
belief in Charlotte's greatness, they can proceed to their only words
on the subject of their marriages — and to the high point of inarticulate communion between them. Adam takes up the basis that
his daughter has offered and pushes it a vital stage further: to the
idea of Charlotte's future greatness as well as her past. And on this
note of a success still to come, away from the far more dangerous
direction of retrospect (no matter how congratulatory), the security
of the bowl is at last almost attained. Adam, taking his half-cue,
accepts the role — or half-role, since he has little need to act it out
— of authoritativeness, of independence of his daughter, and,
above all, of 'possession and control'. The thrill Maggie feels on
hearing him toss off, with an almost arrogant confidence, the re-
joinder 'Oh, but naturally!' to her 'You know her best' comes from
speculating how far he must already have built upon her offered
basis: 'she found herself lost, though with a finer thrill than she had
perhaps yet known, in the vision of all he might mean'. Then she
realizes what he must mean: that they are parting, father and
daughter, on the imaginatively projected fiction (which is accumulating more and more truth as it grows) that his marriage with
Charlotte has not only been a success but will be an even greater
success in the future, especially when focused on the great plan for
American City which Charlotte's 'value' will irradiate and
energize. All this success will come from Charlotte's 'value'. The
word is almost shrilly insisted on and ecstatically repeated, with all
its various semantic resonances: meaning intrinsic quality; meaning
(at the very opposite) material worth in terms of exchange (that
'rare power of purchase' once again); meaning colour tone, as in
a painting (early Florentine or some other, more secular); meaning
latency, the power to go on projecting some particular quality in
new conditions, such as a new land, a new city; meaning, perhaps,

something even of the French, *'faire valoir'*, which James uses elsewhere more than once to sum up his own aspirations in writing – that is, to make something count, to realize and dramatize, to make the most of oneself or one's idea, to assert one's claims, one's talent, one's self. The word 'value' throbs with all these associations, as though the whole of James's *oeuvre*, with his plots of self-fulfilment or self-betrayal, is struggling to emerge from it: it clearly signifies far more than a simple criticism of Adam as financier. Charlotte as mere adulteress is almost lost in the glow of these meanings; though not totally and not for long. And on this climax of celebration, genuine discovery, and consciously enacted delusion the remarkable departure to America quite casually takes place, brushing tragedy aside; and the great tension, which had fuelled and necessitated the vision of Charlotte's 'value', subsides on her exit into a stillness so great as to seem newly 'created' rather than simply 'restored'. Out of this pristine silence, like the atmosphere of waiting in which the scene began, is to be shaped the final critical exchange which will either justify or negate all that has just passed between Maggie and her father. After the social event, with its outward geometry of place and movement, its fictions of politeness and, on a balcony, its exchanged vision, comes the ultimate intimacy on which the completion of the bowl (and the *Bowl*) depends.

At the end of so long a book, it is remarkable how much excitement and suspense can be generated in these closing paragraphs. Everything, we are made to feel, still hangs by a thread. All the proliferating ambivalences of the narration to this point, scene by scene and phrase by phrase, have built up their contrapuntal stresses to this last excruciating test. The very act of interpreting, identified with Maggie's consciousness in the narrative even more closely than was the act of knowing with Maisie's, is now openly referred to as part of the scene, part of its structure and topography. First, there is a surrounding blank area beyond interpretation, even hers: the solemn, new-created silence that is waiting, a little ominously, to give 'remarkable salience' to whatever meaning is about to take shape from her mind. Outside, where Maggie's father and stepmother have disappeared, London, which throughout the chapter has been a backdrop of season's end and desolation, is only a 'great grey space, on which, as on the room still more, the shadow of dusk had fallen'. Then, against this, 'the unheard chorus swelled' for Maggie's mind; and her consciousness, unexhausted, must pull itself together (like Mrs Ramsay's) in order to interpret, to understand, and to communicate understandings: to build her structures of intuition and of intelligent love against the void of London, her father's loss, and the underlying chaos that perpetually threatens their lives. So we follow her processes. She perceives, as she waits in quivering suspense, 'the meaning most disengaged'; she pieces together, out of the twilight 'where it lurked', 'her reason for what she had done'. She is close to knowledge, and to 'the golden fruit' of her 'reward': that is, her husband's response that will consummate – or may not: she feels a 'terror' at that – all her loving manipulations and pained withholdings.

Consummation, hermeneutic, aesthetic, spiritual, and sexual, is expressed to us – at a high risk – in the Jamesian vocabulary, once again, of money and commerce. It is to be for Maggie 'a reward', 'the certification of the amount', 'a wild speculation', the throwing of a 'dice'. The sight of Amerigo, sexually charismatic as always, is 'a view of the number' on the dice; by that sight alone she begins to be 'paid in full'; and in an ultimate, almost grotesque elaboration of the metaphor: 'So far as seeing that she was "paid" went, he might have been holding out the money-bag for her to come and take it.' Clearly there is a risk of the bathetic in such a conceit, not only in its simple incongruity but in its potential reintroduction of the Adam Verver motif of a reifying financial power; but only, I think, when taken out of its context. Within the compressed dramatic movements of these paragraphs, the progress from 'stillness' to 'meaning' to 'reward' to 'amount' to 'dice' to 'number' and then, in sudden flow, to 'paid' and 'money-bag' takes on a certain rhetorical fitness. The anticlimactic and even distasteful associations of 'money-bag' are largely pushed aside by the effect of the crescendo. The elaboration of the figure to a pitch beyond the normal decorum of metaphor is paralleled by the mounting emotional tension of the scene, its concentrated switches of mood, such as here, from a 'terror' of personal failure to 'concern' for another's anxiety. One extremism encourages the other. As in parts of *What Maisie Knew*, the pursuit of the image becomes an expressive, even an expressionist, gesture; and floridity of language, no matter how it reminds us of a narrating 'presence' (indeed perhaps because it so reminds us), becomes part of the almost melodramatic theatricality of the episode, which, in its turn, belongs to the theatricality and nervous mannerism of the whole preceding narrative. Even when Maggie's more-than-half-sexual sense of coming fruition and justification suddenly drops – again, the emotional switch is disconcerting – into a new 'horror' that the Prince will now at the last moment ruin everything by crudely 'confessing' his guilt, the same metaphor of payment is carried over successfully on the complex wave of feeling: 'This, in turn, charged her with a new horror: if *that* was her proper payment she would go without money.'[36]

Near the beginning of this final chapter, Maggie exercised sharp authority to prevent her husband's wish to be forthright with Charlotte from destroying the 'equilibrium' she had almost succeeded in constructing. Now at the end, to prevent another such possible shattering by 'the uttered word' – a fatal, unretractable articulation of a past reality too painful to redeem by confronting – she offers to him, as she did to her father, the alleviating half-fiction of Charlotte's 'greatness'. This is the device that must be their 'help'. But this last-minute invocation of Charlotte's 'mastery of the greater style' has a very particular effect, which in its final paragraph turns the ending of the book in on itself in a series of sudden movements that almost surpass, even while they dazzlingly epitomize, the complex dynamic of the whole. For in so quickly tossing off her evasively conventional trope – 'Isn't she too splendid?' – Maggie reminds us of how she, too, has come to share in 'the mastery of the greater style', and has become, so socially, so manipulatively, a mistress of indirection.[37] Her complementary and equal mastery of the direct, the natural – 'That's our help, you see', she adds, unCharlotte-like, to explain to the Prince her own use of that greater style – seems to be no more perceived by her husband than her mode of artifice. In his intention to possess her physically – as we have seen him on the point of doing several times in this very sexually-aware novel – the Prince merely echoes, emptily, the greater style she holds out to him: 'Oh, splendid!' And equally, her direct explanation, 'That's our help, you see', shows us his failure quite to 'see'; since he turns her clarifying words in the only direction he can follow: '"See"? I see nothing but *you*.' Their final embrace, therefore, passionate and consummating as it is, encloses a continuing incomprehension: at the very least a reminder of their disparity. The fact that his vision is filled by the intimate presence of Maggie is a partial triumph for both of them: she has made herself count totally (*'faire valoir'*) in his eyes, to the exclusion of Charlotte, and he has grown into a more complete and passional realization of who his wife is. But outside that triumphant physical embrace, masterfully taking, masterfully yielding, in the very last sentences there still exists the 'greater style' that has made it possible: the greater style, based on silence, elegance, and evasion, that Maggie has adopted in emulation of the doomed Charlotte, and that the Prince at this climax can still not fully comprehend.[38] The implications of that style − of its creativeness and of its destructiveness − are left hanging unresolved in the air. And while the 'pity and dread' that Maggie feels at the sight of his intent eyes − filled, to a fault, with the image of her alone − are not really an echo of the classic tragic emotions, as it is tempting to suggest,[39] but rather the traditional pity and fear of a woman at the displayed sexual desire and sexual possessiveness of a man, nevertheless they are strangely unexultant emotions with which to seal her love. Similarly, the strange light that fills the Prince's eyes is not just a light of partial new insight but also a light of merely single vision, of partial blindness. When Maggie finally 'buries' her eyes in the Prince's breast, the precarious doubleness of this whole narration is caught in that single word 'buries': a word signifying submission to a desired power, the eyes' 'vision' having been achieved and their lucidity no longer needed; but a word also of extinction, hardening, and loss, a reminder of what must always be 'paid' in life for any gain, and of some endemic flaw, some perpetual process of unmaking, even in the most 'enclosing', the most plenary of golden bowls.

This ultimate stage in James's sophistication of the art of narrative has also been a Jamesian stage in another sense, that of a slow-moving but meticulously directed theatre of language, mime, setting, figures in stylized collision and interplay, and of dangerously protean values. It has all been borne along by a powerful inventive urge to build intricately and build well, to allow no single divergent or confirmatory detail to escape rendering; and by the urge also to decorate, to indulge the creative self by following out the vagaries of image and metaphor, and frequently, in Paul Klee's phrase, simply to take a line − of prose − for a walk. The effect of vulnerability and excess, amid so much confident building, is paradoxical but integral: the art of the stage often ends by drawing attention to the hollowness within its own gestures, its shadows and gilded masks, and in this case its preternaturally knowing conversations that forever skirt, defy, and declare the brink. The precarious, self-scrutinizing, yet self-vaunting art of *The Golden Bowl* remains human and implicating. It is as social in its bearings as *The Bostonians*, and is as concerned with the minutiae of casual behaviour as *The Europeans* − as well as presenting the dauntingly esoteric and the near-apocalyptic. It still sees life, like art, as being not just a perpetual struggle of the articulatable against wordlessness and erosion, but equally as a moral struggle of a certain difficult decency against certain cruelties and perversities. As with Conrad and Forster, its night-fears and its aesthetic, self-mirroring virtuosity are still strongly ballasted by a humanist anguish. But in terms of indirection and ambiguity of narrating, it might seem to be something of a *ne plus ultra*. Where next could the modern novel go? At this final stage − this highest Jamesian pitch − of the creative consciousness moving and weaving like a shuttle, inexhaustibly, obsessively, and ultimately without delusion, it is significant, and perhaps even a relief, that Maggie Verver should end such a narrative of hyperawareness by the overburdened gesture of burying her eyes in darkness, and therefore in a willed closure of vision.

II · *Conrad's breaking strains*

Conrad is so much more obsessively than James a confronter of the abyss, so much more pessimistic an explorer of the dark places of existence, that we are perhaps more surprised to discover any eddies of strengthening consolation than of the reverse within the complex currents of his writings. Surprise, however, of one kind or another, hidden or overt, restorative or destructive, is integral to their vitality as narrations and as performances. For Conrad's fiction exists and affects the reader as a performance, for all that the control is less clearly theatrical and manipulative than in the case of either James or Forster, and so often suggests a more profoundly instinctive, even unbalanced and neurotic, working-out of personal pressures and contradictions. At certain points of his narratives – certain pressure points – something often rises up to challenge the progress and even decorum of what has already gone before, or what seems to have established itself as the governing mood or concept of the whole. For example, in *The Nigger of the 'Narcissus'* (1897), which I have already placed alongside *What Maisie Knew* as signalizing a new dimension of sustained ambiguity in the English turn-of-century novel, we find a typical version of the kind of conceptual dilemma that Conrad creates for himself time and time again and dramatizes – that is, *performs* – by the textural surprise of an outburst of invective or of celebration, or some almost wilful ironic overturning. There, alongside some of the most successfully descriptive narrative he ever achieved, having shown us a crew and a ship almost wrecked, literally as well as figuratively, by the debilitating influence of a self-flaunting sick man, James Wait, appealing to a crew's sympathy and hence to their self-pity, he finds himself in the complex position of having demonstrated that the power of human tenderness (in which narcissism is always entangled) can be seen as inimical to communal loyalty, efficiency, and survival in a stormy world[1] – an impasse not dissimilar to the one that destroys Heyst on his tropic island in

93

Victory. Conrad uses the paradox to intensify and irradiate his material, and we can hardly ask him also to resolve it intellectually. But at one point — there are others, too — he testifies to the size of the problem he has created by a telltale and disruptive excess of rhetorical glorification. Wait dies, is buried at sea, his incubus (the weight of the paradox?) is lifted from the becalmed ship, and suddenly the prose soars into its famous invocation of England and the English Channel:

> The lofty headlands trod masterfully into the sea; the wide bays smiled in the light; the shadows of homeless clouds ran along the sunny plains, leaped over valleys, without a check darted up the hills, rolled down the slopes; and the sunshine pursued them with patches of running brightness. On the brows of dark cliffs white lighthouses shone in pillars of light . . .
> A great ship! For ages had the ocean battered in vain her enduring sides; she was there when the world was vaster and darker, when the sea was great and mysterious, and ready to surrender the prize of fame to audacious men. A ship mother of fleets and nations! The great flagship of the race stronger than the storms! and anchored in the open sea.[2]

There is far more to the ending of *The Nigger of the 'Narcissus'* than this, and the unexpected effusion has to be seen and judged within the fluctuating movement of the whole story — exactly as with a rather similar, though more complicated, patriotic outburst in *Howards End* which we shall be looking at later. But Conrad's narrative textures are always exceedingly sensitive to their own burdens: here, the just-lifted nightmarish burden of Wait and the growing burden of the moral and intellectual dilemma that has grown around him, the dilemma being that the most creatively cohesive force of feeling known to man can also destroy him individually and corporately. And the sensitivity declares itself in one sudden deviation of style and feeling that suggests, by its excess, a note of panicky compensation — which might then be argued either to break the tale's coherence or, on the contrary, to catalyse its open-ended drama.[3]

Conradian indirection, then, while it raises more problems of critical judgement than in the case of James and Forster, is no less integral to the drama of his writing. What might often seem to be slowness of plot movement, or mere heaviness, or uncontrolled rhetoric, can take on a new viability and a new doubleness, or more than doubleness, of meaning when responded to with at least some of the analytic and imaginative alertness in reading that we have seen demanded by the later James. The texture of ambiguity in Conrad may be less dense and seamless than in *The Golden Bowl*, but it is also more abrupt, more uncomfortably self-opposing – and unlike James at times, it is never bland. Conrad is more of a purported moralist, judge, and direct philosopher than James, and by the same token a more strikingly unconscious subverter, or qualifier, within the actual performance of his texts, of what their surface argument tries to establish in other terms. The variation of linguistic and generic modes by which James reveals and copes with the treacherous instabilities of the human situation is much greater over his career than in Conrad, who strikes me as changing very much less in his technique and outlook between *The Nigger of the 'Narcissus'* and *The Shadow-Line* (1917) than does James between *The Europeans* and *The Golden Bowl*. Partly for this reason, it might be more helpful to focus closely on certain problematic areas – surprises, pressure points – in most of the Conrad texts under discussion than to aim at a comprehensive account of each that would indicate development in the pattern of an *oeuvre*. By doing so, it should be possible to detect narrative movements in certain of them – *Heart of Darkness* (1899), *Lord Jim* (1900), and *Nostromo* (1904) – rather more diverse than the 'dark' readings of Conrad would normally allow: and certain reversals and surprises, in the endings of *Under Western Eyes* (1911) and *The Shadow-Line*, for example, and in specific sections or aspects of all of them, that alert us to how the reading of Conrad, differently from James but no less disturbingly than in James, is a vital act of changeable participation rather than a conclusive act of grasping or abstracting.

1. *Heart of Darkness*: a surprise for Marlow

Just before the halfway point of *Heart of Darkness* there is a typical surprise. It has been a narrative so far of accumulating surprises and strangenesses: a series of little or big enigmas; things turned upside down, concealed or transposed, and mostly menacing. Now, above a woodpile on the river-bank, a tattered flag is flying, an unrecognizable flag 'of some sort'. The writing on a board needs to be 'deciphered'. The signature is 'illegible'. The message itself can be read in different ways. What does it mean by 'Hurry up'? What does it mean by 'Approach cautiously'? This irritates Marlow: 'We commented adversely upon the imbecility of that telegraphic style'[4] — though the far-from-telegraphic style of his own narrating so far has been equally enigmatic and disturbing. What is more, there is a coverless, much-repaired book, with its interlinear cipher that reduces the practical concerns of its text to nonsense: the gloss is a kind of book-within-a-book-within-a-book; enigma upon enigma. Towson's *Inquiry into some Points of Seamanship* rapidly becomes 'extraordinary', 'amazing', 'wonderful', 'astonishing', and 'an extravagant mystery'. There is something just on the verge of comedy about the extremism of Marlow's reaction here, his almost Jamesian hyperboles. But at this stage we are far more alert to how the discovery of Towson adds to the distinctly uncomic series of discoveries that has structured the narrative this far: the discoveries that there is a cipher of darkness underlying and shadowing all the 'surface-truth' of human conduct and the values and codes, 'points of seamanship', that make for practical survival. Seen as a culmination of so many similarly unsettling events downriver, this extreme response to Towson's enquiry 'into the breaking strain of ships' chains and tackle' begins almost to suggest the point of breaking rather than of enduring. Marlow would prefer to cling to the nostalgic solidity of Towson's plain lines without their gloss; but is soon fretting that 'my speech or my silence, indeed any action of mine, would be a mere futility. What did it matter what any one knew or ignored?' Darkness falls; and a white fog, impenetrable as a tattered flag or an unknowable cipher, ushers in the narration's last day of journeying towards Kurtz.

The fullest surprise of the incident, however, is delayed until twenty-three pages later, when the actual arrival at the Inner Station as a narrative event — *the* narrative event we have been waiting for — is introduced, and somewhat obfuscated, by the figure of the Russian trader who proves to have left the flag and the message and who wrote the cipher — not, after all, as a cipher but merely as his helpful Russian gloss on Towson. The retrospective change in our reading of the event, and the apparent dodging of the climax of encountering Kurtz — we now have eleven pages mostly centred on the Russian before Kurtz makes his appearance, rather cursorily,

borne on a stretcher – are deeply characteristic of Conrad's manner
in this book. The Russian's innate gaiety, and the prompt simplicity
of his explanation of the 'extravagant mystery' of the book on the
river-bank, suddenly make that little episode seem comic, and send
us back to the half-traces of comic excess we suspected there in the
beginning. '"You made notes in Russian?" I asked. He nodded. "I
thought they were written in cipher", I said. He laughed . . .' (p. 124).
For a moment Marlow – even the whole dominant narrative mode
of mystery-making – is made to seem a little foolish.

There are other aspects to this episode of the Russian which
typically seem to test, by their resistance, some of the book's most
authoritative movements, introduce a momentary new tone and
direction, and yet by creating an entirely different mode of 'mystery'
end by energizing, as well as deflecting, the progress of complex
narration and the deepening play of concepts. Characteristic of
Conrad's intentness, even obsessiveness, as a plot-maker and a
thinker, there has been very little way out of *Heart of Darkness*. We
are all prisoners on the *Nellie*, waiting for that very sluggish tide to
turn, and firmly in the grip of Marlow's harshly brooding loquacity
('Try to be civil, Marlow', is the single growl of relieving discontent
allowed from one of the listeners – p. 94). But this unexpected and
potentially irrelevant Russian is a harlequin. He is free, or almost
free: certainly a wanderer. At the very moment where Marlow (to
whom we, the listeners–readers are riveted) is about to meet the
long-withheld object of his narration's search and speculation a
clown is allowed to dance into the foreground, and to fill the
foreground for some time. Of course he has various more logical
plot-functions, among them that of *preparing* for Kurtz, of offering yet another commentary on that soon-to-be-revealed figure of
power and enigma. To that extent, the Russian is part of the
straightforward linear movement of the story: as a disciple of Kurtz
he can offer interesting anticipatory descriptions of the master.[5]
But he also works in a quite other way. He blows away the mystery
of the cipher in incongruous laughter. And he introduces an un-
Conradian movement of irresponsibility, of escape from the toils
of Darkness, a movement of unforeseeable variety. He is a little
fantasy, strayed into a tragic moral parable. When first seen, he is
'a white man under a hat like a cart-wheel beckoning persistently
with his whole arm' (p. 121): does this mean that his hat is as

wide as a cart-wheel or that swinging his arm makes him look like a cart-wheel? Either way, it is a little comic. He is always waving his arms, this clown, gabbling animatedly, staring wide-eyed with excitement or indignation, rising and falling in his moods. His wildly inappropriate clothing is insisted on by a disapproving, fascinated Marlow:

'His aspect reminded me of something I had seen — something funny I had seen somewhere . . . Suddenly I got it. He looked like a harlequin. His clothes had been made of some stuff that was brown holland probably, but it was covered with patches all over, with bright patches, blue, red, and yellow — patches on the back, patches on the front, patches on elbows, on knees; coloured binding around his jacket, scarlet edging at the bottom of his trousers; and the sunshine made him look extremely gay and wonderfully neat withal . . . smiles and frowns chasing each other over that open countenance like sunshine and shadow on a wind-swept plain.'

(p. 122)

The dominant claustrophobia of the narration is suddenly lifted, and there appears a vignette of sky and space and pleasant oddness: a benign transformation of the perpetual enigma. The efforts quickly made by Marlow to control this oddness and absorb it back into the mode of pessimism and of sombre judgement are quite striking. Marlow's self-conscious words brood and swell around the figure of the harlequin in familiar fashion:

'I looked at him, lost in astonishment. There he was before me, in motley, as though he had absconded from a troupe of mimes, enthusiastic, fabulous. His very existence was improbable, inexplicable, and altogether bewildering. He was an insoluble problem.' (p.126)

Stress becomes evident from self-contradictions. Marlow confesses to 'something like admiration — like envy'; he 'almost envied him the possession of this modest and clear flame'; but in one short sentence he moves significantly from the Russian's 'glamour of youth' to 'the essential desolation of his futile wanderings', without being able at all to support the contention of futility. Indeed, the harlequin even becomes an odd version of a Conradian hero, seeking privation and the chance of self-testing, a perpetual master mariner:

'Glamour urged him on, glamour kept him unscathed. He surely wanted nothing from the wilderness but space to breathe in and to push on through. His need was to exist, and to move onwards at the greatest possible risk, and with a maximum of privation.' (p. 126)

98

It is the combination of these positive and dynamic qualities with the Russian's unreflecting admiration for Kurtz that so threatens and distresses Marlow. The narrative moves more livelily for the introduction of the harlequin; then, as suddenly, pulls itself back to everything that opposes his untrammelled and ever-wandering mode of existence. It is when the harlequin throws wide his arms and expresses his transport at Kurtz's visionary power ('He made me see things – things'), and at the strange expansiveness and even 'glamour' of Kurtz's inspiration, that Marlow is moved to pull the oppressive landscape most firmly around him, epithet by constricting epithet:

'. . . I don't know why, but I assure you that never, never before, did this land, this river, this jungle, the very arch of this blazing sky, appear to me so hopeless and so dark, so impenetrable to human thought, so pitiless to human weakness'.   (p. 127)

The effect is exactly repeated two pages later when the Russian's enthusiasm and 'amazing tale' only make Marlow point out that all around 'The woods were unmoved, like a mask – heavy, like the closed door of a prison'. Are we to take the fact that to the harlequin the actual and metaphorical landscape has been the opposite of 'impenetrable' or 'a prison' as simply proving his amoral gaucheness? No doubt he is partly categorized and controlled by such an explanation; but the energy released by his encounter with Marlow, and with the dominant Marlow style, defies being harnessed quite so tightly. In those regular clauses of despair – 'so hopeless and so dark, . . . so pitiless', etc. – is there not something wilful detectable in Marlow's words, a touch of self-pity born of his confessed envy of the Russian and still unsubdued to his mature judgement? So much of the logic of commentary, scene, and image in the story impels us to accept Marlow's contention that the Russian's devotion to Kurtz is 'dangerous'; and retrospectively, we will recognize the analogy between Kurtz having demonically 'kicked himself loose of the earth' and the Russian's rootlessness and blithe openness to impression. That is, the Russian can be taken as partly confirming Marlow's progress towards horror and the judgement against horror. But when he exits from the narrative, nervous and tired at the crisis he has been involved in, he leaves with a wink, a borrowed handful of tobacco, a pair of shoes, and a few cartridges to help him in his 'renewed encounter with the wilderness'.

And the last impression he provides – highlighted at the end of the episode – is once again of his eccentric dress and equally eccentric connection with the codes of practical seamanship: 'One of his pockets (bright red) was bulging with cartridges, from the other (dark blue) peeped "Towson's Inquiry"' (p. 140). And as a response relevant to his unconstrainedness of dress, manner, and fate there is his final disturbing comment on the diabolic Kurtz: 'He rolled his eyes at the recollection of these delights. "Oh, he enlarged my mind!"' So he vanishes from Marlow: perhaps rather as the disturbing Leggatt swims off into the night from *his* 'other', more responsible, and narrating self in 'The Secret Sharer'.

The episode of the harlequin is itself one of the telltale 'breaking strains' of Conrad's narrative: a point of pressure where something foreign, something incongruously liberated, momentarily challenges the forward progress of the tale; a point where the direction of interest swerves suddenly, runs counter to expectation and dramatic decorum (like the swerve of Mrs Wix offering herself to Sir Claude). The whole dynamics of the narration are based on similar alternation: that of slow progression and retreat, conjunction and dispersal, hard-edged action and misty hallucination. The desire to 'place' intellectually, politically, morally is sustained throughout, but is perpetually accompanied by something opposite to it: the brooding over an 'enigma', great or small, until the movement towards understanding and ethical placing ceases and the 'inexplicable' seems to take on an ultimate, irreducible status of its own. Individual scenes contain ironies that work in both of these ways: an irony that sets the scene firmly within an interpretative pattern, and an irony that resists extrapolation and turns in, spiral-like, on itself. And it is the continuing energy and tension generated between these two unreconciled functions of irony that matters most: not the illuminating and ethical function to the exclusion of the darker, more self-subverting function; nor, on the other hand, the vortex to the exclusion of the line.

For example, the 'political' reading of the ironies in the first part of the tale – the criminal folly of the French man-of-war shelling a continent, the oppression by foreign 'white' laws of the black chain gang, the dying workers in the 'grove of death', the mechanical and inhumane efficiency of the white accountant – notably fails to exhaust the potential significance that the writing offers us, or to be true by itself to the full experience of reading the text. It is the surreal absurdity of the warship that affects us first of all; and even after we have properly deduced its moral and political bearing by reading it in the context of Marlow's opening discussion of imperialism, then of the Brussels episode and the scenes of white rapacity and heartlessness about to be described, our initial 'surreal' reading of it remains partly valid. This is confirmed by the quality of incongruous humour (which is not just moral satire) in Marlow's words: 'Pop, would go one of the six-inch guns', 'a tiny projectile would give a feeble screech', 'a sense of lugubrious drollery in the sight'; and by his equally incongruous tone of expressionist excess: 'It was like a weary pilgrimage amongst hints for nightmares' (p. 62).

Similarly, the vignette of the dying negro with the 'bit of white thread from beyond the seas' around his neck – so easily seen as a straightforward emblem of white imperialist control – makes an obvious and powerful point within the story's line of moral indictment. But Marlow's obsessive focus, and his over-insistent questioning of the episode, also take away from its moral clarity and introduce something that is either greater or less than moral clarity: a provocative sense of disturbance, an excitement as at the opening of an unexpected and only half-understood vista. The one paragraph that contains the encounter begins in open indignation – 'They were dying slowly . . . They were not enemies, they were not criminals . . .' – but ends in a simple evocation of incongruity that comes close to depoliticizing the symbolic white thread:

He had tied a bit of white worsted round his neck – Why? Where did he get it? Was it a badge – an ornament – a charm – a propitiatory act? Was there any idea at all connected with it? It looked startling round his black neck, this bit of white thread from beyond the seas.   (p. 67)

Again, what are we to make of that which immediately follows in a very formal counterpoint: the apparition of the elegant and efficient accountant, 'a sort of vision', 'amazing', 'this miracle', 'wonderfully odd'? Marlow's hyperboles seem tangential to the immediate effect in the reader of moral and political condemnation; then they are strangely supported by Marlow's unexpected praise for this 'hairdresser's dummy': 'I respected the fellow . . . in the great demoralization of the land he kept up his appearance' (p 68). The praise is of course partly ironic, supportive of the line of moral condemnation. But when our thought of the respect Marlow expresses elsewhere in the story for efficiency and hard work begins to act against the ironic denigration of the accountant, and incongruously to set him up as a partial positive value against the 'grove of death', the complex to-and-fro movement of the narration, both in little (in a paragraph, in a choice of epithets) and in the large (over a scene, or over the whole plot), declares itself once again. The judgement does not disappear *into* the ambiguity: what we are left with is more a sense (narrative and aesthetic, as well as intellectual) of interplay. We watch the moral assessment at work, and continue to respect its animadversions; but we also see the gap between the moral idea of the scene and the power of our full sensation of the scene − that is, our sensation of its flow of changes in mode and mood, and of the unexhausted (because not fully interpreted) tension and colour-contrasts of its oppositions.

The whole central issue of the book − its vision of the ubiquitous 'darkness' of the jungle-Absolute, of ineradicable primitive instincts, of Kurtz's Nietzschean reversion, of the dream-reality underneath the mere 'surface-truth' of everyday life − is presented within this contradictory rhythm, in the reading-experience, of evaluation with imaginative feeling or sensation, a rhythm that in itself can become as claustrophobic and implosive as anything else in the narration. At the Central Station, Marlow morally deplores the 'imbecile rapacity' of the white men and associates the unreality of the scene around him with that human rapacity. Yet the jungle is also invoked as a 'reality' in a way that seems to deny any link between moral value and reality, and at times almost suggests that the evil of rapacity, however anti-real in itself, can be a mode of entry into a supreme 'evil' that is also a supreme reality:

'The word "ivory" rang in the air, was whispered, was sighed. You would think they were praying to it. A taint of imbecile rapacity blew through it all, like a whiff from some corpse. By Jove! I've never seen anything so unreal in my life. And outside, the silent wilderness surrounding this cleared speck on the earth struck me as something great and invincible, like evil or truth, waiting patiently for the passing away of this fantastic invasion.' (p. 76)

When 'evil' and 'truth' can be so casually linked, in that almost throwaway phrase; when the unreal is rapacious and the real may be evil (evilly rapacious?); then the play of concepts has clearly become dangerously congested.[6] As usual, it is the act of questioning, Marlow's unanswerable rhetorical questioning, that expresses this tendency of the story to crowd itself into an intellectual impasse — an impasse that is only partially relieved by the 'opening-up' gestures of what he asks:

'What were we who had strayed in here? Could we handle that dumb thing, or would it handle us! I felt how big, how confoundedly big, was that thing that couldn't talk, and perhaps was deaf as well. What was in there?'

(p. 81)

Even the climax — or, rather, especially the climax — of Kurtz's portentous cry, 'The horror! The horror!' (p. 149), in which Marlow detects 'supreme knowledge', is essentially and fittingly a supreme equivocation. Is it a judgement on reality or on his own backslidings? Is such a cry really a judgement at all, an 'affirmation' and 'moral victory' as Marlow at one point proposes to us, or is it, more frighteningly, an invocation, a testimony, even an agonized but still worshipping cry? But while such deathbed 'victories' of ethical judgement seem pyrrhic and partial at best (as pyrrhic as Lena's in *Victory*), it is nevertheless still preferable to resist any single summing-up of the tale even in terms that are nihilistic and blackest of black-Romantic. An equivocation is different from a negation. There is much to argue on this score, and it has been argued back and forth a thousand times before.[7] More important than to look for a summation or summing-up is to bear in mind what we have experienced of the tale's actual unfolding, not just whatever conclusiveness one might try to read into the death of Kurtz or the 'saving' (or damning?) lie to the Intended. The very movement of the narrative, and the expressively eddying rhetoric of the narrator, have come to involve us in an imaginative response more complex and more new than the conclusion-seeking responses we have to foster in our ordinary lives, and a response that because it evokes a form of energy and self-awareness within the reader must also modify radically the whole debate about the book's nihilism or redemptiveness. The pressures and indirections of the text must remain operative within our total perception of it — we cannot arrest it or freeze it into some aphorism, consoling or destructive, or into any controlling image, either of some psychic rebirth-by-night-journey or of a terminal descent into an abyss of

103

self-cancelling relativism. As a token of this openness one might look finally not at Kurtz's last equivocal utterance, or at Marlow's participation in the duplicity of words in his encounter with the Intended,[8] but, less familiarly, at the effect of certain small modulations of narrative viewpoint in the very last paragraphs of the tale – its final and entirely representative 'surprises'.

The concluding movement is a brief one: a return of narratorial stance from Marlow to the almost-forgotten 'I' on the *Nellie*. Typically, the transition comes on an act of questioning and the tailing-away of a voice, Marlow's voice:

'Would [the heavens] have fallen, I wonder, if I had rendered Kurtz that justice which was his due? Hadn't he said he wanted only justice? But I couldn't. I could not tell her. It would have been too dark – too dark altogether . . .' (p. 162)

The switch then from the inner narrative to the outer narrative ('Marlow ceased, and sat apart . . .') is quite startling. The scene with the Intended has just been very vividly and empathetically given to us in the form of dialogue; and we have almost 'been' Marlow for a great length of time; so that the change to our seeing Marlow from outside, static and even statuesque ('indistinct and silent, in the pose of a meditating Buddha. Nobody moved for a time.') produces a momentary dislocation. For a second it is as though we are watching ourselves, our suddenly silenced narrative-spinning selves, as we fall silent and sit, in meditation – it is a piece of narrative sleight of hand that we shall find again, in *Lord Jim*. The reintroduction of the 'I' who has been listening to Marlow is almost bewildering, so completely has 'he' been forgotten. So that there is something of a double shock (both of them small, but not negligible). First, having half-forgotten that Marlow is narrating, there is the shock for us to be told suddenly that we are now watching him as he sits apart. And secondly, as soon as the Director has announced the losing of the first of the ebb, we read 'I raised my head', which makes us recoil for the second time, and see a second unexpected 'other' between us and the scene. The transition is effected by the reference to darkness. Marlow ends by saying, 'too dark altogether'; and at once we are made to see him 'apart' in *indistinctness*, as though the darkness of his own last words is now made tangible around him, projected into the narrative frame. And the original 'I', whom we are surprised to rediscover still so broken off from ourselves, ends the whole tale by looking back into darkness – the 'black bank of clouds' towards which the river is now flowing.

That the tale, however, should end on the phrase 'the heart of an immense darkness' would seem only to confirm its aphoristic and conclusive possibilities: we have a concept and a key to interpretation suddenly underlined by the self-conscious repetition of a symbolic title (the effect is a little different from the less conceptual, more aesthetically ludic repetition of the title in the last words of *What Maisie Knew*).[9] But everything is still in movement around this seeming closure, since our relationship to the whole 'event' of the tale, never a secure one ('Do you see the story?', Marlow has asked before now. 'Do you see anything? It seems to me I am trying to tell you a dream.' – p. 82), has just been further destabilized by the culminating double-switch in the point of view: from Marlow to the 'I', then to 'us', as listeners and readers, suddenly reminded of that intermediary 'I'. The repetition of the key phrase, 'heart of darkness', as well as stimulating us to an act of interpretation, also emphasizes the aesthetic self-reflexiveness in the paragraph by making us see the whole story formally, by its title, from outside – as does the designed return to the opening frame of the listeners on the *Nellie*. And in addition, the flowing of the river eastwards, into the darkness, impinges on us not only as a meaning-bearing symbol of our tragic destiny, or of the falling-away of all human values, but also, in a secondary and contrary way, as something unfinished, still in process, and still demanding a response of action. The Director's words, beneath what we first of all interpret as their symbolic threat of loss – 'we have lost the first of the ebb.' – are also, in their common sense, an urge to get on with the business of sailing. 'Let's not lose the rest of the ebb' is another of their unvoiced implications.[10] The river certainly leads into the barring blackness of the sky, but the waterway is also 'tranquil' and does lead expansively outwards, 'to the uttermost ends of the earth'. By all these residual hints, these continuing oppositions, the ending paradoxically queries finality – and therefore to some degree, though certainly not a cheering degree, modifies the finality of the moral and epistemological impasse that Marlow has articulated *vis-à-vis* Kurtz and the Intended. In its partial veering, the ending, like the narration as a whole, manages at least to flex itself against the threat of stasis and nothingness; and by enforcing on us such participative acts of close attention to the texture and changes of language – acts of alerted imagination as well as of analysis and extrapolation – it evokes something that resembles the energies of personal self-renewal and the related energies of taletelling itself, however self-doubting, to set against the fixity of a single conclusion or the totality of a universal darkness.

2. The jump to Patusan

Having argued that any reading of *Heart of Darkness* that sums it up as a prose poem of directly mounting despair is inadequate without paying due attention to the narrative multivalencies and obliquities that would challenge, and therefore at least modify and enrich, such an emphasis, I want next to look at how an awareness of Conrad's narrative indirections over the much larger compass of *Lord Jim* provides a basis for dealing with the familiar criticism of that novel – quite opposite to the usual account of *Heart of Darkness* – that it evades complexity by the romantic escapism of its second half, turns to the simplicity of exotic colour and adventure on Patusan, and divides itself unsatisfactorily in two. As with *What Maisie Knew*, the problem is one of modulation – the crossing of a channel of tone and setting that transposes and develops basic narrative patterns rather than abandoning them. And as with James's novel – and indeed as with *Heart of Darkness* – what is transposed subtly in the narrating touches upon basic cognitive issues concerning knowledge of the self, knowledge of others, and how, as readers of shifting nuance and process, we 'know' a novel.

Lord Jim is certainly a book in two halves, and with two movements. Chapter 20, where Marlow discusses Jim with Stein, is at the exact halfway point, and is usually recognized as being powerfully central in more ways than one. But the whole Patusan episode of the second half, which Stein inaugurates and makes possible, is more often than not regarded with embarrassment even by Conrad's favourable critics.[11] The contrast between the mode of each half of the novel is at first striking. The first half begins with three chapters of fairly straightforward chronicle: the opening picture of the mature Jim as a water-clerk is quickly followed, in explanation, by Jim as a boy, with the significant episode on the training-ship, then Jim's arrival in the east, his berth as chief mate of the *Patna*, and the vivid first narration of the *Patna*'s collision. Then the more characteristic movement of the first half takes over (at the beginning of chapter 4): that of retrospection, anecdote, and Marlow's endlessly circling inconclusive evaluations, interspersed with sharply illustrative minor scenes. The one major scene remains, in its varying facets, the events on the *Patna*; and around that scene, in painful recapitulation or in blame or in probing wonderment is woven a dense tissue of talk − one crucial physical event revolving endlessly in a stream of half-explanatory, extrapolatory, or baffled language. The reader soon becomes half-hypnotized by these narrative procedures: by Marlow rhetorically questioning or ironically pontificating about the 'Dark Powers' or 'fidelity to a certain standard of conduct'; by Marlow staring bemused at a faltering, self-exculpating, obsessively narrating Jim; by Marlow describing Mr Jones, mate of the *Ossa*, describing Captain Brierly's suicide while both Marlow and Jones speculate on the meaning of the act; by the concentrative and imprisoning effect of intense colloquies, like that between Jim and Marlow, taking place amid the irrelevant clatter of the everyday, unselfconscious world (as in the touristic dining room of the Malabar House); by sudden exclamations ('Ah! what a chance missed!') or vivid sensory details in an anecdote ('a flake of rust as big as the palm of my hand') standing out abruptly from the current of conversation, only to be drawn into it again for lingering evaluation and maceration; by the dense commingling of direct speech and reported speech, all within Marlow's own speaking voice (for example, Marlow's voice conveying to us Jim's voice conveying his own past dialogue with his fellow-officers on the *Patna*), and occasionally, for further complexity of viewpoint, interrupted by a listener murmuring 'You are so subtle, Marlow'. Actual witnesses and apparently unconnected figures − the Malay helmsman, the French lieutenant, Marlow's friend Mr Denver, Egstrom the ship's chandler, little Bob Stanton who drowned trying to save a lady's maid, Chester the West Australian adventurer who disappeared in a hurricane on his guano island − they all *almost* achieve a relieving irrelevance, a contrasted assertion of the possibilities for action, expansion, and surprise that lurk within character and event, before succumbing to

the vortex of narrative enquiry and the hungry process of un-
satisfied philosophic interpretation that evokes so obsessively the
Jim-shaped enigma of life:

Not a vestige of [Chester] ever turned up; not a sound came out of the
waste . . .

End! Finis! the potent word that exorcises from the house of life the
haunting shadow of fate. . . This is what . . . I miss when I look back upon
Jim's success. . . — [12]

and so we are borne back continually from the anecdote into the
meditative centre.[13]

Up to the halfway point of the book this centripetal movement
of narration is for the most part only confirmed, and made complex, by the failure of the anecdotes and the scenes to do more than
occasionally suggest an alternative direction. The suggestion is
there, however. Accompanying the brooding, circuitous movement, enforced on us by the presence and the manner of Marlow,
and confirmed by the emphasized cognitive impulse of this narration — what can we make of this event? what does it all mean? how
can we cope with the inner mystery of Jim, who is 'one of us'? —
there is also something much simpler. It remains minor at this
point, but it is wrong to ignore its existence within the Marlow-
dominated discursiveness concerning idealism, confidence, the
relationship between selfhood and action, and the possible insubstantiality of human values. This is the simple but vital narrative motive of: What will happen next to Jim? Where will he go?
How will he survive? The presence of this counter-urge, this progressive as opposed to retrospective thrust, partly prepares us for
the change at halfway, where the dominant mode of interpretation
is succeeded by a dominant mode of action. Figuratively, the whole
second half of the novel lies latent — and for the moment held back
— in the incident between Jim and Marlow in chapter 7 where Jim
cries 'My God! what a chance missed!', and Marlow sardonically
watches Jim rush imaginatively forwards into the future — 'With
every instant he was penetrating deeper into the impossible world
of romantic achievements. He got to the heart of it at last! . . . He
had penetrated to the very heart — to the very heart.' — before
sternly pulling him backwards into the authoritative mode of conscience and agonized recollection: 'If you had stuck to the ship, you
mean!' (pp. 104–5).

Much has been written about the role of Stein in *Lord Jim*, and about the possible bearings of his famous exhortation, 'in the destructive element immerse' (p. 200).[14] But to all that can be gleaned from the deliberate moral chiaroscuro of the scene this should be added: that Stein is also the most simply heroic and exotic man-of-action we have yet encountered in the book, as well as an elegiac *mage* and a gazer on butterflies; that his history is one of actual achievement and daring action; and that though he is as rueful as Marlow about human potential – 'Sometimes it seems to me that man is come where he is not wanted, where there is no place for him; for if not, why should he want all the place?' (p. 195) – he is also deeply concerned with practicality and with *doing*: 'How to be! *Ach!* How to be!'; and, 'in the morning we shall do something practical – practical'. Stein sees the dreamlike quality of life, and the perpetual betrayal that lurks in it, waiting to destroy friendship, love, and prosperity (and Marlow's 'standards of conduct') like a match blown out. But his advice is 'To follow the dream' (p. 201) – to go onwards to the end, not backwards or in a circle. Marlow characteristically drapes his own orotund pessimism over Stein's words, and tries to pull the narrative back towards circuitousness and darkness, rather as we have seen him try to blot out the expansive, activist suggestions of the Russian harlequin figure in *Heart of Darkness*:

'The whisper of his conviction seemed to open before me a vast and uncertain expanse, as of a crepuscular horizon on a plain at dawn – or was it, perchance, at the coming of the night? One had not the courage to decide; but it was a charming and deceptive light, throwing the impalpable poesy of its dimness over pitfalls – over graves.'

His effort of introspective negation is strengthened by the mirroring effects in the room that seem to reduce all action to somnambulism and futility:

'[The lights] glided among the waxed floors, sweeping here and there over the polished surface of the table, leaped upon a fragmentary curve of a piece of furniture, or flashed perpendicularly in and out of distant mirrors, while the forms of two men and the flicker of two flames could be seen for a moment stealing silently across the depths of a crystalline void.'

(p. 201)

But out of this void, abruptly and paradoxically, rises a triumphant assertion of Jim's reality, and of the personal existence of all of them — as though in the very moment of the crystalline void, of the fall into the inertia and loss of self that is always Conrad's particular vision of hell, the direct opposite, on which the second movement of the book will entirely depend, is generated by necessity: an image of Jim's 'imperishable reality' that suddenly, a little feverishly, springs into Marlow's mind, under the influence of Stein's own perceived 'reality'; an 'absolute Truth', however 'obscure', that now declares itself 'with a convincing, with an irresistible force' in the form of that observed personal identity (p. 202).[15]

The scene between Marlow and Stein, then, with its inner stresses, is a fulcrum in the book — one of Conrad's points of breaking strain. In its evocation of the reductive crystalline void, in Stein's own partial pessimism and Marlow's scepticism, it looks backwards, hypnotically, paralysingly; but in its almost arbitrary discovery of a moment's faith in individual identity achievable through search and pursuit it signalizes the new energies, which are also the narrative energies, of Patusan. And in narrative terms the subtle swing in direction within the Stein scene is generally reinforced at this midpoint of the book by the reader's need for Patusan in ways that are not just inductive, following the logic of sign, symbol, and commentary, but are also forceful ways of feeling, which remain relevant to the book's ideas: the desire (as just before the halfway switch of setting in *The Bostonians*) for change and for the relief of pressure, the excitement of gratified curiosity concerning action and event, and, not least, an impatience with Marlow's restrictive repetitions and his necessary but increasingly inadequate and self-vexing modes of seeking knowledge.

However, we are far from rejecting Marlow, or from leaving him behind. The mode of question-and-enigma, and of an articulate, half-apocalyptic pondering, remains intrinsic to the novel, part of its unity, and will still run through the very different textures of the Patusan affair. Marlow remains our authority, even for Patusan; and pays his one memorable visit to the island. But in the second half there is now a sense of Marlow transmitting something that stands much further away from himself, something more foreign to both his practical and his philosophic cast of mind. This change not only freshens the narration aesthetically, it also illuminates Stein's definition of human destiny as a pursuit of the realization through heroic action of an ideal image of the self. All the previous hints of imaginative liberation offered by exotic settings, all the sense of energy expressed in the liveliness of anecdotes and in the sketches of eccentric, unforeseeable characters, everything that has pointed hypothetically in the direction of a totally fulfilling and expansive *act*, are now concentrated and fully developed in Patusan. As Marlow says at the outset, talking explicitly of Jim but virtually also of the fictional 'new set of conditions' for the reader and for the reader's 'imaginative faculty' of knowledge 'to work upon':

'. . . had Stein arranged to send him into a star of the fifth magnitude the change could not have been greater. He left his earthly failings behind him and what sort of reputation he had, and there was a totally new set of conditions for his imaginative faculty to work upon. Entirely new, entirely remarkable. And he got hold of them in a remarkable way.' (pp. 203–4)

What is unchanged in Marlow's function is that he still preserves, by ironic reference, the echoes of the *Patna* affair, and thereby partially subverts the power of this new escape-into-action. Typical is his comment about Jim's arrival in Patusan:

'That's how he ascended the Patusan river. Nothing could have been more prosaic and more unsafe, more extravagantly casual, more lonely. Strange, this fatality that would cast the complexion of a flight upon all his acts, of impulsive unreflecting desertion – of a jump into the unknown.' (p. 212)

But what is new is that we are now aware of a slightly contrived note to some of Marlow's deflating remarks. In this particular instance there is in fact little or nothing in his description of Jim's arrival – 'prosaic', 'unsafe', 'casual', 'lonely' – to suggest 'flight' or desertion. Marlow seems to be wilfully imposing 'the complexion of a flight' upon 'a jump into the unknown', since the latter suggests the positive and challenging rather than the evasive. And if Jim's jump over the Rajah Allang's palisade is reminiscent of his jump from the *Patna* – as some critics have suggested, though even the ironic Marlow does not – it is only by contrast, since the second leap is entirely the opposite of a self-betrayal. It is a plunge by Jim not into the conscience-stricken inertia of the *Patna*'s lifeboat but into the meaningful action of self-assertion against Rajah Allang, choosing Doramin, and preparing the way to his proper headship of a people.

The narrative of Jim's arrival, his acquiring of status with

Doramin, the successful attack on Sheikh Ali's hill fortress, Jim's skirmish with his would-be assassins, and above all the climactic episode of Gentleman Brown, are among the most vivid pieces of narration in the book – perhaps among the best of all Conrad's pieces of narrated adventure. And what is narrated, quite unlike the first half, diverges by its content and by its dramatic realization from the Marlow who is still narrating it – so that an interesting new tension begins to fill this part of the novel. The scenes are so vivid, the events so 'real' to the imagination – like that 'reality', that absolute existence of the individual so suddenly perceived by Marlow at the end of the Stein chapter – that Marlow's usual rhetorical commentaries seem forced by contrast into a new extreme, in which they take on an uncertain note. Indeed, extremism would seem to become a keynote of the Patusan episode, as part of its accelerated tempo of narrative and interest – culminating in the intensity of the tragic conclusion that in itself casts so contrasted and so modifying a light back into the maintained sombreness and judicial mode of the first half.

Within this new tension, Marlow's commentaries pose us a new problem – or rather, pose us an old problem with a new possible response. The reader is often not quite sure what to make of Marlow's orotundity, even in the first half of the book. If we could see it as slightly ironized, or at least distanced from us within a more objectified area of the narration, it would be easier to accept its laborious cadences and abstractions. But there is not really enough evidence for this in the text, certainly in the first part where the style seems on the whole authoritative and even authorial. In the second half, the rhetorical comments are not necessarily more numerous, but they do seem to take on a quality of excess that comes strangely close to redeeming them. An almost expressionist and nightmare quality begins to infuse them here and there, as if stimulated by the new tempo of contrasted action and by Jim's increasing escape into a heightened reality of action and passion unknown to the courtroom, the hotel dining room, the after-dinner colloquy, the world of commentary. We usually expect the worst when Marlow-Conrad meditates on the Woman Question; and here is an example quite unredeemed by any of the interestingly feverish quality I have mentioned:

'I ask myself with wonder – how the world can look to [women] – whether it has the shape and substance *we* know, the air *we* breathe! Sometimes I fancy it must be a region of unreasonable sublimities seething with the excitement of their adventurous souls, lighted by the glory of all possible risks and renunciations.' (p. 247)

But by contrast, Marlow's effusions can at times develop a rather more suggestive note, even when directed at Jewel, in this case her plea to him for reassurance that Jim will never abandon her:

'I would have given anything for the power to soothe her frail soul, tormenting itself in its invincible ignorance like a small bird beating about the cruel wires of a cage. Nothing easier than to say, Have no fear! Nothing more difficult. How does one kill fear, I wonder? How do you shoot a spectre through the heart, slash off its spectral head, take it by its spectral throat? It is an enterprise you rush into while you dream, and are glad to make your escape with wet hair and every limb shaking. The bullet is not run, the blade not forged, the man not born; even the winged words of truth drop at your feet like lumps of lead. You require for such a desperate encounter an enchanted and poisoned shaft dipped in a lie too subtle to be found on earth. An enterprise for a dream, my masters!'[16]
(p. 276)

The increased intensity and bizarreness of the writing (it still has its simple flaccidities, of course, like 'the winged words of truth') produce an effective and dreamlike disturbance within the rhetoric of such outbursts that makes them more interesting underneath than on the surface – where the meaning tends to be familiarly elegiac, philosophically sceptical, and Olympian. That is, the reader now responds more to the indirect, even personal note of anxiety than to the direct argument about the instability of human values. The anxiety of this new disjunction between commentary and event, surface and depth, can suddenly break through the tenor of narration – rather like the self-consciousness forced on the reader so quickly in the last paragraph of *Heart of Darkness* – to produce as significant an appeal as this:

'I suppose I must have fallen into a sentimental mood; I only know that I stood there long enough for the sense of utter solitude to get hold of me so completely that all I had lately seen, all I had heard, and the very human speech itself, seemed to have passed away out of my existence, living only for a while longer in my memory, as though I had been the last of mankind. It was a strange and melancholy illusion, evolved half-consciously like all our illusions, which I suspect only to be visions of remote unattainable truth, seen dimly. This was, indeed, one of the lost,

113

forgotten, unknown places of the earth; I had looked under its obscure surface; and I felt that when to-morrow I had left it for ever, it would slip
out of existence, to live only in my memory till I myself had passed into
oblivion. I have that feeling about me now; perhaps it is that feeling which
has incited me to tell you the story, to try to hand over to you, as it were,
its very existence, its reality – the truth disclosed in a moment of illusion.'

(p. 281)

The weird 'illusion' that he is 'the last of mankind', forced on
Marlow by his excessively melancholic mood, becomes linked with
the 'illusion' of art itself. Art discloses a 'truth' through its use of
'illusion'; and 'all our illusions', which apparently are not mere
dreams but remain compatible with consciousness and will, are
visions of a remote truth. There are many levels to this arcane insight so suddenly precipitated within the flow of Marlow's self-
communing. It seems even to contain the consoling suggestion that
the 'illusion' of human values – the 'fixed standard of conduct'
– which so much of the action and, above all, of the commentary
has been intent on exposing *as* illusion must, by being illusion,
reflect some higher truth, however unattainable. Yet the whole is
delivered in unrelieved sepulchral tones that convey the feeling, if
not the sense, of an entirely opposite perception: a perception of
absolute isolation, oblivion, and the 'crystalline void' at the heart
of the 'destructive element'. At such moments of strain, contrary
to the usual effect of Marlow's musings, an unexpected intimacy is
established: not with Marlow-as-character, or even with Conrad-
as-revealed-author, but more like a quick sense of intimacy with
ourselves. It is as though Marlow, in abruptly addressing the
listener–reader in order to refer to the very act of telling his tale –
'that feeling which has incited me to tell you the story, to try to
hand over to you . . . its very existence' – makes us suddenly con-
flate the 'me' and the 'you' in our awareness, since they are both
aspects of our one reading self in any case, and only temporarily
kept apart by the conventional needs of the fiction. And in this moment of complicated 'intimacy' with our reading self we are, just
for this brief instant of narratorial anxiety, made conscious of our
self-making, self-abnegating duality of posture within the process
of reading – as within the to-and-fro of any imaginative process
of knowing; or even, as in Jim's case, of climactic commitment to
an action.[17]

The unexpected degree to which this narrative, by its manipulation of anticipation, retrospect, and escape, by its unsettling tempi, its uneasily varying rhetoric, its movement between modes of objective visualization and of intense self-awareness, has enmeshed us within its essential fictional processes constitutes in itself a response to the critical question of its structural unity – and also to its thematic questioning into the validity of human action, the egotism of heroism, the delusions in the image of self, and the workings of nemesis. That thematic, more abstract questioning is not to be avoided. We cannot resist (Marlow-like) brooding over the proliferating ironies that the novel's own philosophical and analytical mode presents to the intellect. We scrutinize and categorize Jim into an emblem – 'one of us'. We extrapolate conclusions from the devastating flash of recognition that is exchanged between him and the squalid Gentleman Brown, whose very name seems a mere transposition of the name Lord Jim. We inevitably attempt to hold the whole book and the whole enigma of Jim rigid and perfected in memory and in diagnosis, caught in their own presented net of significant repetitions, contrasts, patterns, and analogies. But on the other hand, *Lord Jim* as we have performed it in our minds up to the point where Jim proudly takes Doramin's bullet in his chest, and Stein utters the inconclusive last word of valediction to his butterflies, also defeats such stasis, resists its own diagnostic urge, and goes on immersing our natural wish to know, to extract, and to judge within the richer flow of its narrative indirections.[18]

3. On and about the Golfo Placido

Conrad clearly had a great horror of inertia – or rather, one might say that his innate sense of horror often expressed itself in images of inertia. That failure of the will so well known to James and Forster too, and endemic in their analyses of a flawed maleness and a flawed universe; the retreat into solipsism and sardonic apathy; the loss of belief in the values that make individual action (as well as communal solidarity) possible; the inanition that accompanies the life-is-a-dream syndrome, the self-paralysing effect of certain exercises of the imagination – Jim's trance before he jumps from the *Patna*; the hypochondriacal withdrawal of James Wait; Marlow's struggle to carry the two incubus-like weights (Waits?) of the dead helmsman and then Kurtz himself; Verloc's laziness; Heyst, Hamlet-like, hiding in his nutshell-island; the dead calm that besets the nameless ship of *The Shadow-Line* – all of these are the very lineaments of hell, or the temptation to hell, in Conrad's vision. So that when *Nostromo* opens with such memorable vividness on the imprisoning windlessness of the dark gulf, equally walled off to landward by a barrier of mountains under 'moving draperies of cloud', with a headland haunted by the futile ghosts of treasure-seekers, and diabolic black nights when life seems smothered by the impenetrable black poncho of the sky, then we think we know what we are in for.[19] But *Nostromo*, even more than *Heart of Darkness* and *Lord Jim*, never quite goes in the direction we expect. That first chapter, rendered with the hallucinatory power and the confidence of a keynote, a dark omen of dream-realities to come, is at once contradicted by the harbour-bustle of chapter 2, and by the rattling, pragmatic voice of Captain Mitchell describing the animated scenes of the overthrow of Ribiera. Indeed, the whole of the first half of *Nostromo* is extraordinarily active and crammed with incident, for all the accompanying groundswell of irony and portent. It is among Conrad's most virtuoso performances in plot-handling, and vibrates with the energy of what it describes – revolutions, counter-revolutions, individuals like Nostromo and Gould successfully asserting themselves, a whole society, from its patricians down to its stevedores, convulsed with the need to act, to band together, to oppose and challenge. The energy also comes from the manner of its unfolding. Much has been made of Conrad's elaborate a-chronological handling of this narrative; but while there may be dark suggestions of symbolic disturbance, of historical and personal inertia, in its convolutions, its circularity, its prolonged withholding of completion,[20] there is also a contrary and distinctly positive effect that comes from its flagrant confidence in such elaborate constructing. By the narrations-within-narrations and the abrupt foreshortenings of time we are forced, without much real trouble or reluctance (the events are intrinsically interesting), to share in the creative excitement of piecing together the multiform image of Costaguana. The very size of the panorama, social, historical, geographical, seems simultaneously a challenge and a reward to the mind of the reconstructing reader, to the degree that the first chapter, with its underlying hints of inanition and despair, can seem on rereading to be as much picturesque as symbolic, a chiaroscuro set piece swiftly controlled and then left behind by the jostle and throb of the subsequent chapters. The history of Costaguana, as it is circuitously revealed, is obviously one of instability and injustice; but the energies displayed in it — to echo Keats on the sight of a quarrel in the streets — are fine. Typical of how the expected Conradian irony — which by diminishing its object evokes the central void or inertia that morally it deplores — is at once offset by the energies of a scene too active to be diminished, is the following:

On this memorable day of the riot [Giorgio Viola's] arms were not folded on his chest. His hand grasped the barrel of the gun grounded on the threshold; he did not look up once at the white dome of Higuerota, whose cool purity seemed to hold itself aloof from a hot earth. His eyes examined the plain curiously. Tall trails of dust subsided here and there. In a speckless sky the sun hung clear and blinding. Knots of men ran headlong; others made a stand; and the irregular rattle of firearms came rippling to his ears in the fiery, still air. Single figures on foot raced desperately. Horsemen galloped towards each other, wheeled round together, separated at speed. Giorgio saw one fall, rider and horse disappearing as if they had galloped into a chasm, and the movements of the animated scene were like the passages of a violent game played upon the plain by dwarfs mounted and on foot, yelling with tiny throats, under the mountain that seemed a colossal embodiment of silence. Never before had Giorgio seen this bit of plain so full of active life; his gaze could not take in all its details at once; he shaded his eyes with his hand, till suddenly the thundering of many hoofs near by startled him.

A troop of horses had broken out of the fenced paddock of the Railway Company. They came on like a whirlwind, and dashed over the line snorting, kicking, squealing in a compact, piebald, tossing mob of bay, brown, grey backs, eyes staring, necks extended, nostrils red, long tails streaming. As soon as they had leaped upon the road the thick dust flew upwards from under their hoofs, and within six yards of Giorgio only a brown cloud with vague forms of necks and cruppers rolled by, making the soil tremble on its passage.

Viola coughed, turning his face away from the dust, and shaking his head slightly.

'There will be some horse-catching to be done before to-night', he muttered.[21]

It seems to me that this description is exactly dual. In the first paragraph the wild antics of dwarfish men are judged sardonically against the aloofness of Higuerota, 'a colossal embodiment of silence', and it is as though the reductive strain of the first chapter, powerful and bleak, has returned – figuratively, the direction seems downwards, towards a 'chasm'. Then in the description of the horses the opposite effect is suddenly produced: beside the exciting ferocity and energy of the horses the mountain fades from view, and with it Conrad's focus of pessimism, leaving instead a real human voice and a practical human task to be done.[22]

Similarly, on a personal level we are impressed by the *terribilità* of old Giorgio as much as by the lostness of his Garibaldino cause or by his isolation in a foreign society; and by the theatrical swagger of Nostromo more than by any ironic shadow that as yet encroaches on his glittering and fulfilled egotism. Again, the story of Don Carlos and the Gould concession is for some time one of revival and achievement; and there are remarkably few omens of disaster or of Gould's later loss of personal feeling. He falls under a spell, we are told, and the 'fatal spell' that afflicted the doomed treasure-hunters of Azuera might appropriately come into our minds. But this Conradian tendency to evoke the generality of human futility (seen from the Higuerota point of view, as it were) is also strongly countered by everything that is not futile, not self-deluding or solipsistic, in such schemes as Gould's:

. . . it was another form of enchantment, more suitable to his youth, into whose magic formula there entered hope, vigour, and self-confidence, instead of weary indignation and despair.   (p. 59)

And even when Higuerota is once again specifically used as a presence to ironize the activities of those in the Gould mould – in this case the engineers building the new railway, with Sir John representing the financial power of the European entrepreneur – the short paragraph again doubles back on itself in a way that more than half undoes the scathing irony:

. . . the voice of the engineer pronounced distinctly the words – 'We can't move mountains!'
Sir John, raising his head to follow the pointing gesture, felt the full force of the words. The white Higuerota soared out of the shadows of rock and earth like a frozen bubble under the moon. All was still, till near by, behind the wall of a corral for the camp animals, built roughly of loose stones in the form of a circle, a pack mule stamped his forefoot and blew heavily twice.   (p. 41)

Higuerota seems introduced in order to stare down transcendently, from another realm, upon the petty self-delusions of men. But when the transcendent is also only a 'frozen bubble' our imaginations – and our sense of values – are quickly attracted to the greater reality of the wall of the corral, made substantial by the wilful detailedness of 'built roughly of loose stones in the form of a circle' and by the precision of what the pack mule does. In two sentences, the narration moves from a symbolic picturing of the infinite, devaluing human ambition, down to a small celebration of the everyday world of men (and pack mules). And to confirm the change, we then see the heavy Biblical reverberation of 'We can't move mountains!' completely taken away by the humdrum explanation of *why* the engineer had used the phrase and the practical point that, anyway, tunnelling the railway under Higuerota 'would have been a colossal undertaking'.[23]

The actual descriptions of the San Tomé mine similarly press hard against that current in the book which would judge the mine adversely (but does so in surprisingly covert and subdued fashion). For example, if the mine suggests dehumanization and mechanization,[24] this is more than counterbalanced by the way it is also shown to teem with individual and collective vitality (e.g. in such men of practical deed and courageous gesture as Don Pépé and Father Roman). We have this description of the Indians coming to seek employment:

Father first, in a pointed straw hat, then the mother with the bigger children, generally also a diminutive donkey, all under burdens, except the leader himself, or perhaps some grown girl, the pride of the family, stepping barefooted and straight as an arrow, with braids of raven hair, a thick, haughty profile, and no load to carry but the small guitar of the country and a pair of soft leather sandals tied together on her back.   (p. 101)

And the uncritical and dramatized descriptions of the silver mine itself:

It was a time of pause. The Indian boys leaned idly against the long line of little cradle wagons standing empty; the screeners and ore-breakers squatted on their heels smoking long cigars; the great wooden shoots slanting over the edge of the tunnel plateau were silent; and only the ceaseless, violent rush of water in the open flumes could be heard, murmuring fiercely, with the splash and rumble of revolving turbine-wheels, and the thudding march of the stamps pounding to powder the treasure rock on the plateau below.(p. 100)

119

Higuerota and the Golfo Placido are no doubt the numinous elements of Conrad's world. But in this case, and at this stage in the novel, it is the phenomenal and the human that seem to have seized on his imagination most strongly — and therefore on ours, too, as we read.

To take one other significant instant of how the early narration views with complete equivocation the viability of human action, Book 2, chapter 4, ends with a strongly emphasized incident bearing many of the same possibilities as the two briefer examples examined above where the image of Higuerota, almost like the jungle in *Heart of Darkness*, though never quite, comes close to draining the real world of its reality and converting the activities of adventurers and practical moralists to a puppet show, a dream in a white fog. With the overthrow of Ribiera, the interests of virtually all the main characters so far introduced are threatened; the review of the army under the absurd Barrios increases the mood of despondency; and by now Decoud has arrived on the scene to contribute his own weight of faithless cynicism to the gathering darkness. The dream-effect is powerfully created and the void of Conrad's hell comes very close as the narrating begins to undermine the very phenomena it has given such solidity to. But something quite unexpected happens near the end:

The bells of the city were striking the hour of Oracion when the carriage rolled under the old gateway facing the harbour like a shapeless monument of leaves and stones. The rumble of wheels under the sonorous arch was traversed by a strange, piercing shriek, and Decoud, from his back seat, had a view of the people behind the carriage trudging along the road outside, all turning their heads, in sombreros and rebozos, to look at a locomotive which rolled quickly out of sight behind Giorgio Viola's house, under a white trail of steam that seemed to vanish in the breathless, hysterically prolonged scream of warlike triumph. And it was all like a fleeting vision, the shrieking ghost of a railway engine fleeing across the frame of the archway, behind the startled movement of the people streaming back from a military spectacle with silent footsteps on the dust of the road. It was a material train returning from the Campo to the palisaded yards. The empty cars rolled lightly on the single track; there was no rumble of wheels, no tremor on the ground. The engine-driver, running past the Casa Viola with the salute of an uplifted arm, checked his speed smartly before entering the yard; and when the ear-splitting screech of the steam-whistle for the brakes had stopped, a series of hard, battering shocks, mingled with the clanking of chain-couplings, made a tumult of blows and shaken fetters under the vault of the gate. (pp. 171–2)

The symbolism of the shrieking locomotive, at the very point where the futility of the liberal cause – and, in Decoud's words, of any causes in Costaguana – has been most sharply evoked, is powerful and far from banal. The machine, the shrieking, the epithets of war, the theatricality of the 'frame of the archway', the silent footsteps in the dust, then the weird soundlessness of a phenomenon that ought to have been all sound, crowned with the possibly bizarre gesture of the saluting driver – all these seem a confirmation of Decoud's withering criticism. His mode of thought would turn life into a dream of this very kind. Then suddenly, against the odds, in one of those tiny thrills of interest which activate such a book, the paragraph swerves, the silence turns into sound of the most substantial and directly conveyed kind, and what we are left with is not an emblem of futility but on the contrary an expression of energy: 'a series of hard, battering shocks, mingled with the clanking of chain-couplings, made a tumult of blows and shaken fetters under the vault of the gate'. Not even the word 'vault' can stop the movement, the 'series' of those 'battering shocks'; and the fetters are only in the faintest way an allusion to inertia and entombment, since their major effect in the sentence comes from their being 'shaken' under 'a tumult of blows'. Here is energy seeking release, and partly finding it, in the fine clatter and cacophony of the words themselves ('battering shocks, mingled with the clanking of chain-couplings'). And in addition, if it comes to larger echoes and ironic omens, we also have a *positive* omen here, in that this is the locomotive that will before long bear Nostromo on his historic journey of heroism and successful action. The narration, then, for the moment anyway, achieves the complex feat – not uncommon in Conrad – of powerfully summoning up a 'ghost' (of doubt, of perceived futility, of horror) and at once enacting its exorcism through allusion and through the sensuous representation of energy-in-action.

Despite such covertly exorcizing and energizing elements, however, by the time the book reaches its central episode of Nostromo and Decoud sailing the lighter with its load of silver into the Golfo Placido by night there is an accumulative weight of Conradian cold outrage and visionary despair at the world of political corruption and personal self-delusion that has been evoked. But in that famous episode there are certain puzzling aspects which might be clarified in terms of that between-the-lines contradictoriness we have been examining in the narrative up to this point. In its direct narration, the event extends over more than forty pages, not including preliminaries and immediate sequel. It comes spatially at the very midpoint of the novel; has always been recognized as its most reverberative, most imaginatively charged incident; and might be taken, in the sense proposed, as the most revealing pressure point of its various strains and stresses.

The episode is led up to by Decoud's long letter to his sister describing the most recent events in Sulaco: the arrival and flight of the deposed Ribiera, the popular insurrection, the plan to set up an independent Republic of Sulaco, and the desperate trip he is about to undertake with the silver load. The device is a very clumsy one. We have become used to internal narrations and recapitulations in *Nostromo*, but the use of the letter – a letter of about eight thousand words, written at dead of night – is too lacking in verisimilitude and too gauche to carry full conviction. Nevertheless, it is important that Decoud's own words should provide the approach, however awkward, to the central event, in which exploit and inertia are set most concentratedly and tensely in juxtaposition. Almost the whole of the letter is on the side of committed action, supported by its outward-looking narrative and its vivid recreation of scene and dialogue. The famous Decoud cynicism, which seems mostly to reinforce the book's general aspect of disenchantment, seems here to be strikingly in abeyance.[25] Indeed, from Decoud's first appearance we have been as much struck by his energetic and efficient pursuit of the Liberal cause (including his responsibility for ordering the all-important consignment of modern rifles) as by his own attempts to depreciate that pursuit as being attributable entirely to his personal passion for Antonia. What we read later concerning Decoud's death – one of the most significant instances of Conrad's fascination with the suicidal nature of cynicism, apathy, and loss of will – should never totally erase the other impressions of Decoud as passionate lover, plotter, propagandist, and exhorter of others to action – '"Do you know", I cried, "what surrender means to you, to your women, to your children, to your property?"' (pp. 235–6). His letter is full of his own attempts to rouse the flagging spirit of his compatriots and of the practical urgency of his plan to save the silver: '"I am not running away,

122

you understand'', he wrote on. ''I am simply going away with that great treasure of silver which must be saved at all costs''' (p. 244). Only sometimes is there a Marlow-like phrase, 'To each his fate, shaped by passion or sentiment' (p. 245) or (and in context this is more a realistic than a figurative statement) 'I have the feeling of a great solitude around me' (p. 230). For the most part, it is the letter of a man intent on changing, rather than accepting, his fate, contemptuous of loss of will in others, a clear-headed and unsolipsistic critic of the personalities around him, and a man of specifically public and political status, for all his affected intellectual scorn and for all the occasional highlighting of his detachment by a phrase of the narrator: for example, 'the man with no faith in anything except the truth of his own sensations' (p. 229). Decoud is far from being a Heyst — and yet something in the tenor of the novel seems to require to cast him in that role.

The Heyst-role momentarily surfaces, and very abruptly, with the closing words of his letter. Describing the blackness of the night, his isolation, and the presence of Viola's dying wife elsewhere in the house, he concludes:

'And I . . . don't really know whether to count myself with the living or with the dead. ''*Quien sabe?*'' as the people here are prone to say in answer to every question. But no! feeling for you is certainly not dead, and the whole thing, the house, the dark night, the silent children in this dim room, my very presence here — all this is life, must be life, since it is so much like a dream.' (p. 249)

At this stage, I think we note the sudden swerve of the letter into a world-questioning despondency as an acceptable ambiguity: a movement of mood or style in Decoud, even an instance of his affectation. We are also very aware that this is an exhausted man, whose switch of moods can be attributed naturalistically to tiredness, hunger, and strain, as well as being read in terms of some general principle of world-loss and vacuity.

Then comes the voyage:

A great recrudescence of obscurity embraced the boat. The sea in the gulf was as black as the clouds above . . . [Decoud] didn't even know at times whether he were asleep or awake. Like a man lost in slumber, he heard nothing, he saw nothing. Even his hand held before his face did not exist for his eyes. The change from the agitation, the passions and the dangers, from the sights and sounds of the shore, was so complete that it would have resembled death had it not been for the survival of his thoughts. In this foretaste of eternal peace they floated vivid and light, like unearthly clear dreams of earthly things that may haunt the souls freed by death from the misty atmosphere of regrets and hopes. Decoud shook himself, shuddered a bit, though the air that drifted past him was warm. He had the strangest sensation of his soul having just returned into his body from the circumambient darkness in which land, sea, sky, the mountains, and the rocks were as if they had not been.   (pp. 261–2)

The sense of dream and shifting is very powerfully conveyed, and with a suddenness of contrast that makes the narrative at once show signs of stress. It is not that the new trance-like mood has been imposed crudely – many other hints that human action is imperfect, motive unreliable, ambition a folly, and ideal value an illusion, have prepared us for such a climax. But there is also a sense of dislocation, rather as in Marlow's outbursts in the second half of *Lord Jim* – dramatic or melodramatic, or possibly neurotic – which comes from the suddenness of the movement and the new extremism of the rhetoric, and which now fully engages our attention on all the indirections and peculiarities of Conrad's rendering of the scene.

For one thing, although many readers retain an image of the episode as one of listlessness, paralysis, and descent-into-darkness, it is in fact filled with talk. The darkness does, very impressively, weigh upon the characters – and on us – 'like a stone'; but still the impulse to talk, to analyse, to explain, and to complain persists, especially in the loquacious Nostromo. Decoud's sudden mood of inertia takes on something of a hallucinatory quality – 'Decoud lay on the silver boxes panting. All his active sensations and feelings from as far back as he could remember seemed to him the maddest of dreams' (p. 267) – but we are nevertheless quite strongly aware (as before) that the mood is partly caused by the physical facts of his exhaustion and hunger; and his replies to Nostromo, however weary, however reflective of the fact that inwardly he can imagine 'the lighter sinking to the bottom with an extraordinary shudder of delight', nevertheless are strongly argumentative and practical. When Nostromo dramatically puts out their only light on hearing the steamer bearing Sotillo's troops, and disaster seems at hand, Decoud's momentary *goût du néant* is ousted by a keen sense of self-preservation and an awareness of his pressing political motives:

124

Decoud, with careful movements, slipped off his overcoat and divested himself of his boots; he did not consider himself bound in honour to sink with the treasure. His object was to get down to Barrios, in Cayta, as the Capataz knew very well; and he, too, meant, in his own way, to put into that attempt all the desperation of which he was capable.   (p. 282)

'He did not consider himself bound in honour to sink with the treasure' could be made to reverberate with a pronounced Conradian irony in view of Decoud's subsequent suicide-by-drowning with ingots of the treasure to weigh him down. But that possible irony seems to have very little imaginative pressure behind it. The narration, indeed, far from seizing the opportunities offered by the tension of the situation and the symbolic potentialities of the darkness, seems at this point to go out of its way to stress the unexceptionableness of Decoud's reaction, even at the cost of some very pedestrian prose:

The prospect of finding himself in the water and swimming, overwhelmed by ignorance and darkness, probably in a circle, till he sank from exhaustion, was revolting. The barren and cruel futility of such an end intimidated his affectation of careless pessimism. In comparison to it, the chance of being left floating in a boat, exposed to thirst, hunger, discovery, imprisonment, execution, presented itself with an aspect of amenity worth securing even at the cost of some self-contempt.   (p. 282)

It is very peculiar, at such a structurally emphatic crisis, where all the book's accumulating references to human futility would seem to be about to find their most concentrated expression, that Conrad's language should veer away from the direction offered by that crisis and become so anticlimactic and practical – should so turn back towards the life of the shore, as it were.

A similar problem arises in the handling of narrative stance. The intensity of the scene would seem to demand a close focus on Decoud and his sensations, since he seems to be cast in the exemplary role of the book's most vulnerable and revealing figure. But the concentration on Decoud at his breaking-point – or on Decoud *as* breaking-point of the intellectual and imaginative stresses of the whole narrative – is regularly disrupted. Firstly, there is the discovery of Hirsch, with a two-page narrative flashback to describe his experiences during the riot and how he came to be on board. Then, more startling still, as Decoud and Nostromo wait in dead silence while the steamer approaches in the darkness, there is an abrupt switch of point of view not just from the lighter to the steamer but to Sotillo's past experiences in Sulaco, including his behaviour in the Gould drawing room, his conduct in Esmeralda, and his plans for the future. It is six pages before we are returned to Decoud and Nostromo, still standing in the darkness. After the steamer strikes the lighter – another critical moment, if ever there was one, that can ill afford any loss of dramatic immediacy – we are distracted by the account of how Hirsch has fared. And only then are we back with Decoud and Nostromo again, beaching the holed lighter, and finally with Nostromo alone – for the first time in the episode – making his way back to the mainland. Is this a mere botched dissipation of dramatic effect, or does the partial forswearing of the expected effect alert us to areas of narrative counter-suggestion and epistemological tentativeness that are incompatible with traditional patterns of climax and denouement?

Similarly, what is the function of Hirsch in this scene? As a whiner, a coward, and not least as a merely mercantile man he is grotesquely foreign to the heroic mode of both Nostromo and Decoud – the heroic and operatic leader-of-the-people and the heroic and cynical boulevardier. Whenever he appears, speaking cringingly to Gould in chapter 5, or bizarrely stowed away on the lighter, and then, fatally, in his confrontation on shore with the enraged Sotillo, Hirsch seems destined to be employed as a grotesque. He is an obvious foil to the others; but it seems also that the violence of the events, and the strains in the narrative, find some correlative, some strange satisfaction, in the provision of Hirsch as victim – and while it may be an embarrassment to the reader for some of its implications, it is noteworthy that Conrad has made Hirsch a Jew. Hirsch's function is in a way to be a whipping boy. His torture and eventual death, and the great play with the shadow of his hanging body in the night scene between Monygham and Nostromo, express something unbalanced in the text – something that arises from its indecisions, its switches of mood and feeling, its need, here and there, suddenly to throw up an energizing extreme. It may be that Hirsch fulfils a role structurally similar to that of the Russian (the harlequin) in *Heart of Darkness*, but morally in inverse: not an embodiment of irresponsibility, escape, and imaginative innocence but, on the contrary, a focus for contempt, a catalyst of the destructive instinct that has been held off by those countering 'positive' features in the narration that I have concentrated on. Hirsch is a black spot − or, more appropriately, a black, dangling shadow − in the narrative; but one that it apparently stands in need of, as an intensifier of its rhythms and chiaroscuro. And there is some disturbing connection between our contempt at his antics, our compelled sense of disgust and fascination at his killing, and the malaise that has been trying to formulate itself in the lighter episode through Decoud's very muffled urge towards loss of identity and extinction.[26]

Extraordinarily, almost two hundred pages now elapse before the narrative confronts us directly with Decoud's fate − after the prolonged (and really rather slow) account of Monygham's part in the Sotillo-Montero crisis, the entry of Pedro Montero into Sulaco, and the typically virtuoso switch of narrative chronology from Nostromo about to undertake his saving exploit to Captain Mitchell's prosy account of the exploit some years in the future. Only after we have been taken into that future standpoint are we then returned directly to Nostromo in the 'past', to his discovery of the telltale floating dinghy, and then, by another barely alleviated transition, back to Decoud himself contemplating suicide alone on the Great Isabel. And after such extravagant postponement the narrator is peculiarly forthright, even brisk, about the causes of the suicide:

the truth was that he died from solitude, the enemy known but to a few on this earth, and whom only the simplest of us are fit to withstand. The brilliant Costaguanero of the boulevards had died from solitude and want of faith in himself and others . . .
. . . in our activity alone do we find the sustaining illusion of an independent existence as against the whole scheme of things of which we form a helpless part. Decoud lost all belief in the reality of his action past and to come.   (pp. 496–7)

And in a distinctly cursory epitaph:

A victim of the disillusioned weariness which is the retribution meted out to intellectual audacity, the brilliant Don Martin Decoud, weighted by the bars of San Tomé silver, disappeared without a trace, swallowed up in the immense indifference of things.   (p. 501)

It would be facile to say that the refusal of the lighter episode to fulfil our expectations represents ineptitude on Conrad's part. There are certain detailed aspects of the novel – the tragic end of Nostromo, for example, or the overall presentation of Antonia – where Conrad's gaucheness could be asserted more forcibly. And it could also be wondered whether much of the second half does not tend to become a little mechanical in its knotting and unknotting of narrative strands, its ironic parallelisms of character and situation that go on repeating what has already been established. But there is something more interesting and potentially more meaning-bearing about the narration's anticlimaxes, its switches, anticipations, and postponements, its alternation of vivid scene and energetic adventure with slow-moving panorama or recapitulation, its juxtaposing of the conventionally operatic with the wilful withholding of the apposite or the conclusive. The unsteadiness of the narration's mode and direction can become a part of our full imaginative response both on the level of half-articulated but aesthetically shaped feeling and on the level of fully conscious interpretation. On the latter level, we take satisfaction in such an authoritative phrase as the narrator's 'the truth was that he died from solitude', and can place that confident observation within the pattern of similarities and contrasts that the discursive mind un-covers within the flow of the novel. But on the other level of our response, away from moral pattern-making, we find something in the book that acts against the authority of clear judgement: its odd-ness and tension, the progressive indeterminateness that keeps breaking down the narration's traditional promise of decorum, with preparation, climax, and aftermath in the 'correct' order. As we have seen, *Nostromo* perpetually invokes disillusionment and despair, only to offset this immediately by a surprising jump in nar-rative point of view, a seizing on a firm event, a social fact, a vivid natural phenomenon, even a moment of relieving grotesque comedy. A train almost becomes a spectre, but is drawn back into the everyday world of sounds and certainties; and vice versa, and on a quite different scale, a figure of unreflecting action, Nostromo, is turned into a haunted man by the very act that firmly establishes his public status. All the explicit moral ambiguities of the story, and many that are more deeply buried, are intensified, made more radically operative and available to more of our faculties, by the indirections of narration, the changes of approach, the shifting of a paragraph, a chapter, an episode. At the very least, as with *Heart of Darkness* and *Lord Jim*, the narration's own uncertainties should make us suspicious of attempts to encapsulate our whole experience of the novel in one aphorism – no matter how aphoristic one mode of the narrative voice tends to be ('the disillusioned weariness which is the retribution meted out to intellectual audacity', 'the disenchanted vanity which is the reward of audacious action', and the like – p. 501). For example, when one famous aphorism is partly dramatized by being attributed to Mrs Gould, as one of her reported thoughts – 'There was something inherent in the necessities of successful action which carried with it the moral degradation of the idea' (p. 521) – there is a strong tendency for that statement to find ratification from so many examples throughout the book of idealism gone wrong and of action defeating itself. But our awakened reaction to the complexity of how the novel actually operates, how it performs itself, makes us see around the aphorism into a much fuller texture of imaginative response that must modify the range of its validity. For example, the immediate bearing of Mrs Gould's aphorism is the hardening effect on her husband of his obsession with the idea of the San Tomé mine.[27] Although this growth of impersonality in Charles Gould is a rather imposed and cursory feature of *Nostromo* – compared, say, with James's psychological presentation of the corrosive force of the pure 'idea' in Olive Chancellor – and remains something externally given rather than convincingly dramatized by showing the man's change internally and in projected scenes, nevertheless the reader – with a quibble, perhaps – accepts that the point is established. But against that point – or rather, all round it, casting a differing play of light and feeling on it – is our experience of having been emphatically involved as readers in Gould's 'necessities of successful action'. We have taken part with relief and excitement in his commitment to political action and his exercise of the will in the building of the mine – in the vivid descriptions of movement, sound, bustle, and triumphant procession – and we have associated with the image of Gould such scenes of *meaningful* organization and efficiency as the negotiations with Hernandez the bandit, the cinematic night scene of the evacuation from Sulaco, the threat to blow up the mine, the interview with Pedro Montero, and so on. Everything else in the book that resists its own disillusioning vision – from the tiny verbal effects of the railway engine and the stamping pack-mule to the larger narrative effect of the lighter episode clumsily but insistently veering away from its now logical direction of loss-of-reality and death — reinforces the positive aspect of Gould, or at least seriously qualifies any simplistic and aphoristic 'placing' of his dehumanization. This felt complexity of the book's local and overall development makes it impossible for the gnomic phrase, 'Material interests' (p. 522),[28] to dominate our response as conclusively as has often been suggested. *Nostromo* as a narrative does not signify 'ideas decline into matter', or 'the best-intentioned of political actions are inadequate and re-create the injustices they seek to overthrow', or 'life is a dream', or 'love, idealism, heroism, justice are all illusions, though necessary and possibly saving illusions' — though all of these significances are precipitated somewhere within our total experience of reading it.[29]

Closer to that experience, perhaps, is a simple colloquial expression. If someone asks, 'What's the meaning of *Nostromo*?', the reader might casually begin his reply, 'Well, it's about . . .' This is not necessarily evasiveness; for *Nostromo*, like any novel, is a fictional to-do that takes place round about its potential meanings, its references to life, politics, love, and action. There is a reminder here of a well-known phrase of Henry James in the Preface to *Portrait of a Lady* — 'The novel is of its very nature an "ado", an ado about something, and the larger the form it takes the greater of course the ado. Therefore, consciously, that was what one was in for — for positively organising an ado about Isabel Archer.'[30] *Nostromo*, too, just like that earlier masterpiece 'about' idealism and betrayal, and completely in accord with James's view of fiction as interplay and pressure, comes to us as an 'ado': a continuing accretion, an organized flow of unclosable possibilities, of relationships and aspects, a living event rather than the deadening inertia of a certainty. In one of those aspects, *Nostromo* gestures in the direction of finality and fullness — for example, by ending as it does in a pattern-making, circle-completing allusion to the Golfo Placido, the ironically hollow triumph of Nostromo, and the emblematic 'white cloud shining like a mass of solid silver' (p. 566). But it does so from within a narration that has all along queried the finality of emblematic utterances and asserted against 'the dark gulf' the energies of its hold on human realities and actions; and now returns us to everything uncompletable, inexhaustible, and contrary that it has been *about*.

4. 'Like a traveller in a strange country'

Heart of Darkness, *Lord Jim*, and *Nostromo*, tested out in only a few of their cruces, their pressure points, have all been seen as narrative processes that partly resist the urge of the exegete — it is one of their own urges, too — to impose the stasis of paraphrase or conceptual interpretation. Complexity of process in each case was confirmed in certain obliquities of narrative and of suggested meaning that went against the strong Conradian drift of pessimism — not to overcome it by any means but only to deny it the status of a governing idea. Better for many artists, perhaps, to have a recurrent bad dream than a governing idea. *Under Western Eyes* and *The Shadow-Line* are both very much of the bad dream variety. They are two of Conrad's most strongly hallucinatory, as well as shifting, narratives, bearing that terror of self-alienation and loss of reality which operates at varying levels in most of his writing and is a more directly disturbing presence there than the same terror, modified into the fear of personal inadequacy and of the chaos of lovelessness and incommunication, within the narratives of both James and Forster. *Under Western Eyes* and *The Shadow-Line* may more immediately suggest a context of Dostoevsky and Kafka; but within their own much less fevered obliquities and indirections, James and Forster, like Conrad, articulate the same sense of human falsity, self-division, and powerlessness before evil — like a bad dream of a caged beast on a terrace at Fawns, a strange pagoda, silence between husband and wife in a drawing-room in Portland Place; an experience of horror for Margaret Schlegel in a St Paul's that desolatingly parodies form, connection, and identity, or for Mrs Moore in a cave, hearing a word, and all words, become a snake.

In *Under Western Eyes* the nightmare of alienation and duplicity is to be lifted by the thunderstorm that is approaching Geneva, 'the sleeping town of prosaic virtues and universal hospitality'.[31] The distant rumble is heavily portentous, and the coming deluge charged with significance. This violence of the elements ushers in the violent ending of *Under Western Eyes*, one of Conrad's most startling and extreme conclusions. It is startling not just because of the highly dramatic scenes of the narrator and Natalia Haldin searching the streets for Razumov, of Razumov confessing to Natalia, then to the other revolutionaries, that he is the betrayer of her brother, ending in his being savagely beaten up, deafened, and maimed. It is startling also because Razumov's confession, his discovery of the redemptive power of love, and Natalia's consequent maturing-through-suffering seem to provide a conclusion of classic moral clarity, powerfully direct in its feelings of physical and moral anguish, then relief and rebirth, and using confession, punishment, and calm-of-mind-all-passion-spent to redeem and consummate the whole preceding narrative of guilt and alienation.

It has a powerful effect, this contrast between a narrative mostly dominated by impressions of phantasmagoria and a fairly brief conclusion that climactically asserts the restoration of reality and of reality-bearing values. There is nothing obviously hollow or forced about the ending: the writing is far too strong for us to feel that Conrad is whistling in the dark for his redemption-effect. The sense of psychological truth in Razumov's 'temptation' to betray Natalia into marriage being overcome by his discovering a real love for her, together with his long-developing emotional urge towards confession, hold the final scenes in perfectly adequate connection, on that psychological level, with what has gone before. And the oppressive intensity of the narrating has by now succeeded in making the reader, almost as much as Razumov, desire such a release (as we desire to be released into action and novelty out of Marlow's inquisitions halfway through *Lord Jim*): we share in the emotional necessity for release at the same time as recognizing its thematic and mimetic aptness. Nevertheless, the movement from a prolonged dream to sudden awakening is an abrupt one, and reveals a characteristic imbalance that can be seen to be expressive in its own peculiar terms: that is, in terms, hardly classic or redemptive, of a still-unresolved tension between the book's two strains of alienation and recovery.[32]

The much-commented-on device of the narrator − the elderly teacher of languages − is typically paradoxical in effect. At times, his studied prosaicism in the face of Russian abstraction, his expressed preference for so-called western modes of clarity − 'Life is a thing of form. It has its plastic shape and a definite intellectual aspect' – provides a certain familiar solidity on which to base our point of view. But just as frequently his obvious inadequacy to deal with the full nature of the moral and psychological issues involved devalues him, and erodes the solidity before we have fully drawn on it. Similarly, a great deal of verisimilitude is gained from his pernickety observations as narrator; but his frequent comments that he has been observing an essentially foreign and mysterious phenomenon across an unbridgeable gap also strengthens the dream-effect conveyed by so much else in the narrative. This latter form of 'observation' – emphasized by the book's title – makes us frequently aware that we watch Razumov and the events of his life from a distance that may not be enormous but is still definite enough to have self-consciousness – our self-consciousness – written into its perspective.[33] There is a subtly operative connection between the reader's (and the narrator's) sense of partial alienation from the events and Razumov's own portrayed alienation from himself and from reality.

Near the beginning of the two central sections of the book (Parts 2 and 3) the narrator meets Natalia Haldin in the promenade of the Bastions and begins a long series of questions-and-answers concerning her experience at the Château Borel. His self-conscious deprecation permeates the already self-consciously judicial and expository account of what she found at the Château in a way that further disturbs the narration:

She rested her glance on me as if to ascertain the degree of my anxiety or the number of my years. My physiognomy has never been expressive, I believe, and as to my years I am not ancient enough as yet to be strikingly decrepit. I have no long beard like the good hermit of a romantic ballad; my footsteps are not tottering, my aspect not that of a slow, venerable sage. Those picturesque advantages are not mine. I am old, alas, in a brisk, commonplace way.   (p. 143)

And again, this time with a further complicating touch of archness on Conrad's part:

Wonder may be expressed at a man in the position of a teacher of languages knowing all this with such definiteness. A novelist says this and that of his personages, and if only he knows how to say it earnestly enough he may not be questioned upon the inventions of his brain in which his own belief is made sufficiently manifest by a telling phrase, a poetic image, the accent of emotion. Art is great! But I have no art. . .   (p. 162)

Slightly distorted by this frame of self-ironizing comments, the narrative point of view then produces other strange perspectives: for example, the perspective created by our hearing the self-aware narrator's voice telling us how Natalia (in the promenade) told him how Tekla (at the Château Borel) described her past life in Russia. As soon as we become engrossed in a piece of dramatized third-person narration, having suspended our knowledge that it is the teacher who is casting his dialogue with Natalia into the form of reported action, we are suddenly drawn up short by an abrupt switch – for example, into the reported thoughts of Razumov, meeting Natalia for the first time:

> She wondered whether her brother's friend had not already guessed who she was.
> I am in a position to say that, as a matter of fact, he had guessed.(p. 167)

The narrator himself also discovers more and more that he is *not* 'in a position to say', and introduces his own faltering sense of unease into the already unstable texture of his narration:

> I could not forget that, standing by Miss Haldin's side, I was like a traveller in a strange country . . .
> Once more I had the sense of being out of it – not because of my age, which at any rate could draw inferences – but altogether out of it, on another plane whence I could only watch her from afar. And so ceasing to speak I watched her stepping out by my side. (pp. 169–70)

The narrator thus watches himself watching Natalia in her foreignness. And what he narrates at second hand, coming from Natalia, concerns further self-watching and self-criticism, especially in the description of her meeting with Razumov, where she is acutely conscious of how she must appear to the narrator when she describes her reactions of self-consciousness while talking to Razumov and being worried and bemused by *his* excessive and distraught self-consciousness – soon compounded by our occasional privileged entry into what lies behind Razumov's surface reactions. It is all a Chinese-box effect, and oppressive in the extreme.

There is one large factor of irony that must also be detected, adding to these entanglements: that is the fact that all this time we half-know, and are occasionally overtly reminded by the narrator, that his own responses are twofold. There is the response he tries to recreate as it was at the time, based on his ignorance (and

Natalia's ignorance) as to the real facts about Razumov; and the shadow-response of interpreting these encounters and events in the light of his (and our) later knowledge that Razumov is the precise opposite of what Natalia imagines: a Czarist police spy and the betrayer of her brother, rather than an exiled revolutionary and Haldin's loyal friend. With our own fuller knowledge, we ourselves also reinterpret these events independently of the few hints of the narrator, and are in a position where it is impossible not ourselves to be creating a further, unverbalized line of narrative between the lines we actually read. For example, *we* know why Razumov should seem 'overcome' when Natalia sobs out her brother's name, though the narrator gives no indication of *his* knowing, and Natalia's explanation is that 'Their friendship must have been the very brotherhood of souls!' (p. 172). These perceived layers of reading may lend themselves to some conceptual formulation of the purport of the book in terms of self-delusion, false appearance, tricky words and the like; but they also have a more intrinsic effect, in that they create an amazingly dense narrative texture through which we move unsteadily − one full of extraordinary gaps, chasms, and awkwardnesses that threaten to undermine its progress with its own ironies, self-reflections, and deliberate disjunctions.

If the narrative, then, creates its own sense of distancing and alienating; if its strategies include making us see Razumov now close, now far off, now in false appearance, now in self-vexing reality; if it makes us look at its events and people as though at the end of a long tunnel, with irony drawing the shape of the tunnel, then suddenly, perturbingly, abolishes all distance − then what of the intensifying effect of also having a character like Razumov as the main object of interest within such a narrative method? For Razumov is himself one of Conrad's most unforgettable portraits of a personality in an acute state of self-alienation; an epigraph to which might well be found in the following, where he is in the Château Borel:

> He felt, bizarre as it may seem, as though another self, an independent sharer of his mind, had been able to view his whole person very distinctly indeed. 'This is curious', he thought. (p. 230)

When Razumov's vivid emotional states, and even his moral analyses of his own position, find an analogue in the functioning devices and structures by which his presence is conveyed to us, then the effect can only be one of quite dizzying complexity.

One of the most notable technical features in the presentation of Razumov's story is the daring – but characteristically Conradian – gap that is created between the close of his interview with Mikulin in St Petersburg at the end of Part 1 and the return, at the beginning of Part 4 (nearly 200 pages later), to what happened immediately afterwards, hingeing on Mikulin's dramatic words, 'Where to?' (p. 99).[34] Part 1 has been essentially direct in its narrative impact, with only very subdued interventions by the narrator – and for that reason, among others, is often regarded as quite the most successful part of the whole novel. We are kept close enough to Razumov to share, even uncomfortably, in the intensity of his first experiences of hysteria, cold despair, paranoiac outrage, and loss of reality which succeed one another with Dostoevskyan extremism. Part 1 has the vividness of dream, heightened by the fact that Razumov, from the moment he is forced into a false position by Haldin's misplaced confidence in him, always *looks* at himself in his own doubleness: looks at his own actions, stares bemused at a Haldin in *his* room, stares at the image of his own uncertain future. Thrashing Ziemanitch is the only moment of actual physical relief for the unbearable tensions that divide him. Only his sudden near-mystic vision of Russia as an absolute and single reality can strengthen him: a Russia like some white Golfo Placido, as immense and as total as snow, with its 'sacred inertia' of blankness and impersonal power; a unitary authority, like a transcendent father, to underpin the panicky self-divisions of the individual consciousness (especially the unsustained consciousness of the illegitimate and isolated Razumov). His conversations with himself, the haunting hallucination of having walked over Haldin's body in the street, the bitter self-scrutinizing, the neurotic observation of tiny details, the approach to breakdown, and the days of somnambulism that follow the betrayal of Haldin are all given a very physical reality in the narration:

He sat down and stared. He had a distinct sensation of his very existence being undermined in some mysterious manner, of his moral supports falling away from him one by one. He even experienced a slight physical giddiness and made a movement as if to reach for something to steady himself with.
(pp. 76–7)

136

And again:

> . . . his head ached terribly. He passed his hand over his brow − an involuntary gesture of suffering, which he was too careless to restrain.
>
> At that moment Razumov beheld his own brain suffering on the rack − a long, pale figure drawn asunder horizontally with terrific force in the darkness of a vault, whose face he failed to see. It was as though he had dreamed for an infinitesimal fraction of time of some dark print of the Inquisition. . . (pp. 87–8)

And when we return to these events at the beginning of Part 4, after a half of the whole book's length has passed, it is as though nothing in the narrative had intervened, so completely resumed is the effect of local and individual concentration − and to the same end, that of the recreation of a life that has become an oppressive waking dream to itself, and to us as readers.

The narrative's recovery of this coldly frantic intensity at the very point where its last movement − the last evening, of confession and violence − is about to begin, is finely energizing after the long conversations and strangely muffled encounters at or near the Château Borel that fill out the central half of the novel, Parts 2 and 3. And yet, though we are very aware of this change of intensity, and of how heavily the central section has hung on us as we read, there is no real sense of lacuna, since so much of what happens in Geneva is in fact like one of Razumov's waking nightmares. And this is another fact we have to deal with in assessing the relation between the final cleansing confession and the rest of the narration. Because if Razumov's hellish experience in Part 1 and in the first chapter of Part 4 remain in our minds with their hallucinatory power, beyond the capacity of confession fully to expunge, then the slow-moving sessions in the grounds of the Château Borel, which seem so contrasted, have a claustrophobic, surrealistic force of their own, and also build up imaginative pressures of guilt, oppression, and falsity that will be difficult to see 'washed clean' (in Razumov's phrase) by the suddenly cleansing rainstorm of the end.

The Château and its grounds are anomalous in the otherwise bourgeois orderliness and neatness of the Genevan ambience that the narrator so scorns. In its dilapidation and strangeness, and in the illogical and futile toings-and-froings of the conspiratorial exiles who so loquaciously inhabit it, the Château seems an emanation from the Russian unknowableness which the narration continually evokes and pushes us towards. Natalia's first visit establishes its tone:

> She observed green stains of moss on the steps of the terrace. The front door stood wide open. There was no one about. She found herself in a wide, lofty, and absolutely empty hall, with a good many doors. These doors were all shut. A broad, bare stone staircase faced her, and the effect of the whole was of an untenanted house. She stood still, disconcerted by the solitude, but after a while she became aware of a voice speaking continuously somewhere.
>
> 'You were probably being observed all the time,' I suggested. 'There must have been eyes.'
>
> 'I don't see how that could be,' she retorted. 'I haven't seen even a bird in the grounds. I don't even remember hearing a single twitter in the trees. The whole place appeared utterly deserted except for the voice.' (p. 144)

The unknown echoing voice, 'lonely and sad', expresses the mystery of the Château. Though we do not know what language it is (there is an interviewer within – the language may be French), it resembles the cabalistic orthography of Russian which the narrator (like Marlow, baffled by the gloss to Towson's *Inquiry*) has just commented on as he sees a letter in Natalia's hand – 'incomprehensible to the experience of Western Europe' (p. 133). And it resembles the effect he detects, from his carefully detached position, even in Natalia's own voice:

> It may be that she thought I understood her much better than I was able to do. The most precise of her sayings seemed always to me to have enigmatical prolongations vanishing somewhere beyond my reach.(p. 118)

Just like the narrator, we can judge the human ordinariness of the abused Tekla, the hollow self-importance of Peter Ivanovitch, and the shrill sensuality of Madame de S—. But there remain 'enigmatical prolongations': echoes in the Château and its overgrown grounds that speak only of the vision of 'an immense, wintry Russia', the 'great white desert' that filled the dreams of Razumov, the would-be son and adherent of the Absolute. We are back with alienation once again. When the Château is so resonant with moral and existential emptiness, and when the world of Geneva outside the Château gates is continually derided by the narrator, even venomously, for its equally futile orderliness and toleration (and even the Jura is 'ugly'), everything, it seems, has been taken away. Almost as for Razumov, facing Mikulin, we have

nowhere to go. Hence the mounting effect for us of phantasmagoria – the Razumov-experience, in little. When Razumov
himself penetrates the Château, Madame de S—, waiting for him
at the centre as the supposed revolutionary inspirer of meaningful
actions, is on the contrary a figure of nightmare and non-being:

The eyes appeared extraordinarily brilliant . . . The rasping voice inviting
him to sit down; the rigidity of the upright attitude with one arm extended
along the back of the sofa, the white gleam of the big eyeballs setting off
the black, fathomless stare of the enlarged pupils, impressed Razumov
more than anything he had seen since his hasty and secret departure from
St. Petersburg. A witch in Parisian clothes, he thought. A portent! . . .

He sat down. At close quarters the rouged cheek-bones, the wrinkles, the
fine lines on each side of the vivid lips, astounded him. He was being
received graciously, with a smile which made him think of a grinning skull.

(p. 215)

As so often in Conrad in such a situation of oppressive doubt, a
certain grotesque comedy begins to flicker in the narrative (as
around Hirsch on the lighter in *Nostromo*, or Marlow in *Lord Jim*
interviewing the *Patna*'s chief engineer in the throes of delirium
tremens). Madame de S— and Peter Ivanovitch play out a stately
black farce before the appalled Razumov – 'She like a galvanized
corpse out of some Hoffman's Tale – he the preacher of feminist
gospel for all the world, and a super-revolutionist besides!'
(p. 215). Even the basically sympathetic and victimized Tekla
becomes macabre when the narrative, for one sentence, suddenly
focuses on an odd detail through its strangely alienating lens:

The shabby woman laughed a little. Her teeth, splendidly white and ad-
mirably even, looked absurdly out of place, like a string of pearls on the
neck of a ragged tramp. (p. 146)

Attention is drawn, time and time again, to the instability of
language and of communication.[35] Razumov's whole existence in
Geneva (like Nostromo's later life of deceit in Sulaco) is a kind of
double entendre or riddle, and we see him play dangerously with
the double meanings of words in his various eccentric and stagily
reverberative conversations with the various revolutionaries, as
when he perversely embroiders on the theme of 'phantom' with
Madame de S—, or announces to an enthusiastic Peter Ivanovitch,
'Here I stand before you – confessed!' (p. 229). And in his

self-consciousness he theorizes on the alienating game of incommunication that he is playing:

It gave him a feeling of triumphant pleasure to deceive [Sophia Antonovna] out of her own mouth. The epigrammatic saying that speech has been given to us for the purpose of concealing our thoughts came into his mind. Of that cynical theory this was a very subtle and a very scornful application, flouting in its own words the very spirit of ruthless revolution. (pp. 261–2)

The narrator, with some understatement, refers to 'this day of many conversations' (p. 237). And when so many of the conversations are built over false assumptions, misleading allusions, and ironic hints read by us but not by Razumov's companions, and the whole obliquity is transmitted to us by the additionally oblique medium of the commenting narrator who is himself a 'translator' but one confessedly baffled by the 'prolongations' of his material into hidden meanings, then Conrad's method begins to approach its own point of breaking-strain. Just as the narrator has to act out a false ignorance about Razumov for the sake of his narrative convention, so for a while it seems that false information will save Razumov from exposure. The untrue report, given within that not-quite-true narration, that the peasant Ziemanitch was Haldin's betrayer seems to be a culminating instance of some universal force of deception that shapes all the words and thoughts of the protagonists. Yet even in this nightmare there are the traces of a mirthless farce. 'This was a comedy of errors', Razumov thinks as the rumour of Ziemanitch takes hold – 'Thanks to the devil' (pp. 284, 283). Just occasionally, in the central section particularly, amid so many futile and bizarre entrances and exits, when words spin in a kind of vacuum and the human will to act has been etiolated into dream or verbiage or habitual irony, it is Chekhov who comes to mind, to join Dostoevsky among the many ghosts that haunt this novel.[36]

Even the chronologically disruptive switch between the Château Borel and St Petersburg, then, seems only to add to this variety of dream-effects and dislocating vistas that accompany, and in so many ways act against, the book's adherence to 'Western' strategies of moral scrutiny and the exposure of folly, and, near the end, its movement towards meaningful transformation, clarification, and restitution. For a book that seems to mark time for so much of its length, and to become as much of a somnambulist as its protagonist, the narration contains current within current of opposed and even violent pressures. So that the storm, when it breaks over Geneva, breaks directly for all those pressures as well as for the formal ushering-in of the climax. To apply the phrase from *King John* that Conrad used, with rather less appositeness, as the epigraph for *Nostromo*, 'So foul a sky clears not without a storm.'[37]

The 'storm' of Razumov's redemptive confession and physical suffering springs out of the whole preceding narrative in two senses of the phrase 'out of'. We detect a straightforward connection in terms of truth-to-life between Razumov's self-alienating anxieties and the experience of confession that will relieve them. Also, we have seen him *imagine* confessing before now, and even play with the word, as a foretaste of the climax to come. And linear connection is further strengthened by two different expectations in our minds, one the traditional generic expectation that tragic 'foulness' will be cleared by 'storm'; and the other, more local to this work, that a narrative movement so irregular and neurotic will fittingly produce an extreme finale. But the other sense of 'springs out of', meaning 'away from', also applies, no matter how contradictorily. The redemptive power of love and the possibility of healing and rebirth, as invoked in Razumov's written confession and letter of love to Natalia, interject a radically new mode for which there seems to be little support in the phantasmagoria of either St Petersburg or the Château Borel. But it is no more disruptive, and no less disruptive, than the other changes of direction that have characterized the book from the beginning. The arbitrariness of a bad dream is now succeeded by the arbitrariness of a good. It is so transformative and so sudden as to bear a value verging on the transcendent − though after all an abrupt gesture in the direction of a transcendent order is not adventitious in a book that has already invoked the Absolute, even though negatively, in Razumov's terrible dream-vision of Russia the longed-for parent, white, austere, and infinite.[38] The mystery of the 'foreign', that which cannot be translated (by a teacher of languages, or any other), or absorbed into univalency or syllogism, but simply has the power of its otherness, its arbitrary power to alienate or, in a storm of rain, to redeem, pervades this novel. This storm-announced finale makes its transcendent gesture in the direction, or indirection, of some infinitely disturbing, infinitely promising vista – and only seems, delusively, to pluck us back to the mundane in the ironized emptiness of Sophia Antonovna's concluding utterance, 'Peter Ivanovitch is an inspired man'. In the hollowness and futility of those last lying words, the translator-narrator, by again drawing our attention at the end to the unreliability of his medium, leaves us contemplating, as in the alienating mirror of a dream, our own words and our own Western eyes.

5. *The Shadow-Line*: 'the moment of breaking strain'

This moment of breaking strain comes near the end, but everything has been leading up to it – not only within this most brilliant of Conrad's late works but everything also in the account we have been following so far of his creative surreptitiousness, his narratives' equivocal combining, up to the breaking-point, of holding on and letting go. As Towson might have defined it (for cables) in that mildewed book on an African river bank, this is the moment when things are just about to break but don't – and it is the movement from stasis to action that prevents the break, 'the abrupt sensation of the ship moving forward as if of herself under my feet'. The relief, as a wind brings sudden motion to the becalmed narrator, is intense – like a clearing storm to a Geneva of lies, exile, and paralysis. *The Shadow-Line* takes stress, especially the stress of enforced inertia and of being overwhelmed, to an almost unbearable pitch; and inevitably even its relieving motion has a final qualifying shadow across it. Its ambiguity as a narration is exasperating; but the recreation in the reader of a sense of bafflement is singularly appropriate to the general burden of the story. And as well as being ambiguous, it is also peculiarly direct in its appeal to our contradictory emotions of frustration, dread, excitement, inspiration, apathy, outrage, self-confidence, and despair. It deploys a whole rhetoric of imaginative manipulation and expression; it offers in a current of commentary its own half-adequate explanations, its fitfully illuminating sententiousness; but above all, even more concentratedly than for the Conrad texts we have seen so far, it is a manifold event, an encounter, a haunting, rather than an allegory or a demonstration.[39]

In uncharacteristically staccato sentences, sometimes offhand and laconic, sometimes tersely gnomic (at times reminiscent of Stephen Crane), we are inducted into a nervous world of inadvertency and chance, offset by instances of order, 'normality', and authority. After a very orderly beginning, controlled by the narrator's wry and worldly generalizations ('One closes behind one . . .', 'One goes on recognizing . . .') and his calm factuality in conveying details like the sight of his ship's owner or the reactions of the other officers to his decision to give up his berth, the sense of unreality quickly begins to grow with the narrator's entry into the Officers' Sailors' Home. As I have suggested before for Conrad, the onset of tension is marked (and continues to be marked throughout the story) by small flurries of grotesque comedy: the harbour official shakes his hand mournfully, 'as one would with some poor devil going out to be hanged'; the stranger lounging on the verandah does no more than open 'one horribly fish-like eye'; the wizened little Chief Steward seems quite Dickensian (one thinks of Mr Venus), muttering 'Oh, dear! What is it now?' in his weird twilit sanctum shrouded by lace curtains and crammed with mysterious cardboard boxes: 'I wonder what the fellow did keep in them? There was a smell of decaying coral, or Oriental dust, of zoological specimens in that den of his.'[40]

The earlier disquisition on the motiveless perversity of youth, a perversity that comes without warning or explanation in 'moments', is now being dramatized in terms of the disconnected incidents in the Sailors' Home, the sense of being threatened by something random and unforeseeable. But what gives complexity to these opening sections is that the growing invocation of some central absurdity – and the 'fascination' of 'absurdity' is admitted by the narrator – is continually countered by the ironic acerbity of his style, by his continuing empirical grasp, and not least by the interesting (and dual) figure of Captain Giles. Indeed, much of the unresolved doubleness of the opening is summed up in the function of Captain Giles. He is like an architect or a churchwarden; a man of moral sententiousness, admired and employed for his unique expertise in local navigation; benevolent, ponderous, and conventional; disapproving of the 'chance' moods of youth; but capable of some quiet consideration even for a dishonest whiner like the steward. With such qualities he looms paternally, bracingly, before the narrator amid the enigmas and the brooding heat of the Sailors' Home. But he also belongs to these enigmas, in the way he affects the narrator and the reader. His authority is also that of someone who knows some hidden truth and withholds it – thereby adding to the narrator's sense of paranoid oppression. 'I think you ought to know that there is something going on here', is his enigmatic pronouncement. And the narrator at one point even suspects the heavily allusive Captain of not being in his right mind.

The fish-eyed stranger is perpetually incoherent and somnolent, a comic but (to the narrator) disturbing reminder of what happens in the East to those who lose self-discipline. When he speaks he cannot be understood: 'it sounded like some horrible unknown language'. The contemptuous Hamilton is equally incommunicative: watchful, restless, but silent with self-importance. And among these strangely ill-assorted five – the shifty, desperately anxious steward, the all-knowing but indirect Captain Giles, the collapsed debauchee, the aloof Hamilton, the touchy, insecure narrator – a peculiar game is played around the significant event of a missing letter, communication gone astray. Even when the narrator arrives at a prosaic explanation of the steward's evasive behaviour – 'my eyes became opened to the inwardness of things' – the insight is partially shadowed by the solemnity and excess of his language; and also by the emphasized fact that the revelation is brought about by chance, that very power of inadvertency that seems to be the central undermining factor in these scenes:

To this day I don't know what made me call after him: 'I say! Wait a minute.' Perhaps it was the sidelong glance he gave me; or possibly I was yet under the influence of Captain Giles's mysterious earnestness. Well, it was an impulse of some sort; an effect of that force somewhere within our lives which shapes them this way or that . . .
No. My will had nothing to do with it. (p. 60)

The excess in the language (and emotional response) is very intermittent, and all the stranger for its suddenly rising up amid the dry spareness of the prevailing style. This, for example, is typical of the little whirlpools of crisis that appear in the flow of the narration, drawing attention by overstatement to their own unexplained depths. The voice, after some fairly banal dialogue with Captain Giles, becomes all at once orotund, self-pitying, apocalyptic:

144

The whole thing strengthened in me that obscure feeling of life being but a waste of days, which half-unconsciously, had driven me out of a comfortable berth, away from men I liked, to flee from the menace of emptiness . . . and to find inanity at the first turn . . .

A great discouragement fell on me. A spiritual drowsiness. Giles's voice was going on complacently; the very voice of the universal hollow conceit.

(p. 58)

Similarly extreme is the alternation in the narrator of inertia with the will to action: those ever-powerful poles of Conrad's imagination. One moment paralysed by his Hamlet-like ennui ('this stale, unprofitable world of my discontent'), the narrator, just as suddenly as Hamlet, plunges into practical action — 'with the magic word "Command" in my head I found myself suddenly on the quay as if transported there' — confirming a narratorial instability which now begins to dissolve every outline and every discrimination in the text almost as soon as it appears.[41]

The resultant play of tone is very complicated. The narrator's headlong rush to the Harbour-Master's office away from the eerily becalmed night-zone of the Sailors' Home, with its mysteries and incongruities (a foretaste of the great becalmedness awaiting him in the Gulf of Siam), provides an encounter full of peculiar interchanges, growlings from Captain Ellis as the bearer of paternalistic authority, elisions, smiles, and dizziness from the insecure narrator. As an initiate, he is first led towards authority — the command-granting authority — by a bearded, olive-hued acolyte whose dark eyes have 'a languishing expression', who leads the way 'with a mincing gait', opens the door 'with a deferential action', and exits 'most delicately'. Then, in an effective touch, a sudden vista of the sea obtrudes itself. The narrator looks through the windows overlooking the harbour before seeing Captain Ellis, and a totally new mode of lyricism and gentleness appears for a few sentences, a spot of calm and of simple, repeated colours that spreads in the narration, pacifies its stresses, and then passes:

Three lofty windows gave on the harbour. There was nothing in them but the dark-blue sparkling sea and the paler luminous blue of the sky. My eye caught in the depths and distances of these blue tones the white speck of some big ship just arrived and about to anchor in the outer roadstead. A ship from home — after perhaps ninety days at sea. There is something touching about a ship coming in from sea and folding her white wings for a rest. (p. 64)

145

The bird at 'rest', as well as opening an unexpected and liberating panorama beyond the oppressive confines of the action so far, also reflects back on its narrative context in two small ways. The image of rest tranposes into another key the prevalent images of inertia and will-lessness. And secondly — though this is a fine point — the 'white wings' are at once half parodied by something else: 'The next thing I saw was the top-knot of silver hair surmounting Captain Ellis's smooth red face . . .' And to confirm the awkward jokiness that so quickly succeeds the idyllic moment of the view of the sea — and is akin to the other uses of humour in the tale — Captain Ellis is jocosely mythologized:

Our deputy-Neptune had no beard on his chin, and there was no trident to be seen standing in a corner anywhere, like an umbrella. But his hand was holding a pen — the official pen, far mightier than the sword in making or marring the fortune of simple toiling men.   (p. 64)

The scene that began with a rush into action, with the gaining of a 'command' in the real world, ends with the new captain oppressed by 'a heaviness of limbs': 'I moved like a man in bonds . . . I opened the door with the sensation of dealing with mere dreamstuff.' And when in turn, kaleidoscopically, the moment of inertia is succeeded by — 'It seems as if all of a sudden a pair of wings had grown on my shoulders. I merely skimmed along the polished floor.' (p. 67) — this is at once thrown back on itself by his choosing the word 'float', three times, rather than 'flew' to describe his movement: 'nothing in the way of abstraction could have equalled my deep detachment from the forms and colours of this world. It was, as it were, absolute' (p. 68). That fastidious singling out (even in the sentence structure) of 'absolute' comes like a knell. It sits strangely with the state of mind it purports to describe, that of being 'uplifted by my aroused youth', and keeps before us the pervasive paradox (well known to Henry James) that action of even the most committed kind can be scrutinized, self-monitored, or aestheticized into an abstraction, or an absolute.

However, from here to the actual boarding of the ship, lying masterless in Bangkok, the tone of excited confidence predominates over the underlying tone of detachment and fear. The prose moves in places from its normal cool staccato to sudden flights of over-intense joyousness, just held in check, however, by the note of self-consciousness:

146

A ship! My ship! She was mine, more absolutely mine for possession and care than anything in the world; an object of responsibility and devotion. She was there waiting for me, spellbound, unable to move, to live, to get out into the world (till I came), like an enchanted princess. Her call had come to me as if from the clouds. I had never suspected her existence. I didn't know how she looked. I had barely heard her name, and yet we were indissolubly united for a certain portion of our future, to sink or swim together!

A sudden passion of anxious impatience rushed through my veins, and gave me such a sense of the intensity of existence as I have never felt before or since. I discovered how much of a seaman I was, in heart, in mind, and, as it were, physically – a man exclusively of sea and ships; the sea the only world that counted, and the ships the test of manliness, of temperament, of courage and fidelity – and of love.

I had an exquisite moment. It was unique also.   (pp. 72–3)

This 'flow of joyous emotion' that dissolves the 'feeling of life-emptiness' survives even the encounter with the disgruntled master of the steamer taking the narrator to Bangkok – the master who complains, sneers, and (as always) enigmatically mocks the narrator. 'He was absurd', reads a significant three-word paragraph, seeking to dismiss the mocker but instead, in that key word, reviving the former existential threat of the Sailors' Home.

Within minutes of boarding his new ship, the narrator is staring into a mirror – what else? – and the voyage, in every sense, has begun. Interestingly – and, as always, going somewhat against our expectations – the first effect of the mirror is to confirm the narrator's new sense of responsibility and conviction. In the mirror he sees a long vista of other skippers stretching beyond himself, and though he looks at his own image 'with the perfect detachment of distance' he falls into no abysses of self-alienation, seeing himself from outside with 'sympathy for this latest representative of what for all intents and purposes was a dynasty' (p. 83). And he re-embraces the sustaining code of 'duty', and 'the blessed simplicity of the dynasty's traditional point of view on life'. But 'detachment' and a vista of 'immensity' can annihilate as easily as they can inspire; and the self-consciousness of the narrator, even as he celebrates his profession, soon begins to perturb him. It is to be a voyage of perturbation; and faced with the grotesque appearance of Mr Burns the mate – green-eyed, red-moustached, and intently staring – the narrator quickly falls into self-questioning and malaise. An 'odd stress', a 'vague feeling' begins to assert itself. And the inspiring dynasty of previous captains that the mirror had celebrated is at once undercut by his discoveries about the dead captain whose place, literally, he is now occupying — and whose own past 'life-emptiness' and destructiveness are now revealed to lurk in the depths of the mirror. The narrator has not, after all, cast off the dragging devil of inertia that was by his side in the Sailors' Home; for the dead captain, whose spectre waits at the Shadow-Line, is the embodiment of it:

'He had made up his mind to cut adrift from everything [Burns tells the new captain, of the old]. That's what it was. He didn't care for business, or freights, or for making a passage — or anything. He meant to have gone wandering about the world till he lost her with all hands.'
(p. 89)

And as always, with the reminder of inertia comes the thought of universal randomness and a chance-driven world:

the end of his life was a complete act of treason, the betrayal of a tradition which seemed to me as imperative as any guide on earth could be. It appeared that even at sea a man could become the victim of evil spirits. I felt on my face the breath of unknown powers that shape our destinies.
(p. 90)

Delay; the lingering tropical illness that debilitates the entire crew; Burns's embittered mania about the ghost of the dead captain; the complete lapse of wind — everything conspires to confirm the 'unknown powers' in their enervating sway. And even the few moments of movement and release are shown to be delusive, undermined by their shadow of ennui:

when the ship's head swung down the river away from that town, Oriental and squalid, I missed the expected elation of that striven-for moment. What there was, undoubtedly, was a relaxation of tension which translated itself into a sense of weariness after an inglorious fight.
(p. 98)

And a key word returns:

The darkness had risen around the ship like a mysterious emanation from the dumb and lonely waters. I leaned on the rail and turned my ear to the shadows of the night. Not a sound. My command might have been a planet flying vertiginously on its apppointed path in a space of infinite silence. I clung to the rail as if my sense of balance were leaving me for good. How absurd.
(p. 99)

As the climax can be felt approaching, fuelled by this intensity of changing moods, it becomes clear that the narrative is by now intent on a process of breakdown and initiation: that is, by its own coilings and rhetorical feverishness to take away the support of everyday realities both from the Captain and from the reader (even the everyday expectation that medicine bottles for quinine will contain quinine). Strangely, the slow, aimless movement of the ship, drawn nearer and nearer to some central and final aimlessness – more and more like the irresistible current of a Poe short story, like 'A Descent into the Maelstrom' or 'MS Found in a Bottle' – is countered by the slow recovery and strengthening of the sick mate. The ship seems to be doomed by its curse of inertia; yet Mr Burns has begun to come back, even if a little bizarrely, to activity:

He asserted himself strongly. If he escaped being smothered by this stagnant heat, he said, he was confident that in a very few days he would be able to come up on deck and help me. (p. 105)

In one sentence we are told the ship is 'bewitched', yet in the next Mr Burns is 'progressing towards the world of living men' – though as yet his 'progress', and the exasperating life-instinct he seems to embody, seem enough only to highlight the overwhelming entropy of the ship and its crew.

Envying Mr Burns his self-possession, the narrator reaches his own nadir, his moment of breaking strain: 'My form of sickness was indifference – the creeping paralysis of a hopeless outlook' (p. 114). And for the first time in the book, ennui takes on itself the burden of a neurotic sense of guilt: 'The seed of everlasting remorse was sown in my breast' (p. 116); and, 'I feel as if all my sins had found me out' (p. 125). The narration, reaching its climax, turns twice, briefly, to the intensifying device of a diary: two moments of submersion in the mirror, where the narrator's prose, freed by the device, emulates the sinking of the self into its own futility, the narcissistic descent that is again reminiscent of Poe's crazed diarists (and, not least, of the Ancient Mariner).[42]

The captain and the ship are drawn back from the maelstrom of self-absorption and windlessness, but not before the sheer repetition of the epithets of despair and horror have pushed the narration to such a pitch of frenzy that the writing is saved from mere melodrama by its excess actually taking it into an area of expressionist insistence just on the other side of melodrama. We have 'inconceivable terror', 'inexpressible mystery', 'a menace from all sides', 'the end of all things', 'that sense of finality', 'a foretaste of annihilation', 'an eternity of blind stillness', 'the sickness of my soul', 'my sense of unworthiness', all of them within less than two pages (pp. 126–7), Then the moment of breaking strain comes, and is relieved by the ship quivering into movement – and by Burns's screaming laugh that dramatically exorcizes his own obsession with the incubus of the dead captain.

The narrative is very physical, as well as nervous, to the end. As memorably as in *The Nigger of the 'Narcissus'* we are made to experience the effort and exhaustion of the crew, the struggling toil to haul up a sail as though it is the very last attempt to overcome the monumental dead weight (as heavy as Kurtz, as heavy as Marlow's helmsman) of a universal lassitude. The narrative is drawn-out, and emulates the pained sense of foundering under a cosmic (and psychological) pressure – the pressure is felt in the head, in the heaviness of the limbs, in the labouring and gasping of the chest. And the relief of the ending is physical, too: a few pages of rushing wind, the creaking and banging of spars and sail, the first white ridge of foam, 'thin, very thin', breaking alongside the hull; then the quick, curt encounters and exchanges that mark the eventual arrival in harbour. But within this conclusive relief, to which all the tensions of the narrative have built up so strenuously, a quite different movement remains finally to be detected: one final characterizing note of Conradian indirection.

Throughout the trials that beset the narrator, the presence of Ransome, the cook-turned-steward, has been an index of certain positive values, something self-contained and serviceable in the combat against the accidie of the Gulf. He is something of a Billy Budd:

Even at a distance his well-proportioned figure, something thoroughly sailor-like in his poise, made him noticeable. On nearer view the intelligent, quiet eyes, a well-bred face, the disciplined independence of his manner made up an attractive personality . . . he was the best seaman in the ship.

(p. 94)

Even his equivalent of Billy Budd's stammer (which Melville called the Devil's 'little card' of reminder),[43] his weak heart, seems to be turned into a source of strength:

he was the only one the climate had not touched – perhaps because, carrying a deadly enemy in his breast, he had schooled himself into a systematic control of feelings and movements. (p. 94)

Throughout the saga of disease, hysteria, and hopelessness, Ransome moves wistfully between cabin and deck, tending the sick, discreetly consoling the captain by his steady, intimate gaze ('Ransome gave me one of his attractive, intelligent, quick glances.' – p. 122), joining in the final physical struggle at great peril to his own life. The essence of the man is a delicately balanced tension: his heart's breaking strain, measured by the balance between cautious restraint and natural vitality:

Ransome flitted continually to and fro between the galley and the cabin. It was a pleasure to look at him. The man positively had grace. He alone of all the crew had not had a day's illness in port. But with the knowledge of that uneasy heart within his breast I could detect the restraint he put on the natural sailor-like agility of his movements. It was as though he had something very fragile or very explosive to carry about his person, and was all the time aware of it. (p. 98)

Ransome's composure formally offsets the anxiety and exasperation of the narrator; and in the scene where the latter discovers the absence of quinine in the medicine cabinets and responds wildly – 'for a moment I must have been robbed of my reason' – Ransome's contrasting calmness is quickly at hand: 'He was, indeed, a reasonable man.' Several times as the climax comes near he is 'the unfailing Ransome' – the lighter-up of extinguished binnacle-lamps, the provider of coffee and quiet words of cheer. The narrator, in his over-intensity (touched by some almost sexual feelings), creates him as his own benign double: the unshadowed secret sharer he would like to identify with:

Here a faint smile altered for an instant the clear, firm design of Ransome's lips. With his serious, clear grey eyes, his serene temperament, he was a priceless man altogether. Soul as firm as the muscles of his body. (pp. 129–30)

But as the physical climax of struggle, rain, and wind restores the narrator (and Mr Burns), so it breaks something in Ransome:

He sat upright on the locker in front of the stove, with his head leaning back against the bulkhead. His eyes were closed; his capable hands held open the front of his thin cotton shirt, baring tragically his powerful chest, which heaved in painful and laboured gasps. (p. 137)

The narrator sees Ransome's last contribution to the saving of the ship as being exemplary of the code he himself wishes to adhere to, despite the diableries of dead calm on the Gulf:

I could hear him panting close to me and I avoided turning my eyes his way for fear of seeing him fall down and expire in the act of putting out his strength – for what? Indeed, for some distinct ideal.

The consummate seaman in him was aroused. He needed no directions. He knew what to do. Every effort, every movement was an act of consistent heroism. (p. 140)

But the ordeal of Ransome cannot be summed up in that heroizing mould. His decision at the end to leave the ship takes us back to where the whole tale began, with the narrator's own abandonment of his mate's berth: an impulsive act, almost a betrayal. The narrator himself seems indeed to have come far from that beginning, and with hindsight he now articulates the aspect of the story which is progressive, educative, and moral: 'It was the last ordeal of that episode which had been maturing and tempering my character' (p. 142). Captain Giles reappears, puffing at his cigar, to draw out the 'lesson' more clearly, as befits his pontifical role in the earlier part of the story: 'a man should stand up to his bad luck', he deduces; and, more stoically, 'Precious little rest in life for anybody.' But it is Ransome who ends the tale, not Captain Giles, and ends it in a very different way. His farewell reveals a terrible, though hidden, irony in Captain Giles's superficially bracing words to the narrator, 'You will learn soon how not to be faint-hearted.' Ransome wants to cling on to life, but he is no longer the composed, graceful figure of the dark days on the voyage.[44] He is 'in a blue funk' about his heart; his eyes have 'a strained expression'; and he is 'a man listening for a warning call'. That is, the story ends in a complicated counterpoint of recovered and lost strength, of maturation and decline, new courage and a new 'blue funk'; and also in uncertainty – 'listening for a warning call'. In Giles's vocabulary – the very estimable vocabulary which the narrator is perhaps on the point of adopting for life – the heart is the source of vitality, action, and values. But in Ransome's 'faithful breast' the heart, by another vocabulary, is 'our common enemy', an organ of fear, inertia, and death. Is the going-ashore of Ransome the narrator's ultimate casting-off of that fear, the release of an incubus, the triumphant end to a story of initiation and revelation? It is difficult to see Ransome, the mainstay and 'grace' of the voyage, reduced to a disposable incubus, like the 'ghost' of the dead captain. Ransome's ending is a reversal of the narration's apparent direction towards enlightenment, throws us back into the past, and casts a large shadow across the tentative 'triumph' and growth of the narrator. The words 'our common enemy' are an elaboration of the phrase, almost the first used by the narrator about Ransome, 'carrying a deadly enemy in his breast' – but the addition of the words 'our common' now makes Ransome's confrontation with death, his loss of confidence, and even his 'blue funk' into a universal experience. It is a reminder, at the end, that the real edge of darkness has not yet been crossed, nor the narrator's deadly burden of guilt assuaged ('Remorse must wait. I had to steer.' – p. 140). And in the ending's characteristic quick change of emphasis and rhythm all the responsive breaking strains of Conrad's art continue to press through, and beyond, the narration's last word, its last shadow-line.

III · *The Forster angle*

Conrad's intensities, dream-effects, and powerful interlinear contradictions may at first make both James and Forster seem models of over-civilized urbanity and control. Certainly they both, in their writings, cross and recross the same shadow-line between world-loss and recovery with far more wit and aplomb than does Conrad, and with only an intermittent reliance on the nightmarish or the highly wrought – James's *Turn of the Screw* and *The Jolly Corner*, for example, or specific scenes and images in his three late great novels; Forster in his short stories and parts of *The Longest Journey*. But control, in both their cases, in no way implies detachment from apprehension, outrage, and grief, or any diminution in the degree to which their narratives, like Conrad's, are involved and involving processes, above all processes of the fullest response to a world that, if it is to be apprehended honestly by the imagination, must evoke, beyond aplomb, the nervously ulterior, the ambivalent, and the indirect. Forster, in particular, has suffered from being seen as a clear-cut essayist in his fiction – 'a truly civilized mind', and the like – rather than as an edgy and elusive explorer-through-process, whose words, even at their most apparently discursive, form part of a larger and qualifying, even twisting, dialectic of plot and image, and are always on the point of being controverted, twitched on to their backs, by his creative mental habit of disclaiming. His novels, as is well known, have a pronounced moral status; but it is their narrative and rhetorical status that deserves more investigation.

At the end of a familiar description by Forster of the poet Cavafy we might catch an unserious, brief impression of the novelist's own stance: 'a . . . gentleman in a straw hat, standing absolutely motionless at a slight angle to the universe.'[1] The impression can only be brief, since such motionlessness – in his own phrase for annunciation, 'the eternal moment' – is only for that moment, and the author, like his narratives, is soon likely to slip off slyly in a

154

direction other than the eternal, leaving behind him – only his slight angle to the universe. Forster's is an art of the tangent rather than of the essay. He moralizes, as do James and Conrad – and like them, though in his very particular way, he deeply distrusts his own, and other people's, moralizings; and his books, in their very narrative movement and self-qualifyings, seem to value the inconsequential at least as much as the reasonable. For all his ironies as a critic (his admiring but self-protective ironies) against James and Conrad, his narration follows the Jamesian mode (as in *The Europeans* and *What Maisie Knew*) of a wittily directed and theatrical interplay, punctuated by gesture and symbol, and takes us, even in the first novels but increasingly through *Howards End* (1910) and *A Passage to India* (1924), by all the developing openness and scrupulous receptiveness of that method, into a Conradian world where treachery or inanition threaten to prevail, and where change and insight, though longed-for, come in from the side (like wind, like a storm) too randomly to be permanent and are always slipping away, at an angle.

Words themselves are always ebbing, for all three novelists; Marlow, waiting with his listeners for the Thames to ebb, and unconfident about the truth of storytelling, confesses that the eloquent Kurtz, whose open mouth devoured the earth, was 'just a word for me' – as Razumov, a semantic blur to himself and lost in a cloud of others' words, is untranslatable to us by his narrator in Geneva. How much of Jim is in the word 'Lord', and of Nostromo in 'our man' – is he, like Jim, 'one of us'? Boston was words, all words, looking for a Word – and finding a Ransom; while Robert Acton lost his chance in life by dangling over the categorical word 'honest', for which a Eugenia is always too large. Maisie comes to 'know' by what lies below and around words, beyond the straight telling, while her entourage make their quibbles on the meaning of the word 'free'; and Maggie Verver, at the end, is 'paid' (or does she pay?) while the Prince learns to 'see' (or is he blind?). So Forster, who as a moralist esteems 'connection', as a narrator and symbolist deliberately follows words into the places where no connection is possible, and where the grammar of relationships and perception fails. And yet – this is perhaps his ultimate and most challenging indirection, his passage to more than India – by taking us to the brink he also paradoxically restores us to a new sense of actuality; which is perhaps all brink anyway. The inadvertency and wordlessness which Forster can evoke (on *his* Gulf of Siam) and can often celebrate, if fearfully, are enough to challenge the formal consolation of art, which has its own dangers too, and keep the contingent – within which we live and know we live – in a state of dissonance with the structured, for which we long. In their varying ways – Conrad's ironies remain more devouring than the others – it is what all three achieve by the very risks their narratives run. By taking nothing for granted, least of all the utility of language, by asking everything of the reader's attention, and by submitting to their own self-contradictions of thought and temperament, they reawaken us to the stresses within art and to how the forms of art – as James always lamented, yet endorsed, in his criticism – are always under pressure, always a compromise at best, an unending open negotiation between the mind's shaping and the world's recalcitrance.

1. *Howards End*: a harvest, a falling

At the very end of *Howards End*, as the book swells a little fulsomely towards reconciliation, the redeeming of Henry Wilcox through Margaret's love, and the symbolic gathering-in of the hay harvest, a single sentence cuts abruptly across this mood of sober fruition. The other Wilcoxes, snarling in defeat, have been summoned from their various suburban villas to hear Mr Wilcox's decision to leave Howards End to Margaret, and from the witless Dolly drops a careless reference to the long-concealed fact that Mrs Wilcox's dying wish will thereby be fulfilled after all. Then we have this:

> From Evie came a sharply drawn breath. 'Good-bye', she said to Margaret, and kissed her.
> And again and again fell the word, like the ebb of a dying sea.
> 'Good-bye.'
> 'Good-bye, Dolly.'
> 'So long, father.'
> 'Good-bye, my boy; always take care of yourself.'
> 'Good-bye, Mrs Wilcox.'
> 'Good-bye.'[2]

The deployment of these sentences is very characteristic. Evie kissing Margaret (keeping up false appearances to the end) focuses our attention on Margaret and makes us associate the next and crucial sentence with Margaret's own consciousness: 'And again and again fell the word, like the ebb of a dying sea.' The allusion is extreme, not quite explicable, and certainly very chilling: the first half of the sentence made resonant with its Biblical echo, and the whole made to stand out not only by being printed on its own but by its quite unprosaic rhythms (five anapaests and an iamb). The following chorus of 'Good-byes' to which it refers (like the same hollow chorus at the end of Section 2 of 'The Waste Land') is a part of triviality and reality – but quite drained of any consolation by that interpolated falling, ebbing, and dying. And when Margaret then gently asks her husband about the incident in the past, he is as always – and despite his 'redemption' – quite unperturbed by any possibility of having been dishonest:

> Margaret was silent. Something shook her life in its inmost recesses, and she shivered.
> 'I didn't do wrong, did I?' he asked, bending down.
> 'You didn't, darling. Nothing has been done wrong.'   (p. 332)

If Margaret's inward shudder is not to be taken as a frisson of that dying sea, an ebbing of her new security at this reminder of unassuageable betrayals, and is no more than a shiver of fearful pleasure at seeing how Mrs Wilcox's wishes have come right in the end, then her 'Nothing has been done wrong' is an egregious self-betrayal and self-delusion. And on the other hand if her 'Nothing has been done wrong' is a tragically conscious gesture of ironic pacification towards the Wilcox crassness, then her shudder is indeed an echo of that momentary cosmic sense of disaster and chaos. Either way – like Maggie Verver burying *her* knowledge of marital treachery in a self-conscious embrace – it is a deathly note to strike amid the celebration of new life, Helen's baby, and the joy of harvest.[3] It seems not quite to be controlled – though the sense of artistic control, in language, tone, and commentary, is one of the most active constituents of our total response to this novel. It is, in fact, a classic and powerful instance of Forster's 'double turn' (as identified by Trilling): one of these moments where a totally different register suddenly declares itself within the bland or witty cadences of his prose, jolts our attention to a quite different line of thought or feeling, and casts a new light of suggestiveness on everything that has gone before, hinting at contradictory combinations or ramifying echoes in the text that has been already unfolded. As a device, the double turn presents sudden new possibilities of meaning; makes us look back differently at comparable 'surprises' in style, scene, or phrase; and keeps us conscious of how this narrative, in its textures and nuances, is to be apprehended as perpetually *at work*.

'At play' is an equally accurate phrase, since the manipulation of tones, from the waggish to the stiffly solemn, makes Forster's writing a notable instance of the ways in which fiction is a game − and a participative game at that. The stance of the manipulator − that 'gentleman in a straw hat' − is a complicated one, and is itself part of the game.[4] For one thing, by drawing attention to itself it manages to give the impression not just of the events and characters being subject to a confidently omniscient commentator but, on the contrary, of their retaining some vital freedom of movement away from that manipulation and evaluation. The novel's very first sentence is of this kind, drawing attention to the conscious act of presentation yet at once preparing the way for what seems to exist in a dimension beyond the presenting: 'One may as well begin with Helen's letters to her sister.' The narrator shrugs nonchalantly and a little ruefully, contemplating the daunting otherness and multiplicity of the 'events' his narration must try to set in motion − and the letters that are now allowed to begin the narrative emphasize this sense of space and opening-up by their own youthful sprightliness of style, and their own description of surprises, false expectations, and vulnerability to a world where values and feelings might be stood on their head at any moment. The narrator's 'One may as well', just like James's 'As I have had the honour of intimating', in *The Europeans*, is a gesture that creates a little leeway between him and these apparently uncontrollable and interesting events.[5] And across that leeway, within that narrated field, characters and scenes can take on a certain independence, and can eventually be seen to cast their own shadow, while the narrator's shadow falls at a slightly different angle − the true Forster angle.

Even when the narrating stance is less self-deprecatory than this, and more assertive, the effect is not necessarily restrictive. For example, in chapter 2 we have this paragraph:

Margaret was silent. If her aunt could not see why she must go down, she was not going to tell her. She was not going to say: 'I love my dear sister; I must be near her at this crisis of her life'. The affections are more reticent than the passions, and their expression more subtle. If she herself should ever fall in love with a man, she, like Helen, would proclaim it from the house-tops, but as she only loved a sister she used the voiceless language of sympathy. (p. 24)

The effect here is interesting, and intensely Forsterian. Having taken us behind Margaret's silence and told us how it might have articulated itself in speech (*le style indirect libre*), the narrator then suddenly expands into a general aphorism. But the generality does not really limit or finally judge the situation. Rather, it seems to detach itself momentarily, in a brooding, self-communing way, from the immediate 'scene' of Margaret's hypothesized inner self, partly by the different angle of self-confidence and abruptness. Beneath the universalized comment – or rather, on each side of it, in terms of the paragraph – her fictional life continues, touched upon by the remark, but only guaranteed and countenanced by it rather than finally 'placed' or subsumed into it.

It is the variation of mode and outlook – as here, between the dramatized intimacy of word and feeling on one hand and a sudden sententiousness on the other – that helps to create the freedom within Forsterian narration that I have called 'play'. Of course the narrator quite frequently asserts something more directly dogmatic: an endorsement of the Schlegel faith, for example, or an uncompromising gibe that seems to leave the Wilcoxes pinned like butterflies to the wall. But such partisanship is in continual interplay with other things and styles, some of them quite irrelevant to the mode of commentary, some of them contradictory of what the commentary has said. Along with the strong sense of masterful control in plot and in general analytic intelligence, there is unsteadiness of an enlivening kind that challenges the reader's attention at every moment. Nuances of tone keep suggesting alternative vistas. The prose sometimes lumbers portentously in one direction, then suddenly darts in another with an almost Wildean glee. Or a sentence progresses towards a shaped conclusion, then in the last words unexpectedly opens itself up, wittily, vivaciously, even ungraspably – like the effect of the word 'possibly' in this: 'Some day – in the millennium – there may be no need for

159

[Henry Wilcox's] type. At present, homage is due to it from those who think themselves superior, and who possibly are' (p. 165). Direct dramatization or solemn authorial adjuration, even occasional flatness of description and dialogue, are all interspersed with jocosity and occasionally falsetto laughter. A sudden lyricism swells up, only to be cut short by a neat irony, a cool disclaimer. The naturalistic and the highly stylized are in perpetual interplay, so that the reader is in a state of surprise and restlessness – a state of aesthetic response that then finds its conceptual equivalent within Forster's view of the world. For example, we find ourselves almost simultaneously noting the narration's realistic grasp of how social types behave – how Charles Wilcox bullies a railway porter, or drives his car in a certain arrogant way – and responding imaginatively and consciously to the more 'de-naturalizing' features of the telling, even tiny stylizations like an occasional arch inversion – 'Most complacently did Mrs Munt . . .' – or the comic reductiveness of 'the form of Mrs Munt, trying to explain things, sprang agreeably up and down among the red cushions' (pp. 28, 31). The narration is liberated by such textual display, gives itself freedom to ramify and to experiment – and, in the end, to embrace more of the area of human experience that concerns it. For its continual modulations, as well as giving pleasure by their own energy and colour, also move in the direction of suggested meaning, no matter how tentative that meaning. And at one level of our reading them these modulations are recognized as repeating, with novelty and clarity, certain modulations that the book wishes to suggest are in real life: in *its* textures of gaiety, surprise, and dismay. As one small example, in the chapter where the Schlegels hear Beethoven we have this modulation:

Helen said to her aunt: 'Now comes the wonderful movement: first of all the goblins, and then a trio of elephants dancing'; and Tibby implored the company generally to look out for the transitional passage on the drum.

'On the what, dear?'

'On the *drum*, Aunt Juley.'

'No; look out for the part where you think you have done with the goblins and they come back,' breathed Helen, as the music started with a goblin walking quietly over the universe, from end to end. Others followed him. They were not aggressive creatures; it was that that made them so terrible to Helen. They merely observed in passing that there was no such thing as splendour or heroism in the world. (p. 46)

The opening voices are comically, 'realistically' disconnected: Helen apparently affected and whimsical in her image of the trio of elephants; Tibby no less affected, even pretentious; Mrs Munt floundering. Then suddenly Forster's absolute seriousness rises up, with the goblins and the universe, in mid-sentence. Mid-sentence is so often the perfect place for Forster's particular view of the tragic, as for Conrad's casual linkage, 'like evil or truth': a devastating observation, in passing, that no values exist.[6] At the beginning normality seems ready to jog on, in its usual syntax – only a little ridiculous. Then a goblin, which began as a girl's whimsy, suddenly becomes real, and with the unforeseeableness of an accident the paragraph as it flows uncovers an abyss of 'panic and emptiness'. This is the way it happens, the manner suggests to us. Visions of emptiness can come like a modulation in a sentence: a sudden horrifying fall, like the ebb of a dying sea, before language, like Beethoven's energy, returns us to terra firma and the Queen's Hall.

Sometimes, such is the unease that lurks below the groomed surfaces of this book, there is an opposite modulation: say, from the scathingly sardonic to the passionately ideal and romantic. These 'positive' outbursts are more difficult to accept than their acerbic opposites: the lyricism is a little frenetic and highly coloured. But they can be seen as part of a larger rhythm, as a rhetorical compensation through which the necessary components of desire and dream can enter into the book's dialectic of feeling, and can serve not only to counterbalance but to define and explain the opposing sense of loss or detestation. For example, chapter 21 is a brief and pungently satirical vignette of the junior Wilcoxes breeding, complaining, and being arrogant. It ends: 'a perambulator edition is squeaking; a third edition is expected shortly. Nature is turning out Wilcoxes in this peaceful abode, so that they may inherit the earth' (p. 187). Then in quite stark contrast, as if to offset such virulence, the next chapter opens in almost dithyrambic mode:

Margaret greeted her lord with peculiar tenderness on the morrow. Mature as he was, she might yet be able to help him to the building of the rainbow bridge that should connect the prose in us with the passion. Without it we are meaningless fragments, half monks, half beasts, unconnected arches that have never joined into a man. With it love is born, and alights on the highest curve, glowing against the gray, sober against the fire. Happy the

man who sees from either aspect the glory of those outspread wings. The
roads of his soul lie clear, and he and his friends shall find easy going.

(p. 187)

These are extreme words for a transcendental goal glimpsed in a
dream, made extreme by fear of the opposite, the vision of the
world's panic and emptiness. And our unease and half-
embarrassment at some of the cadences and epithets − 'the rainbow bridge', 'love is born, and alights on the highest curve',
'Happy is the man', 'the roads of his soul' − testify to the instability of the dream. It is energized by desire, but the suspicion
of hysteria is functional, since it dramatizes for us the hopelessness
that also lies somewhere within such desire, and it therefore belongs
totally to the basic stresses of the narration. And typically (and sav-
ingly), the very next paragraph sinks to a wry irony that half-mocks
the lyrical excesses of the previous sentence: 'It was hard going in
the roads of Mr Wilcox's soul.'

There is a well-known test case in any consideration of the
rhetoric, particularly the extreme rhetoric, of *Howards End*: that
is the celebrative description of England as viewed from the Isle of
Purbeck, at the beginning and end of chapter 19 (and therefore at
the exact spatial centre of the novel). Even a critic like John Beer,
who has defended it against the strictures of Leavis − Leavis considered it Wilcox-like in its immaturity − has had to concede some
embarrassment at Forster's flourishes.[7] But the final flourish cannot properly be considered on its own, only in the full context of
the reader's response: that is, the reader's involvement in the
intricate movement of the whole chapter and in the surrounding
currents of preparation and aftermath. As a test case, therefore, it
will call for some detailed consideration.

In the previous chapter, where Mr Wilcox proposes to Margaret
in his house in Ducie Street, we have encountered the illogicality
and the disturbing impersonality of love. The love between
Margaret and Henry causes the reader problems later in the book,
but at the beginning its sheer unlikelihood becomes part of its
verisimilitude, so much in the book up to this point, at every level
of plot, scene, conversation, and even syntax, having reconciled us
to the advent of the unexpected. Even the casual 'mid-sentence'
quality of their love − 'Just as this thought entered Margaret's
brain, Mr Wilcox did ask her to be his wife . . .' (p. 167) − is a

part of that narrative rhythm we noted in the 'Beethoven' passage, a rhythm that expresses the inadvertency of experience, great or small, and, having already offhandedly ushered in death in the case of Mrs Wilcox ('The funeral was over'), now does the same for love. Not only is the love illogical, unexpected in its syntax, it is also – which may be the same thing – impersonal: a 'central radiance' which 'had nothing to do with humanity, and most resembled the all-pervading happiness of fine weather' (p. 168). There is a strong degree of naturalism in all this, too, of course, and Forster's other level of operation, that of psychological perceptiveness and a knowledge of manners (as revealed, for example, in the decor of a smoking-room, and a woman's response to a masculine room), bolsters and qualifies the invocation of love as a mystery. But the proposal scene nevertheless ends in a ghost, lightly introduced: 'Mrs. Wilcox strayed in and out, ever a welcome ghost; surveying the scene, thought Margaret, without one hint of bitterness' (p. 170). And we are left feeling that love's contingency and impersonality – out of which zone strays a benign ghost – are so beyond our sense of proportion and control that despite benignity there must be a mystery in such a presence.

Out of this complex experience, then – and out of such intimacy of encounter with both the everyday and the unseen – comes the suddenly panoramic and oratorical consideration of landscape that opens chapter 19:

If one wanted to show a foreigner England, perhaps the wisest course would be to take him to the final section of the Purbeck Hills, and stand him on their summit, a few miles to the east of Corfe. Then system after system of our island would roll together under his feet. Beneath him is the valley of the Frome, and all the wild lands that come tossing down from Dorchester, black and gold, to mirror their gorse in the expanses of Poole. The valley of the Stour is beyond, unaccountable stream, dirty at Blandford, pure at Wimborne – the Stour, sliding out of fat fields, to marry the Avon beneath the tower of Christchurch. The valley of the Avon – invisible, but far to the north the trained eye may see Clearbury Ring that guards it, and the imagination may leap beyond that onto Salisbury Plain itself, and beyond the Plain to all the glorious downs of Central England. Nor is suburbia absent. Bournemouth's ignoble coast cowers to the right, heralding the pine trees that mean, for all their beauty, red houses, and the Stock Exchange, and extend to the gates of London itself. So tremendous is the City's trail! But the cliffs of Freshwater it shall never touch, and the island will guard the Island's purity till the end of time. Seen from the west, the Wight is beautiful beyond all laws of beauty. It is as if a fragment of England floated forward to greet the foreigner – chalk of our chalk, turf of our turf, epitome of what will follow. And behind the fragment lie Southampton, hostess to the nations, and Portsmouth, a latent fire, and all around it, with double and treble collision of tides, swirls the sea. How many villages appear in this view! How many castles! How many churches, vanquished or triumphant! How many ships, railways and roads! What incredible variety of men working beneath that lucent sky to what final end! The reason fails, like a wave on the Swanage beach; the imagination swells, spreads and deepens, until it becomes geographic and encircles England.

(pp. 170–1)

This is far more than a romantic flourish or an indulgence; far more, even, than the compensatory outburst it resembles in *The Nigger of the 'Narcissus'*, on England as 'ship mother of fleets and nations'.[8] It is a further attempt, consonant with the discoveries of the previous chapter, to confront and to mediate the impersonal, even the infinite. The narration, with a theatrical panache, is trying to grasp the ungraspable, to know, through landscape, the elemental presence more quietly encountered in Ducie Street by Margaret, and uttered in a different mode by Beethoven's music in the Queen's Hall. The strangeness of love, strange beyond proportion and, despite her hopes, beyond Margaret's capacity to 'connect' fully with the mundane, is being brought by Margaret through this very landscape towards the watchers: towards the waiting, mundane complexity of her family relationships in the shape of Helen, Mrs Munt, and her cousin Frieda, taking in the view. The landscape is a challenge and an entanglement – and, at beginning and end, frames a chapter which is itself dominated by shocks of encounter and revelation. The vision is of an England so extensive, so rich, so ever-receding and beyond proportion, that 'the reason fails', and only the imagination can deal with it by becoming more than personal: that is, 'geographic' (as Maisie's newly visionary knowledge, on the sands at Boulogne, swelled poetically from 'Most' to 'All', and from self to 'sky' and 'air').[9] Like the vision which the whole novel seeks to 'encircle' by the imagination and to re-create, this landscape both baffles the mind and is accessible to it. It has its definite names and colours, its human history, its graspable forms – 'system after system', the stages of the Stour, the implied vistas, beyond seeing, of the Midlands and of London, the Isle of Wight as an 'epitome' of the larger island, Southampton as an entry, the tides as measurably 'double and treble'. Then measurement and formal gradations threaten to break down in the half-ironic, half-hysterical apostrophes at the end, 'How many! . . . How many! . . . How many!' And in the unresolved images in the last sentence − the reason ebbing like a wave, the imagination flowing like an all-encompassing tide, together with the acute sense of anxiety and impossibility, and the straining, oceanic desire to transcend and embrace − we recognize, here, halfway through the novel, one of its most important and persistent symbols (wave, sea, tide, river) bearing its most characteristic burden of irreconcilable feelings.[10]

Whatever is exalted in that first paragraph is at once deflated, and whatever is unsteady in it is elaborated, by the comedy of Frieda and Mrs Munt clashing over the merits of English and German landscapes: a typical Forsterian transposition from the grand to the self-mockingly petty, within which, nevertheless, certain social and even political realities declare themselves. And this alternating movement is confirmed by the way the focus of narration changes throughout the first half of the chapter from the close-at-hand, the personal and domestic chatter of those waiting on Nine Barrow Down, to the panoramic, as we take a bird's eye view of Margaret's train chugging from Wareham to Swanage, and then of the pony-cart bringing her, and her revelation, closer and closer. The emotional exchanges that follow between the two sisters are dramatically and intimately direct, on a distinctly new register, without any of the earlier shiftings of tone:

> 'Look here, sit down.'
> 'All right; I'll sit down if you'll sit down.'
> 'There. (One kiss.) Now, what ever, what ever is the matter?'
> 'I do mean what I said. Don't; it wouldn't do.'   (p. 175)

But in a subtle involvement the landscape still enters parenthetically and frequently, no longer embraceable or an enhancement to the imagination but now − exactly what the opening paean half-feared in its conclusion − irremediably other, shapeless, cold, and indifferent in its elemental impersonality. Despite mid-sentence appeals to it, the landscape only reinforces the darkness, the weight of incommunication and powerlessness that settles on Margaret and Helen. It is the goblin footfall, the ebbing wave, the falling word, with a vengeance: '[Helen] broke right away and wandered distractedly upwards, stretching her hands towards the view and crying' (p. 175). Margaret follows her 'through the wind that gathers at sundown on the northern slopes of hills', and 'suddenly stupidity seized her, and the immense landscape was blurred.' She finds no aid to understanding: 'With her arm round Helen, and her eyes shifting over the view, as if this county or that could reveal the secret of her own heart . . .' (p. 176). Helen 'in her turn, looked outwards'; and Margaret, admitting her knowledge of the spiritual dishonesty of the man she is about to marry, looks down 'at the shining lagoons'; and when she tries to argue for the merits of the Wilcox practicality she adduces the view of England as evidence of those merits: 'She waved her hand at the landscape, which confirmed anything' (p. 177). The effect is to reinforce the sense of division, contrary to that all-unifying vision of the first paragraph, as we hear the subdued, tense voices of two intimates, despairing, pleading, failing one another, high on the crest of a chalk down above an ungraspable and annulling vista.

Then the frame of the chapter closes by returning overtly to the landscape, testing it anew, as it were, for what it can yield and where it resists. We read the peroration with our awareness attuned to what has gone before, and thereby sensitized to the inner turnings that qualify the superficial impression it gives of a performance now in the major key, putting the goblins to flight with a noise of trumpets. It begins with an enigmatic statement and ends in a rhetorical series of questions tinged – like the apostrophes that closed the chapter's opening description – with the possibility of mockery:

There was a long silence, during which the tide returned into Poole Harbour. 'One would lose something', murmured Helen, apparently to herself. The water crept over the mud-flats towards the gorse and the blackened heather. Branksea Island lost its immense foreshores, and became a sombre episode of trees. Frome was forced inward towards Dorchester, Stour against Wimborne, Avon towards Salisbury, and over the immense displacement the sun presided, leading it to triumph ere he sank to rest. England was alive, throbbing through all her estuaries, crying for joy through the mouths of all her gulls, and the north wind, with contrary motion, blew stronger against her rising seas. What did it mean? For what end are her fair complexities, her changes of soil, her sinuous coast? Does

she belong to those who have moulded her and made her feared by other lands, or to those who have added nothing to her power, but have somehow seen her, seen the whole island at once, lying as a jewel in a silver sea, with all the brave world's fleet accompanying her towards eternity?
(p. 178)

At first, Helen's 'One would lose something' is a little unclear. Can she be making a concession, in the pause that follows her argument with Margaret about the Wilcoxes? Does she mean, 'I agree, without the Wilcox values one would lose something'? Or even more limitingly, is Helen partly retracting her angry claim, of a moment before, that 'It makes no difference thinking things out'? Only after pausing – delaying the progress of the paragraph, and emulating the slow return of the tide – does the reader consider that Helen seems to be simply reiterating her position against the Wilcoxes, and above all against Margaret marrying into them: in so doing, a Schlegel would, and will, lose much. Our doubt about the remark is functional. It gives it an added salience, as though the ambiguity had cleared some space around it.[11] The space has created unease, and into the unease creeps the incoming tide. An 'immense displacement' is moving a little ominously, even abstractly in its generality, towards 'the blackened heather', forcing the rivers back on themselves and creating 'a sombre episode'. This is an encounter with a presiding power – inhuman and inexplicable. The sudden change to 'England was alive, throbbing through all her estuaries, crying for joy' is in startling contrariety: a celebration of energy, after the fear of it. The change is imaged further in the reference to the wind, 'with contrary motion', blowing *against* the encroaching sea. The paragraph, true to the overall narrative mode of which it is a part, leaves the two opposite motions deadlocked – or rather, unresolved and unstilled. It is appropriate that a direct questioning should be thrown up from such a situation. 'What did it mean?' sends us straight back into the welter of hints and opposites. If we cannot understand those elemental opposites of land and sea, river and tide, how can we hope to impose a pattern of coherence on such human opposites as Wilcox and Schlegel: practical power displacing sensitivity, sensitivity poeticizing and losing the real world? For that is the minor irony that is now drowned out by the major bravura of the closing cadences. The rhetorical excess and the very literary allusiveness, just touched by

167

cliché – 'A jewel in a silver sea', 'all the world's brave fleet' – more than hints at the incipient dangers of the Schlegel sensibility, which have been touched on often enough in the novel before now. And Forster also tries to distance himself from the purple of the prose by attributing the lyricism to others, to 'those who have added nothing to her power'. The climax is clearly not mock-heroic; and the mingling of tones is perhaps not assured, not quite stable, with the urge to endorse the romantic celebration being almost audibly in conflict with the need to be sceptical. But this instability is not the same as confusion: it expresses clearly, and in other terms, a dilemma that is central to the novel, and gains coherence from the role it plays in that surrounding drama.[12]

If complexity of narratorial stance and stylistic texture is everywhere at work, or at play, in *Howards End*, subtilizing its apparent liberal–humanist overview, the same is true of its larger-scale handling of plot. It is important, if inadequate, to say that this is one of the best-made of novels, which on every rereading continues to please by its cunning orchestration, its entrances and exits, its anticlimaxes, strange conjunctions, and pure excitement of momentum, anticipation, and shock. What is perhaps more interesting is to see how so much deft planning also expresses something that runs counter to the whole idea of arrangement and form – the very doubleness that gave such tension and force to *The Golden Bowl*. The plot's dynamism – its onward flow and energy – is partly dependent on the use of surprise (and the willing suspension of *un*surprise when we read for the second time). There is, for example, the mistaken identity of Charles Wilcox in chapter 3; and the arresting strangeness of Mrs Wilcox on her first appearance, with words that ring down the curtain on this first episode of the action: '"They do not love any longer, if you prefer it put that way", said Mrs Wilcox, stooping down to smell a rose' (p. 37). There is the unexpected encounter in King's Cross station that cuts short the projected trip to Howards End by Mrs Wilcox and Margaret; the shock announcement of Mrs Wilcox's death, 'The funeral was over'; the surprise of the letter, leaving Howards End to Margaret; the surprising encounter with Mr Wilcox on the Chelsea Embankment; the extravagantly coincidental turning-up of Jackie Bast out of Henry Wilcox's past – and so on, chapter after chapter, with hardly a let-up in the succession of changes, revelations, encounters, recognitions, accidents, and coincidences (some of them, like the last mentioned, more than a little strained). Such events affect us in at least two ways. Firstly, by drawing attention to themselves, they advertise the pleasure we derive from detecting and submitting to a clearly articulated structure. They manipulate the reader, but go out of their way to make him aware of the order and cleverness of the manipulation, hence intensifying the aesthetic pleasure. But, secondly, the arbitrariness which surprising events would present to our minds in real life is not entirely removed even when we are made conscious that they come to us in such a well-made fictional system. As simulacra of everyday things, they evoke the unsystematized surprisingness of the everyday, as well as point to their own immediate context in an art world, their ordered function in a fictional game. And therefore they continue referentially to convey something of life's randomness – an effect which the narrative confirms by several of its other less referential operations, not least its explicit commentaries on the need to be open to the unforeseen, to cultivate some redeeming vulnerability to the chance encounters and revelations of experience.[13]

In our reading of plot, it is the combination of our pleased perception of orderliness with our equally pleased response to incongruity that so involves us, by an analogous mental activity, with the doubleness (and more) in the play of ideas. When Margaret accidentally smashes a framed photograph in Mrs Wilcox's flat and cuts her finger on the glass, we easily catch the event as an echo of exactly the same happening to Leonard Bast in his own home only two chapters before. There is no clear symbolism in either occurrence (Leonard dies, but Margaret does not die): there is simply an unexplained echo.[14] The fact that both events have been invented and wilfully conjoined in a narrative does not take away from their strangeness – though it certainly sets limits to that strangeness. What is created by such an echo, I think, is a sense of random correspondences – a distinctly Forsterian feature, and one hardly found at all in James. It is an effect that tends to become an articulated idea only when we place it in the context of our response to the whole narrative. And that eventual idea, for which these brief corresponding events serve as preliminary images, would seem to be that beneath the world of everyday available forms – the forms of reason and of artistic shaping – there exists a world (a tide? a ghost? a central radiance?) that may or may not reveal itself in shapes accessible to our sense of form or to our hierarchical sense of values. It is perceivable to our reason in the shape of repetition; but mysterious repetition, to little or no purpose, also fails to console the reason, and takes away from our sense of form as much as it gives. Such repetition – like the coincidences and echoes on which the whole plot is founded – promises at least as much of flux and arbitrariness as of shape, and therefore as much of loss as of permanent possession. And by doing so, it becomes an idea – or a vision, rather – that goes quite contrary to those other currents in the book that favour harmony and continuity and growth. By offering us the hints of 'connection', then notably failing to fulfil the promise, in any articulable way, these random echoes and repetitions erode the most fundamental positive value which this book has to offer, Margaret's doctrine of 'only connect'. The plot itself, a model of elegance and control, contains, in its partial reliance on inexplicable collisions and appearances, its own shadow-self: something that questions the very meaning of plot and connection. But, as always, it is the relationship and tension between these two aspects that have to be emphasized. The book's perceivable form may cast a shadow of formlessness, but the formlessness only comes to our perception because of the presence of form: it seems there cannot be one without the other.[15]

The reader's consciousness of plotting, then – of the ordering of fictional events – moves quickly into a consciousness of latent or expressed meanings, encouraged by the perception of rhythms and correspondences at every level, from the largest 'blocks' of plot to local turns of rhetoric and shades of narrating tone. But always an almost physical sense of flow is retained: the interplay of ideas, as I tried to bring out for *Heart of Darkness*, *Lord Jim*, and *Nostromo* in particular, is always being borne back into the interplay-movement and the indirections of the narrative. Chapter 23, almost at random, might be taken as an example of this essential dynamic, which is far faster and more variable, far more orchestrated, than in Conrad. It consists of the following: a dramatized debate in dialogue, with narrative commentary; a visit to a business office; an account of a car-trip and of Hertfordshire; Margaret's first arrival at Howards End, with a detailed description of place; and a surprising, almost ghostly, encounter. The initial brief debate, between Margaret and Helen, is basically about – and itself enacts – the dialectic between spirituality and practicality that is one of the sources of intellectual animation in the book. Helen is for the Absolute, Margaret more and more inclines towards the practical; but the overt commentary – typically half-dramatized as though expressing a thought beginning to dawn on Margaret – endorses a dynamic concept of truth:

The businessman who assumes that this life is everything, and the mystic who asserts that it is nothing, fail, on this side and on that, to hit the truth. 'Yes, I see, dear; it's about halfway between,' Aunt Juley had hazarded in earlier years. No; truth, being alive, was not halfway between anything. It was only to be found by continuous excursions into either realm, and, though proportion is the final secret, to espouse it at the outset is to ensure sterility. (pp. 195–6)

How exactly that 'final secret' can be 'proportion', and how this is compatible with a dynamic truth, is left dangling – a hint, a hope, a desire that the novel never really clarifies (nor perhaps could ever clarify finally without itself falling into the 'sterility' of a formula).

Out of such irresolution and tentativeness, the actual physical journeyings quickly ensue; and do so according to the nature of that brief debate. That is, there follow two 'excursions', one into the secular realm of business, then one into the contrasting mystery of Howards End. In the business world of Henry Wilcox's office there are maps, ledgers, polished counters, brass rails, and Wilcox utterances to match: but it has its effective decisiveness, a rattle of giving orders and passing quick judgements. Then the car-journey to Hertfordshire, with a whimsically half-poetic, half-comic meditation on the subtleties of that county to set against ridicule of car-travelling and Wilcox brusqueness – the car creating a caricature of movement, a mere space-cancelling crudity, that Forster always finds antipathetic to the richer, deeper motions his narration explores: 'She looked at the scenery. It heaved and merged like porridge. Presently it congealed. They had arrived.' (p. 199).

The business world is still to be found in the heart of Hertford-shire, and only after the rattling inanities of Dolly and her father does Margaret's journey come to its last stage. After debate, motion, and prattle, the chapter relaxes finally into an extended

171

celebration of a place at rest: flowers, tree, colour; drawing-room, dining-room, hall. An awareness of exact physical dimension and relationship fills Margaret's mind, as it does the reader's: 'The phantom of bigness, which London encourages, was laid for ever when she paced from the hall at Howards End to its kitchen and heard the rains run this way and that where the watershed of the roof divided them' (p. 201). Within this suddenly crystallized sense of place and space, Margaret can perceive the pattern of her own life; and two flashes of memory – one of a phrase of Helen's, one of the map of Africa (she has just seen such a map in Henry's office) – draw the earlier phases of the chapter, as well as the phases of her life, into a moment of climactic wholeness under the watershed of a roof. And at once, spatial harmony, stasis of house and chapter, breaks up; movement returns, as it must; and a devastating reverberation fills the house, above the drumming of the rain. A door must always be flung open; something new must be explored or endured; a shock, a repetition; and old Miss Avery, in a brilliant *coup de roman*, comes through the door with words of reincarnation, mystery, and triviality. Perhaps only in the pleasure taken by the imagination in seeing such transitions, calms, and surprises preserved in the fabric of a dexterous chapter is there any reflex of that inexplicable 'proportion' we were told earlier on was 'the final secret' even of a dialectical truth. What we participate in as readers does not stop moving – the chapter ends in change, with 'the old woman passed out into the rain' (p. 202). But by watching ourselves, unmoving, participate in movement – by adopting that uniquely contemplative relationship to simulated action that the experience of art enforces – it may be that we enjoy 'proportion' and, above our continuing drama, the momentary shape of watershed and rooftree.[16]

The cross-purposes of *Howards End* run at every level of discourse, and through every unit, large or small, of the narration. Even its most significant and solidly realized settings – like Howards End itself, like Wickham Place, and like Oniton – are transitional and under threat. They are in-between places, as befit a book that seems to query fixity, stability, and 'proportion' even as it tries to sustain such qualities. Wickham Place, where the Schlegels build their hopeful liberalism upon a family tradition, is impermanent: it is to be vacated, then demolished. It is 'a backwater, or rather . . . an estuary, whose waters flowed in from the invisible sea, and ebbed into a profound silence while the waves without were still beating' (p. 23) – and there is no sharper expression of the doubleness of Forster's symbols than this ubiquitous one of the sea, which is simultaneously (like the realm of spirit and mystery) a great authority and (like the realm of business mores, panic, and emptiness) a force of erosion and hopeless flux. Howards End, too, is situated in an in-between place. Its village, Hilton, is 'indeterminate', neither true England nor true suburbia. And the house itself, for all its aspect of mystic continuity, is partly dependent on (and thereby vulnerable to) Wilcox practicality; is extended and altered by Wilcoxes, as well as being preserved by them; and, in the end, is as much threatened by the encroaching 'red rust' of urban living as it is sustained by the meadow and the hay harvest. And Oniton, a place of 'romantic tension', where crucial revelations come separately to Margaret and to Helen, is transitory, for all its delusive promise to Margaret of security and ownership: it is a halfway place, subtly between England and Wales, with rumours of the absolute (the Unseen) in the waters that flow through it from the mysterious Welsh mountains, but travestied, betrayed, and quickly abandoned by Wilcoxes, the bearers of fragmentation and disconnection.

At the level of ideas, the transitions and cross-purposes of the novel can perhaps best be seen as a perpetual process of self-testing: a concern, almost an obsession, in which Forster, Conrad and even James become as one. Time and time again, clear statement signifying hopefulness as to the human lot is challenged, often on the spot, by some scene of futility or disaster. Margaret and Mrs Wilcox go Christmas shopping together, and as against the commercial tawdriness of the season, its distortion of a divine event, we have this:

But in public who shall express the unseen adequately? It is private life that holds out the mirror to infinity; personal intercourse, and that alone, that ever hints at a personality beyond our daily vision. (p. 91)

It reads like a credo – what some readers have taken to be the credo of the whole book, with its Schlegel epigraph of 'Only connect'. But within the space of a few pages incomprehension and offence have fallen across the 'personal intercourse' of the two women, as the London fog envelops them:

The city seemed satanic, the narrower streets oppressing like the galleries of a mine. No harm was done by the fog to trade, for it lay high, and the lighted windows of the shops were thronged with customers. It was rather a darkening of the spirit, which fell back upon itself, to find a more grievous darkness within. (p. 94)

The expressed conviction that intelligence and culture, such as the Schlegels', have the capacity to redeem personal and social life is usually quickly countered by the satiric gloom of a scene like that of Leonard Bast at home with his Jackie, in the parody-opposite of Wickham Place, being bullied (and quite unredeemed) by reading Ruskin. In chapter 12, a meditative chapter after the death of Mrs Wilcox, Margaret moves from reflecting how Mrs Wilcox, in dying with dignity, 'kept proportion' and 'took the middle course', and emphasizing the need for 'hope' and for 'reconciliation', to a final realization that life is an affair of chaos, for which no proportion helps, and to which a deliberate incautiousness is the only response. As usual, the two contrary ideas of 'proportion' and 'unmanageableness' are allowed to flow into one another within an apparent harmony of meditative style that nevertheless fails to mask the unresolved intellectual tension beneath. The tension that underlies the basic plot-stratagem of having Margaret marry Henry Wilcox seems connected with this impulse of self-testing: carried, in this instance, to a degree that has strained conviction for many readers. Margaret's views, which are endorsed by so many aspects of the narrative, are also continually under test. For example, her sermon on the virtues of the Wilcox work ethic, to a scathingly disbelieving Tibby, has validity (Tibby is effeminate and will-less); but is made to defeat itself by the conclusions Margaret betrays herself into: 'A nation who can produce men of that sort may well be proud. No wonder England has become an Empire' (p. 119). This going against the grain is everywhere in her relationship with Henry Wilcox; and it may be that the unease and inconsistency that elsewhere in the book can be regarded as genuinely creative become too bewildering when applied to a central relationship between two characters presented in a fundamentally naturalistic mode. One accepts, within naturalism, that love has its impersonality, and therefore its surprises. But when — as one among many examples, right up to the crucial final example on the last page of the book – a demonstration of Henry Wilcox at his most egregiously awful ends thus –

A wave of tenderness came over her. She put a hand on either shoulder, and looked deeply into the black, bright eyes. What was behind their competent stare? She knew, but was not disquieted. –   (p. 194)

then the ironic double turn, reminding us that 'panic and emptiness' are behind his competent stare, does not appease our simple outrage that Margaret has let him off and betrayed herself, quite incredibly, once again. In such an instance, cross-purposes and self-testing perhaps go too far, and ignore the degree to which the reader has already been persuaded to invest his emotional and intellectual sympathy in Margaret. The line between a rich creative tension and a reader-losing incongruity, between a double turn and a false step, is often a fine one.

An example of where the self-testing impulse is more genuinely dialectical is the very difficult and delicately balanced scene in chapter 27 between Helen and Leonard Bast in the hotel in Oniton. It is delicate because the conceiving of a child between the two of them, like Margaret's relationship with Henry Wilcox, is among the most contentious and dangerously forced pieces of plotting in the novel (the reader's nervousness at the consequence of the Helen-Leonard affair is most famously expressed in Katherine Mansfield's jibe that it must have been Bast's lost umbrella, rather than Bast, that managed to achieve the conception).[17] As always, the sense of change and development throughout the chapter is exciting, and is itself a help to persuasion. It begins with Helen prattling in her unconsciously patronizing way, and Leonard, more subtly shown than anywhere else in the novel, trying at first to keep up with his patroness's wish for high-flown talk, then learning to discriminate between the two Schlegel sisters, being sensitive and defensive about his wife (contrasted with Helen's impulsive disparagement), honestly disenchanted about life and romance, and clinging in his growing despair to the 'little things' of his life – like lack of money and a job – as against the large paradoxes and visions that Helen, suddenly carried away by her own anxieties, her rhetoric, her quixotic self-delusion, parades in front of him. Helen talks and poetically philosophizes herself towards a symbolic sexual act of healing generosity. Given the Schlegel cult of talk and idealization, it is perfectly convincing that she should do so, and that Leonard, bewildered and ashamed, should be forced to accept her irresistible charity. But what is fascinating, and typical, is to see how her ideas and arguments flow into the emotional texture of the episode, and, as ideas, become qualified by that texture. Helen, as a romantic, is absolute for Death. She pounces on the suggestive idea that 'Death destroys a man: the idea of Death saves him': that to think of death is to encounter the Unseen, the infinite, which is more 'real' than the world of Wilcox values, businesses, Empires. As the peroration becomes more intense, and Leonard dumbly concentrates on the thought of getting a job somewhere as a clerk, so Forster, too, allows himself to be carried away for a moment into adding a rhetorical curlicue to Helen's vision, urging that love is stronger than death, and closer to the power of the Unseen. It is just for a moment. For one thing, death exists as pure destroyer in too many parts and levels of the rest of the narrative for us to accord more than a very temporary accommodation to this idea. And more immediately, in a characteristic counter-turn, Forster at once puts the very idea he has just passionately endorsed – or rather, that he has just allowed the rhetoric of his narration to endorse – to a withering test:

'So never give in,' continued the girl, and restated again and again the vague yet convincing plea that the Invisible lodges against the Visible. Her excitement grew as she tried to cut the rope that fastened Leonard to the earth. Woven of bitter experience, it resisted her. Presently the waitress entered and gave her a letter from Margaret. Another note, addressed to Leonard, was inside. They read them, listening to the murmurings of the river. (p. 237)

Leonard is fastened to reality: the letters that come from Margaret, brusquely refusing to help Leonard, are part of that reality. And Helen's 'vague yet convincing plan' is left hopelessly entangled with its unyielding opposite, the reality of 'bitter experience' (backed by the psychological reality given by the narrative to Leonard's feelings during the scene). Helen's idea about death is not invalidated; but it is drained of authoritativeness and thrown back into the welter of contraries, shifting facets, and reversals – that is, back into the narrative movement of the chapter, and of the book. Her idealism is now seen to be incapable of passing from the idea to real experience; and the consequent sexual event, which we deduce only later, is then recognized as having, among its other flaws, that of an idealistic and therefore abstract motive. They both read their sobering letters from Margaret, drawn together finally by 'the murmurings of the river'. At the same time, Margaret is shown listening to the same river, drawing from it a different (and perhaps equally half-delusive, equally half-true) message of confirmation in her policy of forgiveness and proportion. What exactly it says to the very temporary pair of lovers, united on one part by charity and idealism and on the other by uncomprehending gratitude, panic, and emptiness, is left unvoiced at the chapter's end. Like the rivers running inland from the sea (in chapter 19), this stream running out of the mysterious Welsh hills carries enigmatic portents, and itself narrates diverse meanings – including a death that will *not* be overcome by love, and knows no proportion.

I do not wish to over-emphasize the darker, more death-haunted aspects of *Howards End*. My point is that they exist in various layers of our response to the novel, and in perpetual entanglement with what is perhaps obvious: the book's Jamesian luminousness of wit and intelligence, and its unwearying motive to go on searching for a redeeming 'connection' within the individual psyche, between individuals in relationships, and between the human consciousness and the infinite.[18] Any close reading of the novel must qualify beyond tenability the idea that this is a liberal-humanist essay, rather than an intricate (and no doubt imperfect) drama in which – again, as with James – many of the features of liberal humanism are set in train, amid much that negates them, or passes them by. It is the pressure among these different currents, the air of challenge and change, the perplexing and at times perplexed movement from a meditative expounding down to an awkward twining of desires and fears, that makes the book what it is. The commentary sometimes recommends change, vulnerability, openness to the flow of experience; but what is narrated (and sometimes the commentary, too) shows a horror of the deathliness that such flux also contains – hence the doubleness that everywhere attaches to the dominating images of sea, river, and tide. Beneath the line of witty, moral analysis that suggests a faith in the prospect of change there is a depth of fear, a touch of panic that is not only Wilcox panic but panic in something of that etymological sense used more explicitly elsewhere by Forster, an extreme and contagious terror caused by the influence of Pan:[19] in the case of this book, the influence of a half-perceived but unapprehendable absolute, far less absurdist than the reductive absolute of Razumov or of *The Shadow-Line*, purposeless but still full of varied signs, sometimes enigmatically confirming the shapes of civility and intercourse, at other times sweeping them away implacably. The force of it comes in surprises, passions, deaths, cruel snobberies, adventitious births, broken photograph frames. It is felt in the book's ubiquitous rumours of war, its overheard political conversations, slight family altercations, a Schlegel German sword, hung up for peace, that inadvertently kills the weakest of Englishmen; Germany and England, person and person, moving towards Armageddon.[20] Even Mrs Wilcox is both truth-bearer and shadow: she values continuity, 'the inner light', instinctual wisdom; but is always dying, inarticulate, even boring; ghostly in characterization even when shown as alive.[21] The unseen world she so insubstantially emanates from, and which is recognized by Margaret, is one that can enrich and take on human or humanistic shape: a house, say, or a dream of harvest. But it is a world equally that devastates; and its emanations — like the memory or the ghost of Mrs Wilcox — can be simply frightening, doors into the darkness, as well as encouragements to the initiate like Margaret. Moments of cosmic fear float through the book, though never quite overwhelming the resistances of wit, hopefulness, idealism, patience, and artistic form. Yet one of the profoundest and most challenging of these moments comes in the very centre — the representative centre — of a great resistant form.

[Margaret] went for a few moments into St. Paul's, whose dome stands out of the welter so bravely, as if preaching the gospel of form. But, within, St. Paul's is as its surroundings — echoes and whispers, inaudible songs, invisible mosaics, wet footmarks crossing and recrossing the floor. *Si monumentum requiris, circumspice*: it points us back to London.

(p. 275)

The misapplication — or reapplication — of the famous epitaph to Wren is brilliant. Where 'circumspice' properly invites the beholder to glory in the ordered structure of the great church all around him, here it breaks through that form to point at the surrounding and interpenetrating chaos of London which is, for the moment, more

178

ultimate than art or rationality. And London, from which Helen has so appallingly disappeared, is the sea, the encroaching unseen, at its most inhuman:

> The mask fell off the city, and she saw it for what it really is – a caricature of infinity . . . Helen seemed one with grimy trees and the traffic and the slowly flowing slabs of mud. She had accomplished a hideous act of renunciation and returned to the One.[22]   (pp. 274–5)

But Margaret's faith goes on with dynamism and energy, opposing such visions of absolute contingency, seeking humane 'connection' even where the adventitious or taunting connections of narrative, like a cleverly annulling echo, seem to deny its possibility. To the very end, in its context of harvest and a new birth, her view rejects the full implications of the Wilcox lie to others, her husband's lies to himself, the deathliness of every falling and repetitive word, and the death – as for Conrad's Marlow – that exists in every act or phrase of dishonesty, including her own final act of connivance:

> And again and again fell the word, like the ebb of a dying sea . . .
> . . . Margaret was silent. Something shook her life in its inmost recesses, and she shivered.
> 'I didn't do wrong, did I?' he asked, bending down.
> 'You didn't, darling. Nothing has been done wrong.'
> . . . 'The field's cut!' Helen cried excitedly – 'The big meadow! We've seen to the very end, and it'll be such a crop of hay as never!' (p. 332)

For a book so often criticized as essayistic and contrived, it ends with surprising – if disguised – tentativeness, far more tentativeness than, say, *The Bostonians*, that other notable diagnosis of a national culture in stress and internecine division, sexual, regional, moral, and psychological. Its options are still open, its opposed feelings brought to a point not of closure but of perfected and communicative strain, and all kept at a pitch of drama. Everything that is expressed and hinted at in such an ending makes it less a conclusion than a just-suspended rhythm of these two things: consummation and loss, a harvest and a falling.[23]

2. Passages to India

One among the many passages to India is the passage by solecism. The walls of the palace at Mau, where Professor Godbole dances before God, testify to error and inadvertency:

The inscriptions which the poets of the state had composed were hung where they could not be read, or had twitched their drawing-pins out of the stucco, and one of them . . . consisted, by an unfortunate slip of the draughtsman, of the words, 'God si Love'.
God si love. Is this the final message of India?[24]

Verbs and prepositions, messages, connectives of any kind, are unstable in this novel. Syntax is a requisite, but breakable. Passages can lead nowhere, or into themselves. A tree might be a cobra, or vice versa, as 'is' turns over into 'si'. The name of an elderly British lady becomes Indianized into a syllabic chant, 'Esmiss Esmoor, Esmiss Esmoor', empty yet full of meaning. India is still there, and we are here, seeking passage and understanding, as we follow out the ways of a narrative; but the route may require a disjunction: some misspelling or reversal or reductive echo, a half-cancellation or sudden indirection.

In the scene at the beginning of 'Temple' where Godbole confronts the misspelling hung comically on the palace wall, language has been jostled from the outset; 'God is not born yet — that will occur at midnight — but He has also been born centuries ago, nor can He ever be born . . . He is, was not, is not, was.' And what the singers are chanting, in a numbing litany, seems as much the willed negation of meaning and discrimination as the celebration of a divinity:

> 'Tukaram, Tukaram,
> Thou art my father and mother and everybody.
> Tukaram, Tukaram,
> Thou art my father and mother and everybody.
> Tukaram, Tukaram,
> Thou art my father and mother and everybody.
> Tukaram, Tukaram,
> Thou art my father and mother and everybody.
> Tukaram . . .'   (p. 281)

And yet syntax and the equivalent of syntax remain: the corridors at Mau are not confused, they open into a formal courtyard, there are hard white pillars, vaulting, detailed chandeliers of pink glass, a pale blue turban on Godbole's head, a gold pince-nez at a slight angle to — not the universe but his nose. We are made to know where we are; and though the simple opening sentence ends in the phrase 'Godbole stands in the presence of God', thus casually encapsulating the eternal, it has begun on a quite different perspective, 'Some hundreds of miles westward of the Marabar Hills, and two years later in time . . .' – that is, laying down firmly the lineaments of material space and time.

The misdirected chaos of the ceremony gives the event its radiance, its escape from syntax:

> They sang not even to the God who confronted them, but to a saint; they did not one thing which the non-Hindu would feel dramatically correct; this approaching triumph of India was a muddle (as we call it), a frustration of reason and form. (p. 282)

But the 'triumph' of such disorder is not in itself an untrammelled revelation of the real. It has power, it brings an access of happiness, but even if it is benign it is not secure or without ambiguity and evanescence. If 'is' has to be broken for radiance to come, 'si' correspondingly tends to collapse back into the all-too-human mode of 'is'. Following the irregularity of 'Chance', either by a 'trick of memory or a telepathic appeal', it does not matter which, Godbole's mind comes into possession of two random images, those of Mrs Moore and a wasp:

> he impelled her by his spiritual force to that place where completeness can be found. Completeness, not reconstruction. His senses grew thinner, he remembered a wasp seen he forgot where, perhaps on a stone. He loved the wasp equally, he impelled it likewise, he was imitating God. And the stone where the wasp clung – could he . . . no, he had been wrong to attempt the stone, logic and conscious effort had seduced, he came back to the strip of red carpet and discovered that he was dancing upon it. (pp. 283–4)

Everything is a movement: a quick passage from the random image, 'a tiny splinter', towards 'completeness'. And then the sudden discovery that effort is inimical to 'completeness', that 'reconstruction' is the normal human mode – like the normal mode of narration itself – and Godbole returns from where completeness might have been ('the presence of God') to those very bounds of time and space ('the strip of red carpet') that have made the effort at completeness possible. It is an ancient dilemma, and one that denotes the full imaginative scope, and the complex method, of *A Passage to India*. Through Godbole, whom for the moment – and only for a moment – we may take as our novelist,

181

there has been an attempt to express, by encountering, the infinite: 'the human spirit had tried by a desperate contortion to ravish the unknown'. But expression itself, without which there is no novel, disperses any full revelation. Even the little 'contortion' of 'si' for 'is' is not enough, nor is the indecorous interweaving of comedy with solemnity:

How can it be expressed in anything but itself? Not only from the unbeliever are mysteries hid, but the adept himself cannot retain them. He may think, if he chooses, that he has been with God, but, as soon as he thinks it, it becomes history, and falls under the rules of time. (p. 285)

The picture of Godbole trying consciously – it being his priestly duty – to adopt the position of God as He loves Mrs Moore, and to express the real, totally, and from outside history, develops the hint of the artist in the extreme direction of the iconic, the symbolist.[25] But even Godbole fails: and this narration is not his, nor is it in itself iconic – though it may use symbols. Like Godbole, narrative must submit to 'the rules of time', while expressing in all its indirections and ingenuities its discontent with those rules: in no other of the novels we have considered is this general insight so made integral to the whole argument and explicit presentation of the text. 'It does not seem much, still, it is more than I am myself', reflects the Brahman at the end of his ceremony (p. 288), commemorating in that discovery of expansion the fact that narrative, while time-bound and syntax-bound, remains true to its energies by always seeking to test its limits through dynamism and change; by at least making each 'is' dance to the cymbals and become a little more than itself, even if the god does not come and literature, like all thought, must return to the conditions of history.[26]

Even the crucial first chapter, which by its carefully judged allusions to cave and sky would seem to be proposing the cosmic at the expense of the mundane, is far from single in its ironies or in its alternations of movement. That quintessentially Forsterian opening – 'Except for the Marabar Caves – and they are twenty miles off – the city of Chandrapore presents nothing extraordinary' (p. 31) – acts both positively and negatively. By withholding the extraordinariness of the Caves, and allowing it to reappear, still in the distance, in the chapter's last phrase, the narrative keeps alive some promise of revelation and richness. And Chandrapore is both judged adversely against that distant promise – the city is made to

182

appear the very opposite of 'extraordinary' – and also allowed to be in many ways redeemed by having the promise still latent within it, and within the allusive, elusive, to-and-fro of the one prose medium that creates for us Chandrapore *and* sky *and* caves. It is a classic instance of a Forster disclaimer that covertly asserts as much as it openly repudiates, and is as much honorific as pejorative – the 'double turn' that Trilling identified. And when the catalogue of Chandrapore's mediocrity and featurelessness comes to a climax in 'The very wood seems made of mud, the inhabitants of mud moving', the subdued extravagance of the conceit – rather like the mud of London in the first paragraph of *Bleak House* – evokes a vitality that the actual itemizing of the catalogue would seek to deny:

Houses do fall, people are drowned and left rotting, but the general outline of the town persists, swelling here, shrinking there, like some low but indestructible form of life. (p. 31)

Mud proves to have a disconcerting – and perhaps 'extraordinary' – aspect, an 'indestructible' force that resists the simple binary opposition between the special and visionary (which is twenty miles off) and the everyday (which is as ubiquitous as mud). Already, the 'eye' of the reader is being led a dance – not to the cymbals of some mystic vision but to the rhythm of a shrewder, more quizzical rhetoric.[27]

Similarly with the description of the civil station that follows in the second paragraph. We expect the opposition again; and indeed in recalling the chapter it is easy to think that as against the shapelessness of the 'real' India of the bazaars Forster simply shows us the soulless regularity of the bungalows and the right angles of the Raj. In fact, the latter comes only at the very end of the paragraph, which is mostly devoted to how the mediocrity of Chandrapore is transformed by a little distance. The bungalow is certainly not a temple or a mosque, but it seems at least to offer a vantage point of some magicality:

viewed hence Chandrapore appears to be a totally different place. It is a city of gardens. It is no city, but a forest sparsely scattered with huts. It is a tropical pleasance, washed by a noble river. The toddy palms and neem trees and mangoes and peepul that were hidden behind the bazaars now become visible and in their turn hide the bazaars. They rise from the

gardens whose ancient tanks nourish them, they burst out of stifling
purlieus and unconsidered temples. Seeking light and air, and endowed
with more strength than man or his works, they soar above the lower
deposit to greet one another with branches and beckoning leaves, and to
build a city for the birds.   (pp. 31–2)

Of course it is delusive — 'disillusionment' comes to the viewer
when he is driven down to investigate the apparent glory of it. But
the image of richness and vitality remains, and unexpectedly
reflects back on the bungalow-world that makes possible the view
and that image. So that when the paragraph ends, gnomically, by
saying of the civil station, 'it shares nothing with the city except the
overarching sky', the now-established manner of glorifying the
mediocre only to take the glory away, then give it back again, confirms the same doubleness in that word 'except' as in the 'except'
with which the chapter began: the throwaway phrase contains an
oblique assertion of value.

And that sky, too, lastly, for all that its 'core of blue' is persistent, by night and by day, more persistent that its slight changes of
cloud and colour, more persistent than the enriching illusion of a
'tropical pleasance' in Chandrapore, must then have its centrality
challenged in two ways. It is challenged by the attempt to go
beyond — to push the prose into conveying an unconveyable, il-
limitable distance beyond colour itself, and therefore beyond the
spatiality of 'core' and the sensuous reality of 'blue'. And the sky
is challenged in a second way, by the chapter returning to the earth,
and therefore to the mud of the Chandrapore bazaar that was
itself, earlier on, an 'indestructible form of life'. The sky, we are
told, draws its size 'from the prostrate earth', and its impression of
infinite space is in fact created for the eye and the mind by the line
of the earth's horizon. The dimensionless, therefore, succumbs as
before to that which alone can express it; the dimension and
measurement of 'curve', 'league after league', 'heaves a little', 'is
flat again', 'is interrupted'. And there, in the 'fists and fingers' of
an irregular, earthly horizon that humanizes the overarching sky,
draws it down measurably to us, we find the Marabar Hills —
which of course in their turn, their Forsterian double turn,
paradoxically contain the caves which are the core, which is the
vault, which will prove to be the very annulment of horizon, dimension, and humanity. If there is something in all this intricacy and

reversal that sounds, in analysis, a little like 'this is the house that Jack built', it may be that Forster would not have objected to the comparison; since he would have been keen to undercut his own brief solemnities and, as part of these expressive alternations, to move on quickly to the naturalistic anticlimax of Aziz running talkatively, anecdotally, on to Hamidullah's verandah while his abandoned bicycle crashes behind him to the ground.[28]

Throughout 'Mosque', the first of the three parts of *A Passage to India*, the cosmic, the 'unseen', cuts across the social, moral, and political strand of the narrative in distinctly varying directions and stylistic registers.[29] The progress of everyday gossip or political arguments among Aziz and his friends, for example, is liable suddenly to be interrupted by an unconnected moment of part-aesthetic, part-religious idealism, as Aziz without warning breaks into words of Persian or Urdu poetry: 'It never bored them, to hear words, words; they breathed them with the cool night air, never stopping to analyse' (pp. 37–8). The sense of pathos, a hint at 'the secret understanding of heart', releases the imagination; the poetry, arbitrary and sentimental, and expressing the human 'need for the Friend who never comes', produces among those who hear it 'a breath from the divine lips of beauty, a nightingale between two worlds of dust' (p. 119), and evokes for Aziz himself a dream of formal harmony and clear, differentiated naming: 'domes whereunder were inscribed, black against white, the ninety-nine attributes of God' (p. 133). These numinous moments of an Islamic vision can be seen as detached from life, from cause and effect − 'never stopping to analyse' − and from temporal narration. Or they can appear as escapist or purely aesthetic dreams − as the delicately overblown phrases about the 'divine lips of beauty' and the 'nightingale', together with Fielding's criticism of such incantatory language, would suggest. But they can also occasionally be made integral to the more secular texture of voices in realistic dialogue and human relations in action, as when Aziz, brooding on religion and exalted in the mosque at night by his own repeating of the Persian phrase, 'those who have secretly understood my heart', finds Mrs Moore there in the shadows, and bases his friendship for her precisely on this understanding of the heart: one of those moments where the Unseen, for once, enters directly into human act and response: 'his heart began to glow secretly. Presently it burst into speech. "You understand me, you know what I feel . . ."' (p. 45).

Similarly, in the chapter that follows Aziz's first encounter with Mrs Moore, the narrative of Anglo-Indian chatter, family discord, and moral exposure of a class and its individuals is interrupted by three passages – passages in more than one sense – where, for Mrs Moore, a different mode of perception suddenly contradicts these processes, and does so in three distinct ways. Firstly, a sight of the moon awakens her from the falsity and stupefaction of life at the club, and brings from outside a vision that is entirely cleansing and value-bearing:

A sudden sense of unity, of kinship with the heavenly bodies, passed into the old woman and out, like water through a tank, leaving a strange freshness behind . . . cocktails and cigars had died into invisible flowers.

(p. 51)

Far from being disjunctive, the numinous moment is transformative, redemptive, and at once offers 'passage' through the thickets of human dishonesty: after seeing the moon, Mrs Moore now sees the mosque where she has just had her significant meeting with Aziz, and in referring to it puts her son's humanity to the test. But in the second such moment, more threateningly, moonlight is itself transformed. As a reflected 'radiance' on the Ganges, the moon belongs 'neither to water nor moonlight, but stood like a luminous sheaf upon the fields of darkness' (pp. 52–3). The vision quickly becomes one of eternal evanescence, rather than of unity and freshness. The sandbank that causes the reflection is unstable; bodies float down that way; there are crocodiles. 'The radiance was already altering, whether through shifting of the moon or of the sand; soon the bright sheaf would be gone, and a circlet, itself to alter, be burnished upon the streaming void' (p. 53). 'Unquietness', a disruption in the mood of the watchers, echoes that small unexpected image of the void; and finds its own prolongation in the rising quarrelsomeness of mother and son. Then thirdly, when Mrs Moore finds a wasp hanging from her coat-peg, the beneficence of the unifying moon *and* the unconsoling power of the 'streaming void' seem to be held equally, in a characteristically unemphasized suspension, within the packed images of randomness, blessing, and unrest that close the chapter. The wasp, unable to make

186

distinctions — or to name attributes: outside or inside, tree or house, brown or white — harmlessly blurs the edge of things, and effects a half-comic passage of unity. But such 'normal growth of the eternal jungle', having comforted and amused in one phase, chills in the next. And Mrs Moore's words, 'Pretty dear' — very British and banal, but still a token of harmony — float out 'to swell the night's uneasiness', and disperse their blessing in that eternal jungle of indiscriminate noises and things: jackals, drums, trees, wasps, houses, all equal, all nothing. Even the word 'floated' echoes, without comfort, the description of the radiance on the Ganges and the 'void' that it so quickly became — though the two benign words she has spoken do remain also in our minds, and on the page, as one response to that ultimate wordlessness.

The Bridge Party — which is so shamefully far from being a bridge between races or individuals — is in one obvious sense an episode unambiguously opposed to discrimination. The values of communication, equality, unity are the bases from which its satire — often quite withering — is directed. Yet at the outset of the episode, within it, and at its end there occur moments, at the more numinous level of narration, that seem calculated to call these very moral bases in doubt. In each case, the image to create this doubt is basically that of an infinite series: gradations of people, of living things, and, most recurrently, gradations of the vault of the sky. The question of invitations to the Bridge Party — invitations to passage and to unity[30] — begins on what at first promises to be an extension of the moral and political note. There are circles on circles of Indians not invited, the poorest and lowliest. And it seems almost too easy for the two missionaries, old Mr Graysford and young Mr Sorley, to be humorously pilloried for the limitations of their woolly-liberal-Christian view, accepting all colours and creeds as guests in God's mansion but nervously drawing the line in the one case at monkeys, in the other, more daringly, as far down as wasps. But the last phrases of the gentle lampoon are very two-edged:

And oranges, cactuses, crystals, and mud? And the bacteria inside Mr. Sorley? No, no, this is going too far. We must exclude someone from our gathering, or we shall be left with nothing. (p. 58)

In one voice, 'we shall be left with nothing' is a parody of the liberal with his back to the wall. But in another voice, somewhere just below the first voice, is the sonorous implication of a darker possible truth, quite Conradian in the intellectual impasse it presents: all-inclusiveness, carried all the way, means the end of consciousness; therefore sanity and survival are based on the bad faith of self-restriction and the restriction of others. Sanity presupposes discrimination, the perception of difference; so that, in a way, a troubling way, not to exclude is to cease to exist – with a vengeance, 'we shall be left with nothing.' And this is the questioning, on a register quite different from the predominant social satire and comedy of manners, that continues just here and there below the surface of the Bridge Party episode itself.

Perhaps just a little too blatantly – it would be an exaggeration to say crudely – Forster brings this other register to the fore as the party gets creakingly under way. As the words of conversation, contemptuous or halting, die into silence, we see the kite hovering overhead, the vulture hovering above the kite, and the sky beyond everything: silence carried to the nth degree.

It seemed unlikely that the series stopped here. Beyond the sky must not there be something that overarches all the skies, more impartial even than they? Beyond which again . . .

They spoke of *Cousin Kate*.   (p. 60)

More subtle than this are the allusions to the Marabar Hills, ominously visible to Adela and Fielding 'through a nick in the cactus hedge'; and to Adela's intermittent sense of exclusion – exclusion from some further spiritual knowledge that seems to lie behind the mere tourist 'frieze' of India. And subtler, too, is the final outbreak of the tensions of the unsuccessful party in Mrs Moore's Christian harangue at her impossible son. Her homily can only endorse the narrative's clear ethical angle on the Bridge Party: 'God has put us on the earth in order to be pleasant to each other. God . . . is . . . love' (p. 70). But what might have been, as a climax to the episode, some fusion of the Christianized numinous with the secular and political, fades out at once in the all-negating invocation of the infinite series:

[God] had been constantly in her thoughts since she entered India, though oddly enough He satisfied her less. She must needs pronounce His name frequently, as the greatest she knew, yet she had never found it less efficacious. Outside the arch there seemed always an arch, beyond the remotest echo a silence. (p. 71)

And questions of race, of honesty and justice, the chapter's closing question of marriage ('Would they, or would they not, succeed in becoming engaged?'), questions of action, logic, even of the present narration itself as an act of connection and understanding, are suddenly, for a conclusion, allowed to drop away into futility.

Forster, more than Conrad and far more than James, is a master and a manipulator of the inadvertent. As in Shakespearean comedy, he bases the vitality of his plots on the presence of accident, inappropriateness, good and bad luck, misprision, and malapropism of word and deed ('God si love' being like Bottom's comic epiphany, 'the eye of man hath not heard, the ear of man hath not seen'). Professor Godbole chooses to sing his song at Fielding's tea-party at exactly the wrong moment. Something nameless − a buffalo? a hyena? a ghost? − crashes randomly into the Nawab Bahadur's car. Fielding and Godbole miss their train to Marabar. The caves are anticlimactic, tedious, full of despair, everything that was not expected. A hysterical guest thinks she has been attacked and runs away. The presence of causes is hinted at by apparent effects, then as suddenly contradicted: ripples, reversed, wash out their implied source. Even the overwhelming cosmic power of the Indian sun is not ultimate, but is self-cancelled in its own excess; just as the gigantic Indian darkness, seemingly absolute, is only falsely so ('a spurious unity'), being subject to the inappropriateness, the perpetual solecism of 'the gleams of day that leaked up round the edges of the earth' (p. 103).[31]

Typically, Godbole's delayed song to Krishna, sung just as his fellow guests are all leaving, quarrelsome and embarrassed, affects the reader as being simultaneously tangential and central. Godbole's own personal tangentiality − as a Brahman he eats separately from the others and apparently by accident ('ate and ate, smiling, never letting his eyes catch sight of his hand' − p. 89), and, like 'Ancient Night', deviously avoids answering Aziz's direct questions about the caves − runs quite counter to all the loquacious, well-meaning gestures of ordinary human relationship, the reaching out, touching, withdrawing, reaching again, that exercise the other four at the tea-party, Fielding, Aziz, Mrs Moore, and

189

Adela. And his song, when suddenly it comes, is not only tangential and asyntactical by its awkward occasion of delivery and its musical mode (it ends 'apparently halfway through a bar, and upon the subdominant') but also by its content, which seems to commemorate the failure of relationship and communication: 'Oh no, He refuses to come . . . I say to Him, Come, come, come, come, come, come. He neglects to come.' And yet, most powerfully, the episode also has the force of something other than the merely inadvertent, or a universal refusal. For the reader is drawn empathetically into the song's 'maze of noises' that the suddenly quite intense prose evokes, and especially by participating in the brilliant, concentrative detail of the other listeners:

Only the servants understood it. They began to whisper to one another. The man who was gathering water-chestnut came naked out of the tank, his lips parted with delight, disclosing his scarlet tongue.   (p. 95)

The seeming negation of the song's content – the refusal of Krishna to come – produces, at least for the 'moment of absolute silence' that follows its ending, an effect not of futility but of pregnant expectation and equipoise, as 'No ripple disturbed the water, no leaf stirred.' Very indirectly, with excruciating delicacy and fragility, the narration, at the close of a chapter, has produced the sense of an access of power, something cupped and held, despite the sideways nature – or perhaps exactly because of the sideways nature – of its arrival.

Quite different, however, is the quality of the accident that surrounds the incident of the Nawab Bahadur's car. This accident is in certain ways an emanation of the darkness: whatever has crashed into the car is unnameable, and defies labelling. The need to categorize has occurred elsewhere in the same scene. Ronny and Adela wish to analyse the nature of their relationship, and why it seems to have broken down: no Indians, we are told, would have examined the problem so coolly – 'The mere fact of examination caused it to diminish' (p. 101). Simultaneously, they both want to identify a nearby green-and-red Indian bird as part of this same mental process of examining and naming. But the deficiencies of the name-seeking faculty are subtly suggested to us by a mid-sentence phrase that echoes and in effect negates the one just quoted: 'nothing in India is identifiable, the mere asking of a question causes it to disappear or to merge in something else'. And to complicate matters, when Adela reverses her decision and becomes engaged to Ronny immediately after the accident, some other less rational faculty in her is disappointed: 'Unlike the green bird or the hairy animal, she was labelled now. She felt humiliated again, for she deprecated labels' (p. 109). But if the encounter with the 'animal' is another encounter with 'Ancient Night' — 'certainly some external force had impinged' — it does not simply point to the fact that this other, unseen realm exists: an alternative of pure transcendence, as at the end of Godbole's song. The accidental 'external force', like the echo in the cave, also intersects with the affairs of everyday life and makes them swerve, exactly like the swerving track of the car tyres in the dust (whose 'nicked' pattern will be recalled to Adela's mind as she rejects her love of Ronny — and therefore its false 'labelling' — at the very moment she enters the fateful cave at Marabar). The English couple have almost made up their disagreement before the incident occurs, it is true; but it strengthens their reconciliation, unites them in their search to 'identify' and control the alarming event, and pushes them into their temporary and (like the darkness around them) 'spurious unity'. And if the more aloof quality of the accident — its transcendental mystery, randomness, unidentifiableness — is then separately brought out in Mrs Moore's telepathic 'A ghost!', it nevertheless does not produce a final moment of numinous revelation like that other moment without ripple or the stirring of a leaf. The 'ghost' is simply a horror in 'unspeakable form' — and known as such by the Nawab, whose blood-guilt recognizes the ghost as a man killed in the past by his car — and not at all an equipoise, a sudden luminousness. It is that other mode of the unseen: its refusal to be grand or to solace the imagination — or to give delight to the water-chestnut gatherer. Entering into the shapes of certain human lives and changing them just a little; entering into a narrative and therefore into the structure of planned cause and effect (accident causes engagement, therefore crisis at Marabar); the unseen world also resists structures and attributes, and, being 'unspeakable' can simply cause horror at a roadside, a shiver among the players of patience in the civil lines, or descend arbitrarily and without dignity like — at the end of this long day of accidents — the three annunciating blasts of hot wind out of the sky, 'hard and compact, leaving no freshness behind them' (p. 114).

At the end of the Krishna celebrations in 'Temple' we read: 'Looking back at the great blur of the last twenty-four hours, no man could say where was the emotional centre of it, any more than he could locate the heart of a cloud' (p. 310). It would be almost equally difficult to point to one 'emotional centre' of *A Passage to India*, though obviously the expedition to the caves stands satisfyingly at the centre of the narrative in spatial terms.[32] Mrs Moore's vision of despair – a darkness that wells up devastatingly out of the Marabar into the human world of feeling, personal values, and Western religion – is never quite lifted from the rest of the book, and is active to the very end of 'Temple' itself. But the negation is never complete, and remains vivifyingly at odds with many other temporary 'centres' of feeling. 'Caves' narrates the book's darkest spiritual descent, its most direct penetration into the lacuna that disrupts the syntax of ordinary human affairs. But it also contains the book's most sustained demonstration of the countering urge to go on building relationships and to seek to realize the possibilities of personal honesty and affection.

There is a striking hint of this counter-urge – significantly, it takes the form of implied feeling, lyrical and even erotic, rather than of argument – even within the preliminary chapter to the central section, which powerfully conveys the 'unspeakable' nature of the caves, their insane lack of proportion or of relation to anything else, their mind-extinguishing repetitiveness – timeless, lightless, infinitely self-mirroring. But the striking of a match within this black nothingness produces an unexpected effect: a momentary upsurge, through the prose, of quite contradictory colour, intimate sensuousness, and desire:

Immediately another flame rises in the depths of the rock and moves towards the surface like an imprisoned spirit; the walls of the circular chamber have been most marvellously polished. The two flames approach and strive to unite, but cannot, because one of them breathes air, the other stone. A mirror inlaid with lovely colours divides the lovers, delicate stars of pink and gray interpose, exquisite nebulae, shadings fainter than the tail of a comet or the midday moon, all the evanescent life of the granite, only here visible. Fists and fingers thrust above the advancing soil – here at last is their skin, finer than any covering acquired by the animals, smoother than windless water, more voluptuous than love. The radiance increases, the flames touch one another, kiss, expire. The cave is dark again, like all the caves. (pp. 138–9)

The flame does go out – and anyway, as is implicit, the romantic desire for unity may contain its own penchant for darkness and self-destruction. But, very positively, we are nevertheless left with an enriching sense-impression, a lyrical expression of motion-in-desire, and the image of an active will to go beyond the self that resists for a while the paralysing hollowness of the mirror and of the mirror's syllables: Kawa Dol.[33]

Throughout the expedition itself there is an interweaving of narrative that reflects this same variation in latent feeling. The preparations at the railway station are comic, vivacious, full of Aziz's nervous jokiness, energy and farce, chatter about people and things, unstable moments of affection and worry:

> She was perfect as always, his dear Mrs Moore. All the love for her he had felt at the mosque welled up again, the fresher for forgetfulness. There was nothing he would not do for her. He would die to make her happy.
>
> (p. 144)

Through this runs something different: the allusions to the continuing blighting effect on Adela and Mrs Moore of Godbole's 'queer little song' two weeks before; to Mrs Moore's growing mood ('vision or nightmare?') of disillusion with all matters of human relationship ('she felt this with such force that it seemed itself a relationship, itself a person, who was trying to take hold of her hand' – p. 148); to the train passing, in Adela's words, 'the place where my hyena was'; to the premonitory hidden message in the sound and motion of the train itself, which is without clear purpose or any accessibility to the 'well-equipped mind'. There is desire and fear, but no promise, no definition: only travelling, the endless taking of passage.

The approach to the caves themselves, stage by stage, is in one sense a deeper initiation into this 'message' of the train, the stripping away of qualities, dimensions, and values. The expected grand dawn is an insipid anti-climax; the hills are surrounded by a zone that seems 'infected with illusion', where the identity of objects becomes uncertain, nothing seems to have consequence or origin, and the heat makes the confused landscape 'jump as if it was being fried'. But even in the centre of this disorientation and etiolation – just before Mrs Moore penetrates the horror of this landscape, with its 'glutinous' sky and its 'bland and bald' precipice, and is overwhelmed by the ultimate reduction of life in the snaking 'ou-boum' echo of the cave – even here human conversation nevertheless creates its usual tenuous moment of 'civilization', like 'a desert flower'. Civilization, created by their chattering voices over tea and poached eggs in the very shadow of the lowering hills, consists partly of the human values of nobility, hospitality, and self-sacrifice evoked by Aziz's story of the Emperor Babur; partly of the dream of universal brotherhood associated by Adela with the Emperor Akbar ('how else are barriers to be broken down?'); and partly of the lucid narrative commentary, quintessentially Forsterian, that draws attention to how friendship is only to be built, and to go on being rebuilt, by conscious effort, by patience and recovery, and by the desire to understand:

> Like most Orientals, Aziz overrated hospitality, mistaking it for in-timacy, and not seeing that it is tainted with the sense of possession. It was only when Mrs Moore or Fielding was near him that he saw further, and knew that it is more blessed to receive than to give. These two had strange and beautiful effects on him – they were his friends, his for ever, and he theirs for ever; he loved them so much that giving and receiving became one. He loved them even better than the Hamidullahs, because he had sur-mounted obstacles to meet them, and this stimulates a generous mind. Their images remained somewhere in his soul up to his dying day, perma-nent additions. (p. 154)

It is only as an alternative to such comments, images, and tones of voice that the 'ou-boum' takes on its full force. Since it is 'entirely devoid of distinction' we have to perceive it largely in negative terms of its opposite, the human images and efforts that it reduces and destroys. And conversely, as part of the interplay of opposites, we grasp the emotions and qualities of 'civilization' only by their being silhouetted for us against this presence of a waiting emptiness.

Here, at the book's centre, words fail Mrs Moore; words, a little differently, fail Adela. And out of the failure of words, comes the descent of each woman into her cave – unleashing the verbal Babel of confusion, ill will, and only partial restitution that constitutes the trial and its aftermath, and the elliptical 'hundred voices' from 'God si love' to the 'No, not there' of the book's last words. Mrs Moore's despair comes to her only when she begins to write. Only when she starts her letter with the words, 'Dear Stella, Dear Ralph', does the full power of the caves overwhelm her. The echo drains words, and therefore drains concepts and values, of all content:

If one had spoken vileness in that place, or quoted lofty poetry, the comment would have been the same — 'ou-boum'. If one had spoken with the tongues of angels and pleaded for all the unhappiness and misunderstanding in the world, past, present, and to come . . . it would amount to the same, the serpent would descend and return to the ceiling.

Religion appeared, poor little talkative Christianity, and she knew that all its divine words from 'Let there be light' to 'It is finished' only amounted to 'boum'.   (pp. 160–1)

And in a trance of cold incommunicativeness and horror, Mrs Moore surrenders to that state where, in the chapter's dissolving last phrase, all her past words of human affection are 'no longer hers but the air's'. Between Adela and Aziz, correspondingly, words are half-hearted, talk quickly fades out in heat and detachment. Suddenly the word 'love' in Adela's mind reveals to her the falsity of her coming marriage, then is itself discarded — 'she wasn't convinced that love is necessary to a successful union' (p. 163). Verbal communication fails between her and her companion, who is shocked by her absent-minded question as to whether he has one wife or several. And separated by 'the wrong thing' having been said between them, each plunges, one in anger, one in boredom, into a different cave — and the narrative plunges straight into the disjunction of imagined violence, panic, and communal upheaval: voices raised sharply in questioning, voices that accuse, harangue, whine, and bluster. Mrs Moore's confrontation with the way words become mere air has been mystical and profound.[34] Adela's remains at a different level, more intermittent, even casual: more of a traumatic puzzle and a bad dream than a vision. And though both levels remain operative through the long narrative sequence centring on the trial, the emphasis now falls far more consistently than in any other sequence of the novel on the failure of coherence in social, political, and interpersonal terms, rather than on existential or epistemological dissolution — virtually the opposite case to *Heart of Darkness*, which progresses more directly from the political to the metaphysical. When Adela 'confesses' the truth in court the 'vision' of truth she has is inspired not mainly by any echo from another world — despite the unvoiced possibility of influence from the god-like punkah wallah or from having heard the distant chant of 'Esmiss Esmoor' – but by the very sound of her own voice at that moment and in that place. Under cross-questioning, she has a 'vision' of how it really was at the Marabar, but it is a vision of something solid, precise, and recovered, not of something touched by infinitude:

> The fatal day recurred, in every detail, but now she was of it and not of it at the same time, and this double relation gave it indescribable splendour. Why had she thought the expedition 'dull'? Now the sun rose again, the elephant waited, the pale masses of the rock flowed round her and presented the first cave; she entered, and a match was reflected in the polished walls – all beautiful and significant, though she had been blind to it at the time. Questions were asked, and to each she found the exact reply. (p. 230)

Correspondingly, the focus of the narrative now is on ethical and personal things: the dishonesty of groups and individuals, the wish in a few to be decent and honest, the detailed, drawn-out hesitations and confirmations of friendship between Fielding and Aziz, the Occidental lack of warmth in Adela and Fielding, and the perpetual grim farce, theatrically presented, of the English asserting themselves in arrogance and near-hysteria, and of the Indians half-rebelling, collapsing, turning against themselves – a farce of misdirected words and of endless voices reaching out noisily to one another, then recoiling in recrimination and misunderstanding.

So non-mystical does the register of narration become that when Godbole makes one of his brief and not-quite-congruous appearances, asking an incredulous Fielding about the success of the Marabar expedition and about a name for his new school at Mau, his arcane words concerning good and evil have quite the opposite effect to that of his 'funny little song' to Krishna at Fielding's ill-starred tea-party. There, his voice was succeeded by the most pregnant of silences: a moment of unparaphrasable and otherworldly meaning, cherished and endorsed by the narration. But here, within a more prosaic rhythm of narrative events and voice, Godbole's gnomic words strike us, and the exasperated Fielding, as lapidary and unhelpful:

> 'Good and evil are different, as their names imply. But, in my own humble opinion, they are both of them aspects of my Lord. He is present in the one, absent in the other, and the difference between presence and absence is great, as great as my feeble mind can grasp. Yet absence implies

presence, absence is not non-existence, and we are therefore entitled to repeat, "Come, come, come, come".' And in the same breath, as if to cancel any beauty his words might have contained, he added, 'But did you have time to visit any of the interesting Marabar antiquities?' (p. 186)

This cutting-out of the transcendental seems very conscious, even to the point of parody. Godbole is absurd here, rather than vatic, and his argument, in its compression and apparent irrelevance, sounds partly like an empty jingle.[35] Whatever rich suggestions may lie latent within it, there is no heightening here, no encouraging wave of feeling, to unlock them. And similarly, when the Marabar Hills appear briefly in the distance at sunset, as Fielding exits, half-pushed, from the club, the poetic moment – 'they were Monsalvat, Walhalla, the towers of a cathedral . . . At the moment they vanished they were everywhere, the cool benediction of the night descended, the stars sparkled, and the whole universe was a hill' – is soon highlighted for its negative aspect, its transience and inaccessibility, and is therefore as closed off to us as Godbole's visionary words of explanation. Fielding, seeing the hills, 'experienced nothing himself', and plunges instead into moral self-scrutiny and his characteristically prosaic mode of discontent, doubt, and frustration.

Of course the Marabar echo remains, and its lesson of a dimensionlessness beyond the ethical. For a while, until the sound of her own pragmatic voice gives her a self-restoring purchase on truth and factuality, Adela is haunted by it: 'The sound had spouted after her when she escaped, and was going on still like a river that gradually floods the plain . . . Evil was loose' (p. 200). And for Mrs Moore, the Marabar has struck a gong to mark her final alienation from the world of relationships, judgement, and words like 'duty', 'good', and 'love'. But what is brought out now is not so much the annihilating power of the despairing vision as its strange pettiness – as though to match the narrative's present focus on legal process, political dispute, and social and personal fumblings. This is 'the twilight of the double vision', the doubleness being the simultaneous perception of the horror of the universe and of its refusal to be grand – grandeur being a quality by which even an infinite horror can make at least some appeal to the human imagination. So the echo becomes a maggot rather than a serpent; Mrs Moore, in her twilight, grows merely irritable and unsympathetic; and only the enigmatic repetition of the place called Asirgarh ('I do not vanish') offers an undeveloped hope and presage as against the final shredding of Mrs Moore's India into a chaos of unvisitable, unrelated places, things without either limit or connection, and the jeering laughter, in farewell, of a thousand Bombay palm-trees.[36] But still unextinguished by that echoing laughter or by the heart of darkness from which it comes, rise up the insistent voices of two friends, one brown, one white, on the roof of the Nawab Bahadur's country mansion, seeking unsteadily to clear the passages to understanding and friendship – and after that, the voices of the old misunderstandings again, voices helplessly gesturing from East, from West.

It is hardly to be expected that *A Passage to India* will close in synthesis and harmony, even that concluding sense of aesthetic wholeness which consummates man's 'one orderly product', the work of art, and is allowed to this book by Frank Kermode, among many others.[37] Certainly, the reader's sense of the aesthetic is particularly appealed to in 'Temple', where repetition and transposition – always among Forster's favourite devices – draw attention to themselves, as if to confirm in terms of art the promise that was half-offered earlier by the semicircle Mrs Moore's train described round the arbitrary place name of Asirgarh, only forty miles from where 'Temple' is set. The section is brief – many readers have found it too brief for what it contains[38] – and hence its moments of formal interconnection and discovery are all the more heightened. It comes as the third of three relatedly named sections – from 'Mosque' to 'Caves' to 'Temple' – and even that can arouse expectations in the reader. Even the outline of a triad conventionally suggests a growing intensification, a climax and fusion of elements.[39] And finally, the fact that the section focuses so vividly on the description of a religious ritual enacting rebirth and divine intercession is in itself enough to heighten our awareness of fictional shaping all round, to alert us to any hint of the iconic it may contain, and to make us detect revelation in the very drawing-together of narrative motif and allusion.

On the other hand, the brevity of the section, even its over-brevity, seems also to act against the revelatory and the formally climactic, and, if anything, to endorse that other accompanying

198

note of separation, failure, and unceasing process. The combination of the poetically heightened − the boating-trip that ends in chaotic immersion and a half-comic entanglement of the human with (in clay image form) the divine is certainly as intense as anything in the book − and the perfunctory (especially the sketchiness of Stella and Ralph as figures) gives an instability to the conclusion that need not be seen as mere narrative deficiency, but rather as a final expression of tentativeness and fluctuation that fits the rhythm of the whole novel as clearly as it does the order of Godbole's Hindu ritual:[40]

And those 'imitations' [of Krishna], those 'substitutions', continued to flicker through the assembly for many hours, awaking in each man, according to his capacity, an emotion that he would not have had otherwise. No definite image survived; at the Birth it was questionable whether a silver doll or a mud village, or a silk napkin, or an intangible spirit, or a pious resolution had been born. Perhaps all these things! Perhaps none! Perhaps all birth is an allegory! Still, it was the main event of the religious year. It caused strange thoughts.   (p. 287)

In the cursory drawing of Ralph and Stella, too, there is something of this 'flickering' quality of half-expectation, a lack of 'definite image', which is therefore a cause of 'strange thoughts' beyond the verge and activity of the narration. Stella, according to the half-baffled Fielding, is 'after something', has 'queer troubles', and has now found some kind of benediction for her restlessness in the ritual crisis of Gokul Ashtami. And Ralph, who is beyond Fielding but behind Stella, strikes Aziz as being 'not so much a visitor as a guide'. Forster just avoids portentousness by the brevity of these allusions to the continued search, by these avatars of Mrs Moore, for the divine friend, the one answer, the ground of being. And by them he further unravels the closing edge of his narration and confirms the uncompleted process of passage that is his subject.

'Temple' reverberates, in its compressed state, with sanctity and with secularity. Throbbing Hindu drums, legends of a miracle-working Islamic saint, Godbole jigging, hills 'covered with temples like little white flames', ecstatic white-robed processions, consecrated dancers of 'imitations', a palanquin brimming with godhead − holiness at its most hectic surrounds and percolates the secular events of friends kept apart by acrimony and individuals separated yet not quite separated by race, and precipitates such moments of interfusion as where Aziz's sardonic cruelty towards Ralph is interrupted by the distant noise of the religious ceremonial:

'Aha, you know my name, I see. Yes, I am Aziz. No, of course your great friend Miss Quested did me no harm at the Marabar.'
Drowning his last words, all the guns of the State went off. A rocket from the jail garden gave the signal. The prisoner had been released, and was kissing the feet of the singers. Rose-leaves fall from the houses, sacred spices and cocoanut are brought forth . . . It was the halfway moment; the God had extended His temple, and paused exultantly. Mixed and confused in their passage, the rumours of salvation entered the Guest House.
(p. 305)

When such 'passage' occurs it brings an access of love; but when it is accompanied by the sense of repetition, it is not all gain. Memory may redeem – Aziz now hears, beneath the distant chant of 'Radakrishna Radakrishna', the old 'syllables of salvation that had sounded during his trial at Chandrapore'; and by implication the words are 'Esmiss Esmoor'. But repetition, in experience and also, as here, when imitated in the forms of art, may also suggest the treadmill of futility:

'Then you are an Oriental.' [Aziz] unclasped as he spoke, with a little shudder. Those words – he had said them to Mrs Moore in the mosque at the beginning of the cycle, from which, after so much suffering, he had got free. Never be friends with the English! Mosque, caves, mosque, caves. And here he was starting again. (p. 306)

Repetition – of certain casual words or feelings, or of a chant, or of a place-name ('Asirgarh') – can be a means of passage for 'rumours of salvation' by suggesting the presence of form in the universe; and can also satisfy the harmony-hunger, the form-seeking, of the reader. But, by the same paradox that *Howards End* sketched out, repetition also undercuts by reminding that in a universe of echoes nothing is new, and therefore nothing is redeemed; and that the symmetries of art, equally, can be an imprisoning imposition and a delusion.[41]

Where no passage is shown between sacred and secular, by repetition or by other means, the narration leaves the two in opposition, or pursuing their independent paths. Ronny Heaslop's letter to his new brother-in-law, blaming the Jews for the troubles of India, and Aziz's reaction to this instance of the terrible English closing their ranks, is a brilliantly sharp-edged datum from the novelist, and belongs very much to this world. And the account of Aziz's life since Marabar is prosaic, shrewd, and naturalistic, lucid with Forster's very particular light of satiric, rueful knowledgeability:

> His impulse to escape from the English was sound. They had frightened him permanently, and there are only two reactions against fright: to kick and scream on committees, or to retreat to a remote jungle, where the sahib seldom comes . . .
> Life passed pleasantly, the climate was healthy so that the children could be with him all the year round, and he had married again — not exactly a marriage, but he liked to regard it as one — and he read his Persian, wrote his poetry, had his horse, and sometimes got some shikar while the good Hindus looked the other way. (pp. 289–90)

But quite independent of that style, the sacred runs its own way:

> Seated at his ease, [the Rajah] could witness the Three Steps by which the Saviour ascended the universe to the discomfiture of Indra, also the death of the dragon, the mountain that turned into an umbrella, and the saddhu who (with comic results) invoked the God before dining. All culminated in the dance of the milkmaidens before Krishna, and in the still greater dance of Krishna before the milkmaidens, when the music and the musicians swirled through the dark blue robes of the actors into their tinsel crowns, and all became one. (p. 299)

And different still from either of these, in style and purport, is the full-blown symbolic event described with the kind of unqualified bravura (like the 'peal of thunder' itself) that Forster, no lavish symbolist, reserves for very special occasions in his novels:

> The boats had collided with each other.
> The four outsiders flung out their arms and grappled, and, with oars and pole sticking out, revolved like a mythical monster in the whirlwind. The worshippers howled with wrath or joy, as they drifted forward helplessly against the servitor. Who awaited them, his beautiful dark face expressionless, and as the last morsels melted on his tray it struck them.
> The shock was minute, but Stella, nearest to it, shrank into her husband's arms, then reached forward, then flung herself against Aziz, and her motions capsized them. They plunged into the warm, shallow water, and rose struggling into a tornado of noise. The oars, the sacred tray, the letters of Ronny and Adela, broke loose and floated confusedly. Artillery was fired, drums beaten, the elephants trumpeted, and drowning all an immense peal of thunder, unaccompanied by lightning, cracked like a mallet on the dome. (pp. 309–10)

Where so many elements, old and new, jostle in so brief a space, it is difficult to see 'Temple' as the reconciling third of a triad, or as offering some new synthesis. It rearranges the strands of 'Mosque' and 'Caves', which themselves were always in a state of movement and self-qualification, and concludes on the very pattern of 'God si love', half-making and half-retracting a statement. After the solemnity of ritual storm and immersion, the narrative ends in the loud conversation of two people squabbling yet seeking intimacy. There is a great bustle as Fielding and Aziz ride noisily through the trees, alive with assertiveness, regret, and the desire for some new thing, new politics, new forms, new friendship and love. The contradictory energies of the book run through them in this way, and run beyond them, beyond the last word. Mrs Moore, who saw too far into the inhuman shapelessness and conflating power of the infinite ('like evil or truth', as Marlow saw it), is also converted by Aziz's memory into the opposite of what she heard in the caves: she becomes something that recurs, but gives strength and affection rather than the 'ou-boum' of despair. Which sound is the more true is beyond the novel's scope to declare. Godbole was able to assert with confidence that good and evil, presence and absence, are both aspects of the one Lord; but his words were his own, half in obscurity; and the narrative does not have his confidence. The echo Mrs Moore heard was apparently the final *reductio* of life; but if she herself becomes an echo that is creative in the lives of others, both for the simple Hindus who transpose her into a cult figure, a minor god, and for Aziz, to whom she is the Friend, then reductiveness is far from total. The narrative ends on an echo: a small echo of, and within, those larger echoes. When the Hindu worshippers make their offering of human words and images to God, we are told:

Thus was He thrown year after year, and were others thrown – little images of Ganpati, baskets of ten-day corn, tiny tazias after Mohurram – scapegoats, husks, emblems of passage; a passage not easy, not now, not here, not to be apprehended except when it is unattainable: the God to be thrown was an emblem of that. (p. 309)

And an echo to 'not now, not here' is heard in the novel's very last words, which are the words of everything that is not human answering the human cry for friendship and the Friend:

the horses didn't want it — they swerved apart; the earth didn't want it, sending up rocks through which riders must pass single-file; the temples, the tank, the jail, the palace, the birds, the carrion, the Guest House, that came into view as they issued from the gap and saw Mau beneath: they didn't want it, they said in their hundred voices, 'No, not yet,' and the sky said, 'No, not there.' (p. 316)

The 'passage' to be attained 'not now, not here' has become the passage to be achieved 'not yet, not there': the two aspects of ineluctable opposition being those of time ('now', 'yet') and space ('here', 'there'). This contrived echo, for one thing, reminds us that we are still in the play of art: that consciousness and skill are shaping this experience, drawing our attention, building a delusive but necessary form of control upon the matter of chaos — like Fielding's view of the piazzetta of Venice against the muddle of India. But insofar as that shaped narrative also draws our attention by its echoes to the possible insubstantiality of form and repetition, its pleasing shape, like the dome of St Paul's in *Howards End*, changes into something different — something admonitory, ironic, and self-critical.[42] *Si monumentum requiris, circumspice* — look around, it says, at India. Also, where the conclusion in its series of negations might seem only to confirm division and tragedy, it takes away some of its finality by the unspoken ameliorating questions that are implied naturally within its own words: if 'not yet', then presumably some time; if 'not there', then presumably some other place. Within the final denials, that is, there lie possibilities that point beyond the verge of closure. And very differently, the words 'not yet' and 'not there' can be seen to confront us with time and space not just as obstacles to the spirit (whether permanent or temporary) but as the ultimate determining conditions of mimetic narrative itself. We are back where we began, with Godbole's ecstatic dance succumbing, as it must, to 'the rules of time', and to the rediscovery that his dance to God is taking place on a strip of red carpet in a stucco palace on a specific rainy day:

Not only from the unbeliever are mysteries hid, but the adept himself cannot retain them. He may think, if he chooses, that he has been with God, but, as soon as he thinks it, it becomes history, and falls under the rules of time. (p. 285)

And this discovery — the reader's, as he finally reads 'Not yet, not there', as well as Godbole's when he ceases to dance — contains a certain alleviation of Mrs Moore's annihilating echo and of the simple obstructiveness of the limits that hedge us in. It reminds us that narrative, for all its heightened perceptions in cave or temple that seem to transcend time and space, for all the music of the symbol and the revelatory *dérèglements* of syntax, spelling, and perception, for all that 'slight angle to the universe' that gives any novel its necessary indirection and surprise, also takes place as an act of will within a world of resistant limitation. Godbole's dance – his spectacles askew; everything indecorous, going contrariwise; attaining insight, losing it; loving, being betrayed; building on words, falling into the abysses of words; knowing and unknowing; above all performing, gesturing, trying out steps in the direction of the Friend who can only be glimpsed by indirection, and even then feared and not attained – Godbole has danced for more than *A Passage to India*. It is 1924, and seemingly a far cry from the elegant gesturing of *The Europeans*, or from *Lord Jim*, or even *Howards End*. It is the decade of *Women in Love*, *Ulysses*, and *To the Lighthouse*: new, and possibly even bolder, angles to the universe. But modernist narrative, in its dance of indeterminacy and contradiction, remains as much a performance as ever, and as unassuageable an anxiety and a breaking-strain as it was for James, Conrad, and Forster: an equivocal negotiation and testing-out that for its dynamism ultimately depends, like Godbole's dance, on the pressure between shaping and obstacle – between the words of passage and the rules of time.

Notes

Introduction: narratives of the brink

1. Preface to *The Portrait of a Lady*, reprinted in *The Art of the Novel*, ed. R. P. Blackmur, New York, 1934, p. 50.
2. For an extended, if rather mechanical, comparison of the two novelists see Elsa Nettels, *James and Conrad*, Athens, Ga., 1977. There are some suggestive points of comparison in Gabriel Pearson, 'The Novel to End all Novels: *The Golden Bowl*', *The Air of Reality: New Essays on Henry James*, ed. John Goode, 1972, pp. 301–62.
3. Dorothy Van Ghent writes, 'In James's *The Portrait of a Lady* we watched the creation of a self. In Conrad's austerely pessimistic work, the self stands already created, the possibilities are closed' (*The English Novel: Form and Function*, New York, 1961, p. 233).
4. In *Notes on Life and Letters*, 1905, pp. 13–23.
5. James's review of *Chance* is a model of voluminous equivocation, admiring the 'gallantry' with which Conrad faces up to the difficulties of narrative method he has willed on himself, but leaving a clear impression that the justification for so much effort remains questionable: 'It places Mr. Conrad absolutely alone as a votary of the way to do a thing that shall make it undergo most doing.' The ultimate irony is that James's whole essay, in his most self-proliferating late style, is itself a perfect example of what he cannot quite bring himself to criticize in *Chance* ('The New Novel', 1914, reprinted in *Selected Literary Criticism*, ed. M. Shapira, New York, 1965, pp. 311–42).
6. *The Secret Agent*, ed. Roger Tennant, Oxford, 1983, p. 309.
7. 'Gabriele D'Annunzio', *Notes on Novelists* (New York, 1969), p. 281.
8. Preface to *The Tragic Muse*, reprinted in *The Art of the Novel*, ed. R. P. Blackmur, p. 84; Preface to *The Spoils of Poynton*, *ibid.*, p. 122; letter to Wells, 10 July 1915, reprinted in *Henry James and H. G. Wells*, ed. L. Edel and G. N. Ray (London, 1958), p. 267.
9. The latter phrase occurs in chapter 19 of *The Tragic Muse*.
10. *The Art of the Novel*, p. 41.
11. *Ibid.*, p. 87.
12. *Ibid.*, p. 278.
13. Conrad's use of indirect narration, and especially of Marlow as narrator, has often been seen as influenced by James – see, e.g., Ian Watt, *Conrad in the Nineteenth Century*, 1980, pp. 200–14.
14. Trilling's phrase is in his *E. M. Forster* (1943), London, 1967, p. 17. For the 'mole', see John Beer quoting Leonard Woolf on Forster: 'He was strange, elusive, evasive . . . Lytton nicknamed him the Taupe, partly because of his faint physical resemblance to a mole, but principally because he seemed intellectually and emotionally to travel

205

unseen underground and every now and again pop up unexpectedly with some subtle observation or delicate quip which somehow or other he had found in the depths of the earth or of his own soul' (Beer, *The Achievement of E. M. Forster*, 1962, p. 173). See also P. N. Furbank's graphic description of Forster's conversational manner, full of 'odd hints and tiny surprises', and with a 'perpetual slight displacement of the expected emphasis' (*E. M. Forster: a Life*, ii. 1978, p. 293).

15. *Where Angels Fear to Tread*, Harmondsworth, 1968, pp. 87–8.
16. Forster described the incident in a letter: 'Bodily punishment [for Philip] . . . was necessary too: in fact the scene − to use a heavy word, and one I have only just thought of − was sacramental' (*A Garland for E. M. Forster*, ed. H. H. Anniah Gowda, Mysore, 1969, p. 128).
17. *Aspects of the Novel*, Harmondsworth, 1962, p. 162.
18. Cf. Alwyn Berland, who in his 'James and Forster: the Morality of Class' contrasts James's belief in the redeeming power of 'culture' with Forster's weaker reliance on 'pastoral' values (*Cambridge Journal*, VI, 1953, 259–80).
19. 'Joseph Conrad: A Note', *Abinger Harvest*, 1936, repr. 1965, pp. 159–60.
20. 'Language, Narrative, and Anti-Narrative', in *On Narrative*, ed. W. J. T. Mitchell, Chicago, 1981, p. 205.

Jamesian stages

1. *The Europeans*, Oxford, 1985, p. 120. Future page-references are to this, the World's Classics edition.
2. Nicola Bradbury interestingly analyses the expressive value of silence in James's later novels, and links it with the way his most mature fiction draws attention to its own processes − both functions, expression and textual foregrounding, being, in my reading of *The Europeans*, a feature even of his very early writing (*Henry James: the Later Novels*, Oxford, 1979, pp. 13–35). On a very different register − though still relevant − Merleau-Ponty's famous essay, 'Indirect Language and the Voices of Silence', is an enthralling philosophic disquisition on these issues of silence, physical gesture, and artistic expression (*Signs*, Evanston, 1964, pp. 39–83).
3. Still the most authoritative and sensitive reading of the novel, drawing together its surfaces and depths, is Richard Poirier, *The Comic Sense of Henry James*, New York, 1967 ('James uses the convention that the novel is an entertainment to complicate our experience and to control it. In a word, his stylistic fanciness exists to amuse us, to give us an aesthetic pleasure. But when we agree to that we have agreed to something of importance to the serious themes of the novel . . . James would like us to react favourably not only to literary but to social

manners, to artfulness in the expression of his characters as well as in his own style' – pp. 108–9).

4. See René Girard, *Deceit, Desire, and the Novel: Self and Other in Literary Structure*, Baltimore, 1965, for an extravagant and ingenious working-out of the role of desire in the form of the novel.

5. For a similar effect in Forster see below, p. 158 (cf. James on Trollope: 'He took a suicidal satisfaction in reminding the reader that the story he was telling was only, after all, a make-believe' – 'Anthony Trollope', 1883, repr. in *The Future of the Novel*, ed. L. Edel, New York, 1956, p. 247).

6. Richard Poirier is particularly interesting on the role-playing of Eugenia, *The Comic Sense*, pp. 112–30.

7. Above all, one can find in the narrative something more than the pictorialism and naturalism that have traditionally resulted in half-hearted praise like Oscar Cargill's – '*The Bostonians* is as satisfactory as any French naturalistic novel' (*The Novels of Henry James*, New York, 1961, p. 137) – or disparagement like that of Peter Buitenhuis: 'As a result of James's lack of emotional commitment to his characters ... the novel does not quite live up to its own high promise. The whole is less than the sum of its parts' (*The Grasping Imagination: the American Writings of Henry James*, Toronto, 1970, p. 159).

8. *Autobiography*, chapter 5.

9. Hawthorne's *Blithedale Romance* has long been recognized as one of the sources of *The Bostonians*, and, like 'Ethan Brand', shows the perversion of feeling by idealism and by intellectual manipulativeness, particularly in the characters of Zenobia and Westervelt. See Marius Bewley, *The Complex Fate*, London, 1952, pp. 11–30.

10. Irving Howe, in quite the best discussion of *The Bostonians*, describes 'the perception that lies at the heart of the novel: that somehow, for reasons he cannot quite grasp, the proportions and rhythms of life in America have gone askew ... the idea of what it means to be human had come into question. All that we have since associated with industrial society was moving into sight – call it depersonalization or *anomie*, the sapping of individuality or the loss of tradition' (*Politics and the Novel*, Cleveland, 1957, p. 190). Lionel Trilling sees *The Bostonians* as James's de Tocqueville-like observation of 'the beginnings of sexual disorientation of America ... the sign of a general diversion of the culture from the course of nature' (*The Opposing Self*, New York, 1959, p. 111).

11. *The Liberal Imagination*, New York, 1957, pp. 58–61.

12. *The Bostonians*, ed. Charles R. Anderson, 1984, pp. 251–2. Future page-references are to this, the Penguin edition, which reprints the first book edition of 1886.

13. Cf. Irving Howe: 'Basil Ransom ... is treated by James with a cool and detached irony ... Ransom is as deeply entangled with his

ideology as Olive with hers . . . This, indeed, is the great stroke of *The Bostonians*: that everything, even aspects of private experience supposedly inviolable, is shown to be infected with ideology.' (*Politics and the Novel*, pp. 196–8). Trilling, more sweeping and less subtle in his reading of the character – and of the novel – than Howe, makes nothing of any irony against Ransom: '[Ransom] is akin to Yeats, Lawrence, and Eliot in that he experiences his cultural fears in the most personal way possible, translating them into sexual fear, the apprehension of the loss of manhood' (*The Opposing Self*, p. 113).

14. F. W. Dupee writes crisply, 'The implacably sunny Verena with her queer gift, the wonder of Boston, is a wraith out of Hawthorne (with some assistance from Daudet's *L'Évangéliste*), and not interesting.' (*Henry James*, New York, 1965, p. 129). But cf. David Howard's attractive defence of her as 'a great creation' in '*The Bostonians*', *The Air of Reality: New Essays on Henry James*, ed. John Goode, 1972, pp. 60–80.

15. *Henry James: Letters*, ed. Leon Edel, vol. 3, 1981, p. 121 (letter of June 13, 1886).

16. Cf. Irving Howe, who finds that James's 'free and happy release of aggressive feelings' in *The Bostonians* makes the prose '[race] forward with a spontaneous sharpness and thrust' (*Politics and the Novel*, pp. 184–5).

17. Peter Buitenhuis calls the visit to Memorial Hall 'the central episode of the novel . . . a nodal point' (*The Grasping Imagination*, pp. 147–8).

18. '[Verena's] state of moral tension is one born of a reality in which the truth of experience is seen to be plural rather than single. The union between Basil and Verena telescopes James's vision of the character of reality as one emerging out of experience itself. As such, reality is conceived of as dynamic and changing rather than static. It stands for life in actuality and potentiality. It means freedom to live.' It also means, in William McMurray's term, 'pragmatism'. ('Pragmatic Realism in *The Bostonians*', in *Henry James: Modern Judgements*, ed. Tony Tanner, 1968, p. 164).

19. Last sentence of *Little Dorrit*.

20. The interested reader is referred to my account of *The Spoils of Poynton*, which is of relevance to this section, in *Henry James: the Drama of Fulfilment*, Oxford, 1975.

21. Tony Tanner's excellent account of the novel brings out its elements of the 'phantasmagoric' and the 'comic-grotesque', associating them with the half-formed nature of Maisie's own perceptiveness (*The Reign of Wonder: Naive 'y and Reality in American Literature*, Cambridge, 1965, pp. 278–98).

22. See for example James's review of *John Gabriel Borkman*, published in the same year as *Maisie*, 1897 (reprinted in *The Scenic Art: Notes on Acting and the Drama, 1872–1901*, ed. Allan Wade, New York, 1957, pp. 291–4).

23. *What Maisie Knew*, 1897, pp. 113–14 (chapter 15). Future page-references are to this, the original edition. Both the Penguin and the World's Classics editions are based on the revised New York Edition, and since I have preferred the earlier editions elsewhere, it seems best to refer to the 1897 version but in this case also to give chapter references for the convenience of readers.

24. Philip Weinstein relates this 'shop-front' allusion to two other 'plate glass' images, and reads them as expressing how Maisie is always 'at a remove' from experience (*Henry James and the Requirements of the Imagination*, Cambridge, Mass., 1971, p. 83).

25. Nicola Bradbury writes, of this change of scene, 'It is significant that this takes place in France, for the geographical move, besides establishing appropriate social conditions in the moral world, with the removal from English codes of decorum, also suggests how the child's view of the world changes, becoming "decentralized", with maturity.' (*Henry James: the Later Novels*, Oxford, 1979, p. 22).

26. It is also compatible with James's famous account of the anti-absolutist nature of his own upbringing: 'Thus we had ever the amusement, since I can really call it nothing less, of hearing morality, or moralism, as it was more invidiously worded, made hay of in the very interest of character and conduct; these things suffering much, it seemed, by their association with the conscience – the *conscious* conscience – the very home of the literal, the haunt of so many pedantries' (*A Small Boy and Others*, New York, 1913, p. 216).

27. See Laurence Holland's stimulating comparison between the style of Renaissance Mannerism and James's use of distortion and nervous histrionics (*The Expense of Vision: Essays on the Craft of Henry James*, Princeton, 1964, pp. 57–89); and also Viola Hopkins Winner's succinct discussion of James and Mannerism ('. . . an art of preciosity, of intricate asymmetrical patterns leading to no final solution, of subjects treated from unexpected angles, of "rigid formality and deliberate disturbance, bareness and over-decoration"'), in *Henry James and the Visual Arts*, Charlottesville, 1970, pp. 89–93 (the internal quotation is from Nikolaus Pevsner).

28. E.g. see above, p. 50 and below, p. 77.

29. On the sexual side see, for example, J. C. McCloskey, 'What Maisie Knows: a Study of Childhood and Adolescence', *American Literature*, XXXVI, 1965, 485–513; and H. W. Wilson, 'What *Did* Maisie Know?', *College English*, XVII, 1956, 279–82.

30. *The Golden Bowl*, 1905, repr. 1963, pp. 289–91 (Part 4, Ch. 1). It seems unnecessary to give actual page-references throughout the following analysis of the book's last chapter, which is itself only eleven pages long and is analysed in sequence. I have followed the text of the first English edition as published, then reprinted, by Methuen; The World's Classics also follows this text, but the Penguin follows the revised New York Edition of 1909.

31. On this exchange Ruth Yeazell writes, 'With language – "the right word" – the conscious self resists and controls the psyche's unspoken and only half-conscious demands' (*Language and Knowledge in the Late Novels of Henry James*, Chicago, 1976, p. 20).

32. John Bayley, after similarly describing the momentary attractiveness of the Prince's wish to come clean, wittily glosses Maggie's reproof – 'with her dumpy and somehow Victorian majesty' (*The Characters of Love: a Study in the Literature of Personality*, 1960, p. 234).

33. See, for example, my own account of *The Tragic Muse* in *Henry James: the Drama of Fulfilment*, Oxford, 1975, pp. 79–126.

34. Cf. F. O. Matthiessen, 'James's neglect of the cruelty in such a cord, silken though it be, is nothing short of obscene.' (*Henry James: the Major Phase*, New York, 1963, p. 100). Critics of *The Golden Bowl* have traditionally fallen into two camps: pro- and anti-Verver. For a convenient listing of those on each side, see Ruth Yeazell, *Language and Knowledge in the Late Novels of Henry James*, Chicago, 1976, pp. 131–2. See also below, p. 90, and n. 37.

35. Cf. a rather baffled Philip Weinstein, who comments on this same passage: 'this coyness, or unwillingness, or confusion is what most grates' (*Henry James and the Requirements of the Imagination*, Cambridge, Mass., 1971, p. 194). Dorothea Krook, more firmly, sees the '*le compte y est*' ambiguity as a demonstration of the Jamesian doubleness that catches the doubleness of life and is the essence of his vision (*The Ordeal of Consciousness in Henry James*, Cambridge, 1967, pp. 322, 324). For the similar cut-off, see above, pp. 19–21.

36. Ruth Yeazell, describing what she sees as the Donne-like use of such conceits in *The Golden Bowl*, writes: 'The strangeness of these vehicles resembles the strangeness of dreams – at once distant and bizarre, seemingly far removed from ordinary life, and startlingly immediate in their implications. Denied the ordinary dreams of sleep, James's characters appear to find in their waking imagery an equivalent release' (*Language and Knowledge in the Late Novels of Henry James*, p. 46).

37. Marianna Torgovnick, opposing the 'redemptive' readings of the novel, and analysing this final scene at some length, suggests that Maggie 'has re-won the Prince by adopting and by meeting his aesthetic standards' (*Closure in the Novel*, Princeton, 1981, pp. 154–5). Sally Sears, going distinctly beyond this, sees Maggie by the end as having become 'more than Charlotte's equal' in manipulativeness and pure will: 'in some ways the last part of the book, under Maggie's sponsorship, resembles a sado-masochistic nightmare worthy of the dark dreams of Poe' (*The Negative Imagination: Form and Perspective in the Novels of Henry James*, Ithaca, N.Y., 1968, pp. 210–11). And just as lurid is Marianne Hirsch: 'Maggie is at best a Satanic Christ' (*Beyond the Single Vision: Henry James, Michel Butor, Uwe*

Johnson (York, S.C., 1981, p. 72). For an older, but still helpful survey of the wildly opposing interpretations of Maggie, see Walter Wright, 'Maggie Verver: Neither Saint nor Witch', *Nineteenth Century Fiction*, XII, 1957, 59–71.

38. J. C. Rowe writes, 'The singleness of Amerigo's final vision contrasts sharply with Maggie's refusal to look . . . In this very last moment she seems to give up her power, only to awaken to the reality of her nightmare. The marriages have been preserved by emptying them of all possible meaning.' (*Henry Adams and Henry James: the Emergence of a Modern Consciousness*, Ithaca, N.Y., 1976, p. 223).

39. E.g. R. P. Blackmur, *Studies in Henry James*, New York, 1983, pp. 228–9.

Conrad's breaking strains

1. Cf. Jacques Berthoud, who sees different kinds of compassion being contrasted in the tale, and therefore no paradox (*Joseph Conrad: the Major Phase*, Cambridge, 1978, pp. 33–4). Throughout his lucid and strongly argued book, Berthoud takes issue with the 'panic' view of Conrad.

2. *The Nigger of the 'Narcissus'*, ed. Jacques Berthoud, Oxford, 1984, pp. 162–3.

3. See Robert Foulkes's interesting analysis of the unstable – or destabilizing – rhetoric of the tale in 'Postures of Belief in *The Nigger of the "Narcissus"*', *Modern Fiction Studies*, XVII, 1971, 249–63: 'the reader is left with two impulses at the end of the narrative. One leads him to doubt the celebration of a seaman narrator . . . The other leads him to follow the narrating voice as it becomes excited to the pitch of high rhetoric . . . Both impulses are valid; to deny either distorts the text. One has its source in the naturalistic rendering of life at sea, the other in the hallucinatory world evoked by a fulness of metaphor.'

4. *Youth, Heart of Darkness, The End of the Tether*, ed. Robert Kimbrough, Oxford, 1984, p. 98. Future page-references are to this, the World's Classics edition, which reprints the first book edition of 1902.

5. This is basically how C. F. Burgess sees him: while emphasizing the aspect of Fool, Kurtz's court-fool, he sees the Russian as a prefigurement of Kurtz and of Marlow's horrified judgement of Kurtz ('Conrad's Pesky Russian', *Nineteenth Century Fiction*, XVIII, 1963, 189–93). Ian Watt comments, a little heavily, 'The Russian harlequin thus represents his century's innocent but fateful surrender to that total Faustian unrestraint which believes that everything is justified if it "enlarges the mind"' (*Conrad in the Nineteenth Century*, p. 228). John W. Canario sees the harlequin as 'a representation of aboriginal

man', an atavistic satyr; but also, much more plausibly, as personifying Marlow's own 'lost innocence and boyish love of adventure' ('The Harlequin in *Heart of Darkness*', *Studies in Short Fiction*, IV, 1967, 225–33).

6. 'Reality in this story exists not in the positive but in the negative, for it is all that human disciplines cannot reach, all that lies beyond these disciplines within the center of a man, of a wilderness, and, as Marlow implies, of experience itself. Language too, as all resources of the human imagination, fails in attempting to discover the meaning of Kurtz and of experience' – James Guetti, *The Limits of Metaphor: a Study of Melville, Conrad and Faulkner*, Ithaca, N.Y., 1967, p. 59 (Guetti's is still one of the best accounts of the tale). The interchangeability of 'evil' and 'truth' is reminiscent – like so much else in Conrad – of Melville: see, for example, Leon F. Seltzer, *The Vision of Melville and Conrad: a Comparative Study*, Athens, Ga., 1970; also Guetti, *Limits of Metaphor*. See also below, p. 150 and n. 43.

7. Ian Watt provides something of a compendium – a bulky compendium – on the interpretative problems of the tale and on its techniques, particularly its relations to Symbolism and Expressionism (*Conrad in the Nineteenth Century*, pp. 126–253).

8. H. M. Daleski, though uneasy about the success of the scene with the Intended, sees it in 'redemptive' terms: 'In accepting his mortality, what Marlow in effect accepts is an ultimate loss of self . . . the loss that is a finding . . . it is this dimension of being [the dark reality beneath the cloak of time] that Marlow was intended symbolically to accept and incorporate in a unified self when he pulls himself together and lies' (*Joseph Conrad: the Way of Dispossession*, 1977, pp. 75–6). See also Ian Watt, pp. 241–4 (including footnote 19).

9. See above, p. 73.

10. Cf. George Williams, who sees a moral change in the 'I' narrator repeated formally and emblematically in the turn of the tide producing 'the 180° swing of the *Nellie*' ('The Turn of the Tide in *Heart of Darkness*', *Modern Fiction Studies*, IX, 1963, 171–2).

11. For example, H. M. Daleski (surely unconvincingly?) writes, 'this section of the novel sometimes gives the impression of being an uninspired repetition of "Heart of Darkness"' (*Joseph Conrad: the Way of Dispossession*, p. 98); F. R. Leavis dismisses it as 'eked out' and 'decidedly thin' (*The Great Tradition*, New York, 1954, p. 231); and even Ian Watt sees it 'as a marked falling off' from the first part (*Conrad in the Nineteenth Century*, p. 347).

12. *Lord Jim*, ed. Cedric Watts and Robert Hampson, Harmondsworth, 1986, p. 172. Future page-references are to this, the Penguin edition, which is based on the first British book edition of 1900.

13. Dorothy Van Ghent – as always – writes imaginatively and powerfully on *Lord Jim*: 'Jim is one of the most living characters in fiction,

although his presentation is by indirection, through Marlow's narrative; that indirection is itself uniquely humanizing, for we see him only as people can see each other, ambivalently and speculatively' (*The English Novel: Form and Function*, New York, 1961, pp. 229–30). See also Ian Watt's analysis of what he sees as the major narrative techniques in *Lord Jim*, which he calls 'delayed decoding', 'symbolic deciphering', 'thematic apposition', 'the use of time', and '*progression d'effet*' (*Conrad in the Nineteenth Century*, pp. 270–310).

14. Ian Watt provides a useful summary, *Conrad in the Nineteenth Century*, pp. 322–3.

15. For a different, and rather less sympathetic, reading of the Stein episode, see Daleski, pp. 95–7 ('Stein's sea is productive of a number of red herrings.'). Cf. Frederick Karl, 'Stein's presence, then, is truly the destructive element, for his multifarious activities – his controlled romanticism, his grasp of reality, for example – allow alternatives to Jim's compulsiveness, and the alternatives, had Jim acted upon them and still failed, would have provided the stuff of real tragedy.' (*A Reader's Guide to Joseph Conrad*, New York, 1960, p. 131). See also Albert Guerard's balanced account of Stein (Guerard's whole study of *Lord Jim* is particularly strong) in *Conrad the Novelist*, Cambridge, Mass., 1958, pp. 164–6.

16. Donald Yelton comments on the preponderance of 'spectral imagery' and images of 'cosmic perspective' in *Lord Jim*: 'a sort of saturation of imagery and vocabulary, a rhetorical soaking in solution that might as accurately be termed "metaphysical" as metaphorical' (*Mimesis and Metaphor: an Enquiry into the Genesis and Scope of Conrad's Symbolic Imagery*, The Hague, 1967, p. 171).

17. See Paul Ricoeur's highly intricate and theoretic analysis of the relation between the reader and himself in front of such textual sequence in, for example, 'The Hermeneutical Function of Distanciation', *Interpretation Theory*, Fort Worth, 1976.

18. For a rather different analysis of the dynamic indeterminacy of *Lord Jim*, see Hillis Miller's surprisingly pragmatic and untheoretic study, *Fiction and Repetition: Seven English Novels*, Oxford, 1982, pp. 22–41. E.g., 'The novel is made up of recurrences in which each part of the story has already happened repeatedly when the reader first encounters it, either in someone's mind, or in someone's telling, or in the way it repeats other similar events in the same person's life or in the lives of others. The temporal structure of the novel is open. *Lord Jim* is a chain of repetitions, each event referring back to others which it both explains and is explained by, while at the same time it prefigures those which will occur in the future. Each exists as part of an infinite regression and progression within which the narrative moves back and forth discontinuously across time seeking unsuccessfully some motionless point in its flow' (p. 34).

19. Royal Roussel, for example, sees this opening 'revelation of the darkness' as a portentous symbol and concept that governs the rest of the novel (*The Metaphysics of Darkness*, Baltimore, 1971, pp. 109–31). Robert Penn Warren, in an eloquent essay, also sees the opening as the book's governing 'fable' – 'of man lost in the blankness of nature' (in *Joseph Conrad: a Critical Symposium*, ed. R. W. Stallman, E. Lansing, 1960, pp. 209–27).

20. E.g. Thomas Moser, *Joseph Conrad: Achievement and Decline*, Cambridge, Mass., 1957, p. 43; and Douglas Hewitt, *Conrad: a Reassessment*, 1975, pp. 66–8. A valuable analysis of the chronology of *Nostromo*, and a good defence of its narrative 'surprises' and disruptions, is provided by Keith Carabine in his introduction to the World's Classics edition (Oxford, 1984) – e.g. pp. xiii–xix and xxv–xxx.

21. *Nostromo*, Oxford, 1984, pp. 26–7. Future page-references are to this, the World's Classics edition, which is based on the Dent Collected Edition of 1947.

22. Cf. C. B. Cox, who emphasizes the 'pervading sense of human insubstantiality' in this same description (*Joseph Conrad: the Modern Imagination*, 1974, pp. 62–3).

23. See Cox's analysis of this passage, pp. 60–1 ('In this short scene . . . our visual perspective rapidly changes, and this reflects shifting attitudes to man, society and Nature. The sequence is "fluid" . . .').

24. E.g. Cox, p. 70.

25. See Albert Guerard: 'there is generally a marked discrepancy between what Decoud does and says and is, and what the narrator or omniscient author says about him . . . Conrad may be condemning Decoud for a withdrawal and skepticism more radical than Decoud ever shows; which are, in fact, Conrad's own' (*Conrad the Novelist*, p. 199).

26. Irving Howe, writing from his committedly moral and political viewpoint, comments trenchantly: 'One cannot help wondering whether Conrad's scorn is due entirely to Hirsch's being a coward or perhaps, a trifle, to his not being a gentleman. And one cannot help wondering, as well, whether Conrad does not occasionally indulge in the Elizabethan game of having his Jew sweat' (*Politics and the Novel*, Cleveland, 1957, p. 112).

27. H. M. Daleski makes a briefly suggestive comparison between Gould and Gerald Crich in *Women in Love* (*Joseph Conrad: the Way of Dispossession*, p. 219, n. 16) – his account makes Gould central to the book.

28. This famous summing-up by Mrs. Gould appears as 'material interest' in the Collected Edition but is noted as a misprint for 'interests' by Keith Carabine in the new World's Classics edition, xxxiv.

29. Robert Penn Warren, for example, though trying to avoid the 'gnomic' summing-up, stresses the book as a 'fable', and Conrad as being 'in the fullest sense of the term a philosophical novelist' (in

Joseph Conrad: A Critical Symposium, p. 227).
30. The Art of the Novel, ed. R. P. Blackmur, p. 48.
31. Under Western Eyes, ed. Jeremy Hawthorn, Oxford, 1983, p. 336.
Future page-references are to this, the World's Classics edition, which
is based on the Dent Collected Edition, 1946.
32. Frank Kermode provides an ingenious and subtle reading of the
'awkwardnesses' and self-subverting doublenesses of this text in
'Secrets and Narrative Sequence', in On Narrative, ed. W. J. T. Mitchell, Chicago, 1981, pp. 79–97. In another essay, Kermode says that
Under Western Eyes, by confirming 'the fallibility of all that it seems
to assert' provides in its last pages 'not closure but a hermeneutic
booby-trap' ('Novel and Narrative', in The Theory of the Novel: New
Essays, ed. John Halperin, New York, 1974, p. 173).
33. Donald Yelton, in an effective account of what he calls, in Under
Western Eyes, 'the most complex and closely woven texture of
thematic imagery' in all of Conrad's novels, emphasizes the extraordinary prevalence of 'eye' and 'vision' imagery (Mimesis and
Metaphor, pp. 199–201).
34. 'The terrible plight summed up by Councillor Mikulin's question
"Where to?" is not that of a man to whom all other lands are barred,
but rather that of a man condemned to perceive the whole world
through a fractured and aggrieved mind' (Tony Tanner, 'Nightmare
and Complacency: Razumov and the Western Eye', Critical Quarterly,
IV, 1962, 197–214). Tanner's account of Razumov is a particularly
vivid one.
35. For a Derrida-influenced elaboration on this theme, see Avrom
Fleishman, 'Speech and Writing in Under Western Eyes', in Joseph
Conrad: a Celebration, ed. Norman Sherry, 1976, pp. 119–28.
36. On Under Western Eyes and Dostoevsky see, e.g., Douglas Hewitt,
Conrad a Re-Assessment, Cambridge, 1952, pp. 126–8; and Andrzej
Busje, 'Rhetoric and Ideology in Conrad's Under Western Eyes', in
Joseph Conrad: a Celebration, ed. Norman Sherry, 1976, pp. 110–16.
37. Cf. Frederick Karl, who finds the symbolism of the storm 'an affront
to the serious reader', and the whole conclusion a 'hash' (A Reader's
Guide to Joseph Conrad, New York, 1960, pp. 226–7).
38. Cf. Tony Tanner: 'Conrad's characters live in a remorselessly ter-
restrial world. Razumov's reward is limited to that peace which lies on
the other side of nightmare and which is perhaps all we can hope for
in an unredeemed world' ('Nightmare and Complacency: Razumov
and the Western Eye', Critical Quarterly, IV, 213).
39. Donald Yelton, in a very full treatment of the story, takes issue with
Albert Guerard's tendency to see it, too simply, as an allegory of personal crisis and neurosis: '[Conrad] may . . . give us an overplus of
evoked meaning – or an undercurrent of suggestion – but he does
not give it to us at the expense of the narrative surface' (Mimesis and

Metaphor, p. 301). Yelton is particularly suggestive in his comments on Ransome, and on the story's Baudelairean and Coleridgean features.

40. *The Shadow-Line*, ed. Jacques Berthoud, Harmondsworth, 1986, p. 48. Future page-references are to this, the Penguin edition, which is based on the Heinemann Collected Edition, 1921.

41. Cf. Jacques Berthoud, '. . . the tone of the narration is confidently natural from beginning to end. Its language inhabits a temperate region between colloquialism and artifice; in its clarity, sobriety, energy, and ease, it is systematically unaffected and spontaneously controlled . . . *The Shadow-Line* . . . is nothing if not a school of reality.' (Introduction to *The Shadow-Line*, Harmondsworth, 1986, p. 13).

42. Edward Said's laboriously 'biographical' reading of the tale would go even further at this point: 'We are witnessing also the decomposition of Conrad's old individuality – all his personal history of poses, insecurity, fear, and shame – and, with it, the decomposition of modern Europe' (*Joseph Conrad and the Fiction of Autobiography*, Cambridge, Mass., 1966, p. 192).

43. In atmosphere as well as in theme *The Shadow-Line* seems one of the most Melville-like of Conrad's works, and in its emphasis on darkness, perpetual enigma, and failed communication is especially reminiscent of *Benito Cereno* and *Bartleby*.

44. F. R. Leavis, in an enthusiastic essay, writes: 'And I would remind you that it is on that parting with Ransome that the tale ends, and exhort you to attend very closely to the particulars of the parting. Ransome, who has behaved with recklessly selfless devotion throughout the ordeal, now fiercely demands his discharge: "I have a right". He wants, and wants with a fierce intensity, to live. And he, the exquisitely-mannered ("the man positively had grace") doesn't at first notice the Captain's hand held out for the parting hand-shake' ('The Shadow-Line', in *Anna Karenina and Other Essays*, 1967, p. 110).

The Forster angle

1. 'The poetry of C. P. Cavafy', *Pharos and Pharillon*, 1923 (quoted in P. N. Furbank, *E. M. Forster: A Life*, vol. 2, 1978, pp. 32–3).

2. *Howards End*, ed. Oliver Stallybrass, Harmondsworth, 1983, pp. 331–2. Future page-references are to this, the Penguin edition, which reprints the Abinger Edition of 1973.

3. Cf. Peter Burra, 'at the very end, as tragedy goes off into the past. . . "Nothing has been done wrong", she says to him with the final wisdom of acceptance. For love, she sees, is a greater thing than opinions' ('The Novels of E. M. Forster', 1934, reprinted in the Macmillan Casebook for *A Passage to India*, ed. Malcolm Bradbury,

1970, p. 71). Disconcertingly, Forster said of Burra's essay, 'Burra saw exactly what I was trying to do' (quoted in the same Casebook, p. 61).

4. The stance is much commented-on: see, e.g., Kinley Roby, 'Irony and the Narrative Voice in *Howards End*', *Journal of Narrative Technique*, II, 1972, 119; Francis Gillen, '*Howards End* and the Neglected Narrator', *Novel*, III, 1970, 139–52; J. L. Van De Vyvere, 'The Mediatorial Voice of the Narrator in E. M. Forster's *Howards End*', *Journal of Narrative Technique*, VI, 1976, 204–16; and Paul R. Rivenberg, 'The Role of the Essayist–Commentator in *Howards End*', in *E. M. Forster: Centenary Revaluations*, ed. J. S. Herz and R. K. Martin, 1982, pp. 167–76.

5. See above, pp. 29–30.

6. See above, p. 102.

7. *The Achievement of E. M. Forster*, 1962, pp. 187–9. Leavis's criticism is in *The Common Pursuit*, 1952, pp. 271–2.

8. See above, p. 94.

9. See above, pp. 67–8.

10. See J. S. Martin on the novel's 'many references to seas, rivers, and tides', in *E. M. Forster: the Endless Journey*, Cambridge, 1976, pp. 118–20.

11. The phrase is resonant enough to reappear in Margaret's mind when she later enters Howards End for the first time. Forster, with a fine discretion, slightly misquotes it: 'Now Helen came to her mind, scrutinizing half Wessex from the ridge of the Purbeck downs, and saying: "You will have to lose something". She was not so sure . . . she thought of the map of Africa; of empires; of her father; of the two supreme nations, streams of whose life warmed her blood, but, mingling, had cooled her brain' (pp. 201–2). The connection of the threatened 'loss' with what the landscape suggested in Purbeck is beautifully expanded here – a perfect example of how Forster can use the '*petite phrase*' in the way he admired in Proust (*Aspects of the Novel*, Harmondsworth, 1962, pp. 166–8).

12. An example of the more typical criticism that the instabilities of this passage *are* simply confusion and self-contradiction and not a complicated dialectic is K. W. Gransden's comment: 'the over-writing, the over-ripeness here . . is too like that of a travel advertisement. And the swelling optimism of such words as "but the cliffs of Freshwater it will never touch" is belied by numerous other passages in the book which say the opposite and in which the author's critical and prophetic sense proves a surer judge than his "poetic" one' (*E. M. Forster*, 1962, pp. 58–9).

13. On some of the general implications of this topic, see Morse Peckham, 'Order and Disorder in Fiction' (1966), in *The Triumph of Romanticism*, Columbia, S.C., 1970, pp. 290–317 – e.g., 'I come, therefore, to my final paradox that the telling of stories, and the listening to

stories, is motivated both by the desire for order, for cognitive and perceptual and interpretive continuity, and by the desire for disorder, for cognitive and perceptual and interpretive discontinuity . . . Fiction . . . satisfies our desire for semantic order we cannot experience in our everyday and endless and hopeless task of trying to link language surely and permanently to the world, and this satisfaction permits us to encounter a non-semantic disorder which trains us to endure the slippery instability of the real world, and of interpretation, and of language itself' (p. 317). See also below, on *A Passage to India*, pp. 203–4.

14. John Colmer sees the echo rather differently, and more categorically, by picking on the subject of the photograph in each case: 'it is worth noticing that [Jackie] and the upper middle-class Dolly are drawn into close parallel by similar incidents relating to broken photographs . . . We are thus made to see that both are silly coarse women; class is largely irrelevant' (*E. M. Forster: the Personal Voice*, 1975, p. 96).

15. The effect of 'repetition' in fictional plotting has given rise to much recent narratological and post-structuralist theorizing, often taking Vico, Kierkegaard, Heidegger, or Freud as a starting-point. Not untypical is Peter Brooks's Freud-influenced account in 'Repetition, Repression, and Return: *Great Expectations* and the Study of Plot', *New Literary History*, XI, 1979–80, 503–26. E.g., 'Repetition as return speaks as a textual version of the death instinct, plotting the text, beyond the seeming dominance of the pleasure principle, towards its proper end, imaging this end as necessarily a time before the beginning' (p. 514). See also J. Hillis Miller, *Fiction and Repetition: Seven English Novels*, Oxford, 1982; and Paul Ricoeur, 'Narrative Time', in *On Narrative*, ed. W. J. T. Mitchell, Chicago, 1981, pp. 165–86. On 'repetition' in *A Passage to India*, see below, p. 200, and n. 41.

16. On similar effects see also above, pp. 104–5, and p. 114 (and n. 17).

17. *The Journal of Katherine Mansfield*, 1954, p. 120 (entry for May, 1917).

18. Cf. Alan Wilde, among many others, who finds the two aspects of the book unsatisfactorily fused, the symbolic level pointing to harmony, the realist level pointing to failure and unease (*Art and Order: a Study of E. M. Forster*, 1965, pp. 100–23). Cf., also, more straightforwardly 'optimistic' readings of the novel, like Richard Martin's in *The Light that Failed: Ideal and Reality in the Writings of E. M. Forster*, The Hague, 1974, pp. 105–32. Useful listings of the varied critical accounts of *Howards End* are to be found in the *catalogues raisonnés* by Frederick P. W. McDowell in *E. M. Forster: a Human Exploration*, ed. G. K. Das and J. Beer, 1979, pp. 269–82; and in *E. M. Forster: Centenary Revaluations*, ed. J. S. Herz and R. K. Martin, 1982, pp. 311–29.

19. On 'Pan' and 'panic' in Forster, see, e.g., Alan Wilde, 'The Naturalization of Eden', in *E. M. Forster: a Human Exploration*,

ed. Das and Beer, pp. 196–207.

20. K. W. Gransden sees this universalizing force of the book as pointing to 'a profounder and more drastic breakdown of the whole of nineteenth-century liberal civilisation, and England's fate, so eloquently lamented in Forster's novel, is part of Europe's, as analysed, in vaster allegory, by Thomas Mann in *Der Zauberberg*' (*E. M. Forster*, 1962, p. 56).

21. Lionel Trilling writes very sympathetically and imaginatively about Mrs Wilcox, often regarded with discomfort or disapproval by critics: 'Her "reality" is of a strange kind and consists in her having no reality in the ordinary sense – she does not have, that is, the reality of personality, of idiosyncrasy or even of power. Her strength comes exactly from her lack of force, her distinction from her lack of distinguishing traits. She suggests Shakespeare's "gentle" women, the Countess of *All's Well* or an older Imogen; or she has a touch of Chaucer's Griselda. It is appropriate that we find her kind in the past, for she represents England's past.' (*E. M. Forster*, London, 1969, pp. 104–5). For George Thomson, more than a little bizarrely, Mrs Wilcox 'assumes the role of Demeter' and is 'a Great Mother figure' (*The Fiction of E. M. Forster*, Detroit, 1967, p. 192).

22. John Beer writes of this 'moment of horror', this 'low point in the novel': 'for a moment in St. Paul's, Margaret has had a glimpse of that other absolute, that meaningless fabric of sights and sounds that stretches to infinity and returns only echoes and reflections to the questing human spirit . . . In the central incident of *A Passage to India*, echoes and reflections will again figure the shapeless absolute, in a cave where every sound turns into an echo and every sight is reflected from polished walls' (*The Achievement of E. M. Forster*, 1962, pp. 113–14).

23. Very many critics have found the conclusion less rhetorically complex and less satisfying than I suggest. Wilfred Stone, for example, is led by his sense of dissatisfaction into a strangely insensitive dismissal: '[The Schlegels] make of Howards End a place of sterile quarantine for the best self of England, but there is no indication that these defenders will ever again do battle with the enemy . . . The burden of the book's conclusion is that Forster does not really want connection at all, but only the rewards of connection; he does not want sex, but only the heir. He wants, in short, ends without means' (*The Cave and the Mountain: a Study of E. M. Forster*, Stanford, 1966, pp. 265–6).

24. *A Passage to India*, ed. Oliver Stallybrass, Harmondsworth, 1985, pp. 282–3. Future page-references are to this, the Penguin edition, which reprints the Abinger Edition of 1978.

25. See Reuben Brower's particular use of the concept 'iconic' in relation to *A Passage to India*: 'It would be harder to find purer examples of symbolic expressions than ['Mosque', 'Caves', and 'Temple']. They are obviously "iconic"' ('The Twilight of the Double Vision: Symbol and

Irony in *A Passage to India*', from *The Fields of Light*, 1951, reprinted in the Macmillan Casebook, ed. Malcolm Bradbury, 1970, p. 114). One of the most extended – indeed, extravagant – treatments of Forster as a symbolist is George H. Thomson, *The Fiction of E. M. Forster*, Detroit, 1967.

26. See Molly B. Tinsley, 'Muddle Et Cetera: Syntax in *A Passage to India*', in *E. M. Forster: Centenary Revaluations*, ed. J. S. Herz and R. K. Martin, 1982, pp. 257–66 – an analysis of certain prevalent irregular syntactical forms in the novel – e.g. anticlimactic sentences, comma-spliced sentences, and catalogues – that reflect Forster's rejection of the 'orderly hypotaxis' of European civilization, and are contrasted with the tighter orderliness of the typical syntax in *Howards End*. See also in this connection Michael Orange, 'Language and Silence in *A Passage to India*', in *E. M. Forster: a Human Exploration*, ed. G. K. Das and J. Beer, 1979, pp. 142–60 – e.g.: 'He reconciles an adept manipulation of his verbal structures to the complete unsufficiency of language itself, without finding it necessary to rely upon crudity of utterance to make the crucial disavowal of literary expression's congruence to mystical experience' (p. 145).

27. See Frank Kermode's discussion of the effect of 'except for' and 'extraordinary' in this passage, in 'The One Orderly Product' (1958), in *Puzzles and Epiphanies: Essays and Reviews, 1958–1961*, 1962, pp. 81–2.

28. Cf. the analysis of this chapter by Barbara Rosecrance, '*A Passage to India*: the Dominant Voice', in *E. M. Forster: Centenary Revaluations*, ed. Herz and Martin, pp. 234–43).

29. Most of the influential interpretations of the novel concentrate on this relationship between the cosmic and the mundane, its hopefulness or its tragedy, and its success or failure in fictional rendering. June Levine's *Creation and Criticism: A Passage to India* (1971) contains a helpful, if slightly mind-numbing, *catalogue raisonné* of interpretations of the novel up to the end of the 1960s. Her book is a kind of compendium, with much information about the Indian background and the different MS versions. It can be supplemented by Frederick McDowell's two listings referred to above, n. 18.

30. F. C. Crews picks out, as two important metaphors elaborated by Forster throughout the novel, 'the metaphors of *receding circles* and of *invitation*' (*E. M. Forster: the Perils of Humanism*, Princeton, 1962, p. 147).

31. 'What the city is as metaphor in *Howards End*, India is in *Passage*: a figure for contingency' (Malcolm Bradbury, *Possibilities: Essays on the State of the Novel*, 1973, pp. 111–12).

32. Many interpretations taking the Caves as their starting-point – often in Jungian or in mystic terms – find it difficult to emerge from them. Wilfred Stone is an example, led by his immersion into such comments

as these: 'The sky also harbors the air, without which hearing and breathing would be impossible. The novel is full of breathing, as if it were itself an exercise in yoga – as in a sense it is' (*The Cave and the Mountain: a Study of E. M. Forster*, Stanford, 1966, p. 313).

33. See some words on this passage by John Beer, in '*A Passage to India*, the French New Novel and English Romanticism', *E. M. Forster: Centenary Revaluations*, pp. 140–1. A great deal has also been made of its potential interpretation in Hindu terms ('the merging of Atman and Brahman') – e.g. by James McConkey, *The Novels of E. M. Forster*, Ithaca, 1957, pp. 147–9. Cf. George Thomson's rhapsodic translation: 'Here is the horror and attraction of narcissism: supreme isolation in all its insidious charm and deathlike beauty. The human spirit ravishes the known self, and the lost soul momentarily reflects its own glimmerings then endlessly reflects its own darkness' (*The Fiction of E. M. Forster*, Detroit, 1967, p. 231).

34. K. W. Gransden writes, of Mrs Moore's experience, 'The horror becomes Conradian, becomes . . . the heart of darkness; vision becomes nightmare' (*E. M. Forster*, 1962, p. 94).

35. Michael Orange writes similarly on these words of Godbole's: 'a noticeable feature of Godbole's explanation is Forster's satirical framing of it by Fielding's impatience, tiredness and boredom, and – to be anachronistic – the insistence on Godbole's Peter Sellers brand of near-fatuity and inconsequentiality. The result is not, of course, to deprecate the Hindu's faith, but the process of explanation itself' ('Language and Silence in *A Passage to India*', in *E. M. Forster: a Human Exploration*, ed. G. K. Das and J. Beer, 1979 p. 158).

36. Cf. J. S. Martin, who detects, very differently, an optimism in Mrs Moore's last sight of India, and in the ending of the whole novel: 'The waving palms lining the harbour seem to her to be saying, "So you thought an echo was India; you took the Marabar Caves as final? . . . What have we in common with them, or they with Asirgarh? Good-bye!" Surely the entire passage, taken in conjunction with Mrs Moore's experience in the Marabar Hills, points to the contrast between a world infused with vitality and variety and one that her world-weary soul has reduced to a meaningless boum. The world may indeed be disordered and meaningless, but it still exists and must be experienced for its own sake' (*E. M. Forster: the Endless Journey*, Cambridge, 1976, p. 162).

37. The phrase, '[Art] is the one orderly product which our muddling race has produced', is Forster's own, in 'Art for Art's Sake', *Two Cheers For Democracy*, Harmondsworth, 1976, p. 106. See Kermode, *Puzzles and Epiphanies*, 1962, pp. 79–85.

38. Forster himself was uneasy about this aspect of 'Temple', saying of the description of the ceremony, in an interview: 'It is well placed; and it gathers up some strings. But there ought to be more after it. The lump

sticks out a little too much' (*Writers at Work: the 'Paris Review' Interviews*, ed. Malcolm Cowley, 1958, p. 27).

39. Many accounts of the novel are very influenced by the triad – e.g. Gertrude White, who writes, 'The threefold division of the book . . . represents also a kind of Hegelian Thesis–Antithesis–Synthesis; or, more properly perhaps, the statement of the problem, and two opposite resolutions' ('*A Passage to India*: Analysis and Revaluation', *PMLA*, LXVIII, 1953, 644). Other critics, like Glen O. Allen, have seen the triad in terms of emotion–reason–love ('Structure, Symbol, and Theme in E. M. Forster's *A Passage to India*', *PMLA*, LXX, 1955, 934–54).

40. The use of the word 'rhythm' enforces admiring reference to E. K. Brown's seminal 'Rhythm in E. M. Forster's *A Passage to India*', *Rhythm in the Novel* (1950), Toronto, 1963, pp. 89–115. Brown's sympathetic account of the function of Ralph – despite the sketchiness – is virtually the point of entry for his elegant and sensitive analysis of the novel.

41. Cf. E. K. Brown: 'To express what is both an order and a mystery rhythmic processes, repetitions with intricate variations, are the most appropriate of idioms. Repetition is the strongest assurance an author can give of order; the extraordinary complexity of the variations is the reminder that the order is so involute that it must remain a mystery' (*ibid.*, p. 115). See n. 15 above.

42. See above, p. 169, and n. 13.

Index

Index

16, 37, 38, 131, 155, *179–204*
A Room With a View, 10, 14
Where Angels Fear to Tread,
   10–12, 14
Foulkes, Robert, 211
Furbank, P. N., 206

Gillen, Francis, 217
Girard, René, 207
Gransden, K. W., 217, 219, 221
Guerard, Albert, 213, 214, 215
Guetti, James, 212

Hawthorne, Nathaniel, 34, 207
Hewitt, Douglas, 214, 215
Hirsch, Marianne, 210
Holland, Laurence, 85, 209
Howard, David, 208
Howe, Irving, 207, 208, 214
Howells, W. D., 36

Ibsen, Henrik, 54, 55, 208

James, Henry
   The Altar of the Dead, 4
   The Ambassadors, 7, 33, 70, 74
   The American Scene, 3
   The Awkward Age, 70
   The Bostonians, 15, *32–54*, 55,
      61, 66, 73, 92, 110, 129, 155
   Daisy Miller, 8
   The Europeans, 10, 15, *19–32*,
      42, 44, 54, 59, 61, 73, 75, 79,
      83, 86, 92, 95, 155, 158, 204
   The Golden Bowl, 4, 10, 15, 42,
      65, 70, *73–92*, 95, 131, 155,
      157, 168
   The Jolly Corner, 4, 154
   Maud-Evelyn, 4
   Notes on Novelists, 6
   The Portrait of a Lady, 7, 33
   Prefaces, 1, 7–8, 130
   The Princess Casamassima, 32,
      33, 35, 39
   The Spoils of Poynton, 12, 33,
      54, 70

The Tragic Muse, 7, 32, 79
The Turn of the Screw, 154
What Maisie Knew, 12, 15, 33,
   42, *54–73*, 74, 82, 89, 93, 100,
   105, 106, 155, 164
The Wings of the Dove, 12, 70,
   74
James, William, 38
Joyce, James, 204

Kafka, Franz, 131
Karl, Frederick, 213, 215
Keats, John, 2
Kermode, Frank, 17, 198, 215, 220,
   221
Klee, Paul, 92
Krook, Dorothea, 85, 210

Lawrence, D.H., 204
Leavis, F. R., 162, 212, 216
Levine, June, 220

McCloskey, J. C., 209
McConkey, James, 221
McDowell, Frederick, 218, 220
McMurray, William, 208
Maeterlinck, Maurice, 54
Martin, J. S., 217, 221
Martin, Richard, 218
Matthiessen, F. O., 210
Melville, Herman, 2, 150
Meredith, George, 19
Merleau-Ponty, Maurice, 206
Mill, John Stuart, 33
Miller, J. Hillis, 17, 213, 218
Moser, Thomas, 214

Nettels, Elsa, 205

Orange, Michael, 220, 221

Pearson, Gabriel, 205
Peckham, Morse, 217
Poe, Edgar Allan, 2, 149
Poirier, Richard, 206, 207
Proust, Marcel, 217

224

Index